# ATOMIC
# HARVEST

# ATOMIC HARVEST

## Hanford and the Lethal Toll of America's Nuclear Arsenal

# MICHAEL D'ANTONIO

Foreword by Stewart Udall

CROWN PUBLISHERS, INC.
NEW YORK

Published by Crown Publishers, Inc., 201 East 50th Street, New York, New York 10022.
Member of the Crown Publishing Group.

Random House, Inc. New York, Toronto, London, Sydney, Auckland

CROWN is a trademark of Crown Publishers, Inc.

Manufactured in the United States of America

Library of Congress Cataloging-in-Publication Data

D'Antonio, Michael.
Atomic harvest: Hanford & the lethal toll of America's nuclear
arsenal / by Michael D'Antonio.—1st ed.
p.  cm.
Includes index.
1. Hanford Nuclear Reservation.   2. Nuclear weapons plants—
Environmental aspects—Washington (State)—Hanford Reach Region.
3. Radiation—Toxicology—Washington (State)—Hanford Reach Region.
4. Pasco (Wash.)—History. 5. Richland (Wash.)—History.
6. Kennewick (Wash.)—History.   I. Title.
TD898.12.W2D36 1993
363.17′99′0979751—dc20
93-10590
CIP

ISBN 0-517-58981-8

10 9 8 7 6 5 4 3 2 1

First Edition

*For Toni, Elizabeth, and Amy, of course.*

# CONTENTS

# ACKNOWLEDGMENTS

Many people offered support for this work and helped me understand Hanford, the American atomic complex, and the history of the Columbia Basin region. Tom Bailie and Casey Ruud, the two men who inspired this book, gave freely of their time and energy. Lynn Stembridge and Jim Thomas of the Hanford Education Action League lent me both their files and their wisdom. Kenneth Morgan of the Department of Energy and Michael Lawrence, Hanford's former manager, were equally generous. And several reporters—Karen Dorn Steele, Eric Nalder, and Keith Schneider—selflessly shared their stories. I am also deeply appreciative of my editor, David Groff, whose judgment is matched only by his kindness. Finally, I am most indebted to my wife, Toni, for her unending patience and encouragement during a project that at times was all-consuming.

# FOREWORD

IN CHILLING DETAIL, *Atomic Harvest* recounts the most tragic chapter in American Cold War history and reveals the pattern of deceit that infected the entire nuclear weapons industry. Michael D'Antonio paints a vivid picture of the citizens who long suspected that they had not been told he truth about the Hanford nuclear-weapons complex and its effect on their health and their environment. In the end, they discover their government had betrayed them with both radiation and lies.

While some proudly proclaim that America won the Cold War, it was a far more costly victory than most of us realize. Each side spent trillions of dollars developing and deploying nuclear weapons. Ultimately, the former Soviet Union's mismanagement and excessive military spending bankrupted its economy. Similarly, in the 1980s the United States piled up a gargantuan deficit that will hamper economic growth for years to come.

But the price of the arms race goes beyond the money spent on weapons. In the United States both people and the environment have suffered from astounding levels of lethal contamination. Atomic weapons facilities have created massive pollution problems in many areas of the United States. After years of study, experts still don't know exactly how to handle the mess. They do know, however, that the clean-up will cost more than the weapons themselves and will last for decades.

The legacy of the arms race includes damaged people, too. I first encountered the human victims of America's nuclear program in 1978, when I agreed to represent those who had been exposed to high levels of radiation during the testing of nuclear weapons in Nevada. After fifteen years of investigating, I have concluded that the U.S. government's atomic weapons industry knowingly and recklessly exposed millions of people to dangerous levels of radiation.

Nothing in our past compares to the official deceit and lying that took place in order to protect the nuclear industry. In the name of national security, politicians and bureaucrats ran roughshod over democracy and morality. Ultimately, the Cold Warriors were willing to sacrifice their own people in their zeal to beat the Russians.

Anyone describing the awful reality left behind by the arms race would have to make the story of Hanford, as told in *Atomic Harvest,* Exhibit A. The single most polluted place in the Western world, Hanford is home to 177 waste tanks, each of which holds as much as a million of gallons of radioactive chemicals. As I write, sixty-eight of these tanks are known to be leaking. And several have the potential to explode. Officially the most urgent environmental emergency in the land, Hanford has already polluted the nearby Columbia River and it threatens local groundwater. Over the years, the complex secretly emitted about million curies of radiation, which entered the environment where hundreds of thousands of people lived.

Perhaps the most disturbing aspect of this tragedy is that an elite corps public officials were so willing to violate the basic rights of their fellow human beings in order to fulfill the reckless goals of the nuclear establishment. From 1955 to 1960 I served as a member of Congress. I was Secretary of Interior from 1960 to 1968. During my time in government I listened to experts say that weapons plants such as Hanford did not pose risks to local people, and that they could "handle" the waste products pouring out of the reactors and processing plants. Of course, they knew at the time that the health of the downwind folk was being put at risk and that they were creating horrendous environmental problems. Sadly, this is a burden my generation is thrusting upon our children and grandchildren.

The nuclear arms race must be seen as the most important, and destructive enterprise of the Cold War. An intricate mythology was developed to support the nuclear weapons build-up. The scientists and politicians declared that no one was being harmed, that everything was under control. Today, new truths about what really happened at places like the Nevada test site, Los Alamos, Rocky Flats, Savannah River and Hanford reveal that our leaders and our experts lied.

Future generations will be forced to deal with the bombmakers' legacy of contamination. It is up to us to understand the deception that poisoned the dialogue of democracy. The frightening story told in this landmark book punctures the atomic myth that has demeaned American democracy.

*Stewart Udall*
*Santa Fe*

# ATOMIC HARVEST

# INTRODUCTION

A YELLOW PENCIL is the focus of Tom Bailie's sharpest recollection of childhood. In this memory it is 1952, and he is five years old. He has been taken out of his wheelchair and is sitting on the kitchen floor in a farmhouse in Eastern Washington. He is trying to grab the pencil with his toes. It is an excruciating chore for a boy whose legs have withered during a year of paralysis. But with great effort he struggles across the sloping wooden floor, stretching for the pencil. When he makes contact, it rolls out of reach. But he keeps on trying and at last manages to clutch it. He is exhilarated.

The pencil chase was an exercise that helped young Bailie recover from a mysterious bout of paralysis, which had kept him in a wheelchair for much of the previous year. It is also a symbol of his lifelong struggle to find out why he was so sick as a child, and why he is sterile as an adult. Bailie was joined on his quest by neighbors, citizen activists, and journalists who wouldn't stop asking questions. In the end, they and the rest of the world would discover that Bailie and thousands of other "downwinders" had been unknowingly showered with poisonous radiation from the nearby Hanford Atomic Reservation—now innocuously renamed the "Hanford Site"—a top-secret government facility that made plutonium for America's nuclear weapons.

The Hanford downwinders are among the most irradiated people on earth, and the little-known reservation is arguably the most polluted place in the western world. More than 440 billion gallons of chemical and radioactive liquid waste have been poured into the ground at Hanford, including enough lethal plutonium to build two dozen nuclear weapons. Uranium, cesium, strontium, americium, plutonium, neptunium, and other deadly radionuclides have been

1

discharged into the soil, the air, and the Columbia River. Almost all of the pollution, including massive airborne releases of radiation that reached civilians as far away as Spokane, 125 miles to the east, was kept secret. Indeed, whenever anyone asked if Hanford was safe, they were assured by federal authorities that there was no danger.

Hanford is not the only federal nuclear installation that silently fouled the environment and threatened public health. At Rocky Flats, Colorado, at Savannah River, South Carolina, at Oak Ridge, Tennessee, and at Fernald, Ohio, the government-owned atomic bomb industry has dumped tons of radioactive materials into the earth and the air. Radiation-related illnesses have been documented among workers and/or neighbors at all of these sites. And at ten other locations, from New York to California, similar but smaller pollution problems have been revealed. Reliable estimates set the price of cleaning up after the government bomb factories at more than $200 billion, but some analysts say it could go as high as $1 trillion. (Hanford alone could cost $50 billion.) It is certain, whatever the final amount, that cleaning up the nuclear complex will cost more than the savings-and-loan scandal of the 1980s, more than the cost of the entire Vietnam War.

Although we can make some estimate of the price of cleaning up Hanford and the other sites, the human toll of four decades of pollution and deceit has yet to be tallied. Studies on the health of the downwinders and Hanford's workers may one day confirm just how much physical suffering was inflicted. In the meantime, there is little doubt among scientists that tens of thousands of people were hit with enough radiation to increase their risk of developing cancer. Excess thyroid disease has already been noticed in the downwinder community. (Thyroid tumors are commonly associated with iodine 131, one of Hanford's most plentiful by-products.) And experts know that anyone who ingests even the tiniest particle of plutonium is all but guaranteed to develop a malignancy. Perhaps no civilians in America are more at risk of this kind of poisoning than people like Tom Bailie, who grew up close to Hanford, and the Indians who lived on the river, drank its polluted water, and ate its radioactive fish.

By 1993 the possible illnesses caused by Hanford and many other

atomic weapons facilities were the subject of landmark epidemiological studies, which hold some promise of a reasonably accurate
accounting. But it would be impossible to measure the shattered
faith of thousands of loyal citizens who were deceived and betrayed
by their own government. Recently declassified documents, and the
testimony of those who were there, reveal that authorities were
aware of the dangers posed by Hanford's emissions. They knew the
long-term ecological implications of their failure to take care of
Hanford's waste. Worst, they knowingly placed the downwinders
in harm's way. Even when scientists suggested issuing warnings to
protect the public—from radioactive air, water, food—they were
overruled by those intent on protecting the secrecy of the weapons
program.

It was in a newspaper article published in 1988 that I learned of
farmer Tom Bailie's struggle to uncover the truth about Hanford.
With further research and a telephone call to his farmhouse in the
little town of Mesa, I discovered that Bailie's struggle, and the story
of Hanford, constituted an important piece of Cold War history.
But it is not, as some might believe, a story about science or technology. Rather it is a political drama. Bailie and the others involved
confronted a government that had hidden the truth from its citizens
so that it could conduct the arms race without the interference of
those who had to pay for it with their taxes and, in the case of some
downwinders, with their health. Just as surely as Richard Nixon
violated the public trust with a secret war in Cambodia, those who
ran the bomb factories violated the public trust with secret experimental releases of radiation and forty years of virtual silence about
the environmental catastrophe they were creating.

This book tells the stories of the many people who demanded to
know what Hanford had done to them and to the environment of
the Columbia River Basin. Tom Bailie had many allies, including
neighbors like Juanita Andrewjeski, who kept a map of the cancer
and heart disease in an area near her house that became known as
the "death mile." He was also joined by citizen activists from the
nearby city of Spokane, who were organized by preacher Bill Houff,
a veteran of the civil rights struggle who found his conscience
stirred by the Hanford issue. All of these key figures were helped by

reporters like Karen Dorn Steele of the Spokane *Spokesman-Review,* who was the first to reveal the downwinders' fears and the truth about Hanford's past.

But as this book reveals, the scandal of Hanford is not confined to the past. Even as Tom Bailie and Karen Dorn Steele and the Spokane activists waged their struggle over Hanford's history, a brave young inspector inside the nuclear reservation was uncovering improper dumping of radioactive waste, dangerous flaws in the design of key facilities, and numerous violations of safety and security regulations. Casey Ruud fought to resolve these problems within the Hanford system. But he came to believe that safety was being sacrificed to the demands for more plutonium, and that only a major accident would lead plant managers to change their ways. Eventually he would turn to Eric Nalder, an investigative reporter for the *Seattle Times.* Nalder's articles led to an immediate shutdown of the key plutonium factories. Days later, Ruud was in Washington, D.C., to tell what he knew to congressional investigators.

Hanford's shutdown was followed quickly by the collapse of the entire nuclear-arms–making industry. Here again, reporters—especially Keith Schneider of *The New York Times*—played a key role. So did a stubborn veteran nuclear expert named Richard Starostecki. Starostecki was hired as a kind of super-inspector by energy secretary John Herrington. His alarming discoveries of mismanagement, ineptitude, and crumbling facilities hastened the end of dangerous operations at many sites.

*Atomic Harvest* presents all of these figures—from the downwinders to the Secretary of Energy—and reveals their roles in events that could only have occurred at the end of the superpower arms race. To make clearer how the Hanford scandal could have happened, I have tried to describe it in the context of its time and place. Like most of the major nuclear weapons facilities, Hanford was born in the urgency of the Manhattan Project and grew exponentially during the Cold War. Its community—the so-called Tri-Cities of Richland, Kennewick, and Pasco—became almost entirely dependent on Hanford's payroll, and came to identify completely with its mission. Hanford's rise and decline unfold against this backdrop of almost unanimous community support.

Indeed, most of the nation loyally supported the atomic weapons buildup during most of the Cold War era. But this support was based in large part on ignorance. Only now is the public becoming informed about the dangers associated with the bomb factories and the deceptions practiced to keep them operating. These deceptions included the "missile gap" of the 1960s, which former Secretary of Defense Robert McNamara would later admit was a myth, and the inflated reports on Soviet strength issued in the 1980s. In 1992, McNamara explained that in the early 1960s, as President Kennedy had thundered about the Russian threat, the Soviets had possessed only a few working rockets. "But myths are sometimes more important than reality," he would observe. In part because of the power of these official myths, the United States would eventually spend more than $1 trillion on atomic weapons per American.

Those who supported the arms race would say that it ultimately caused the disintegration of the Soviet Union and freed Eastern Europe from communism. After spending more than $1 trillion on nuclear weapons, the USSR did collapse, and freedom movements have produced independent states in the former Soviet republics. But it also may be argued that the Cold War helped the tyrants of the old Soviet system hold their empire together longer than they could have without it. After all, it is easier to command loyalty when there is a fearsome enemy to rally against. Freedom might have blossomed sooner if the Soviet people had not felt threatened from without.

Although questions about the wisdom of American policy may never be resolved, there can be no doubt about who "won" the Cold War. No one did. With this war ended, the economy of the former Soviet Union is a shambles, and the people of the independent states face years of privation and dangerous political turmoil. Likewise, the U.S. economy is burdened with $4 trillion worth of debt, part of which can be attributed to the cost of building thousands of highly sophisticated weapons that became obsolete the moment the arms race ended. At the same time, precious scientific and financial resources that were poured into defense programs have robbed the private economy of important intellectual and financial investments. The Cold War was a tragedy for everyone involved.

The legacy of the arms race, the atomic harvest left to the American people, is bitterly ironic. For forty years American children lived with the nightmare fear of Soviet missiles that never flew. Now it seems certain that in the process of building our own nuclear weapons arsenal, we have killed and wounded many of our fellow citizens. The threat to the health of downwinder populations at many sites will continue for generations. The millions of tons of waste created by weapons production will remain toxic for thousands of years. Ultimately, it was our own fears—and the nuclear arms complex we built to soothe them—that did us harm, not the Soviet Union's bombs.

The price of nuclear fear can be found on the windswept desert of the Hanford Site, where huge pools of highly radioactive toxic sludge wait in steel tanks. Beneath the tumbleweed and the prairie grasses, millions of tons of contaminated earth hold plutonium and other deadly radionuclides. No one knows, yet, how to clean it all up. In the meantime, radiation continues to leak into rivers and the groundwater system. Animals spread the deadly particles across the landscape, and the tanks full of atomic waste threaten to explode before they can be emptied. In April 1993, a similar tank exploded in Russia, spreading contamination across a mile-wide area. Fifty years after Manhattan Project leaders decided to use "temporary measures" for handling nuclear wastes, the bomb's lethal by-products still awaited a final resting place.

A deadly harvest also waits in the lush, cultivated farmlands outside Hanford's fence. Thousands of people who were bombarded with radioactive pollution already claim to be suffering the effects—miscarriages, deformed babies, benign and malignant tumors. Thousands more must wonder if a radioactive time bomb ticks inside of them and will one day explode into a life-threatening illness.

Finally, the atomic harvest includes a lesson for the future. Hanford and the other bomb factories were allowed to endanger their neighbors and foul the environment because government scientists and officials didn't trust the people they served. Coming out of World War II, the government maintained its wartime claim to extraordinary secrecy. Elected and nonelected authorities didn't believe that, given all the facts, citizens would make the right choices. So they simply declared the facts secret, and retained the power for themselves. For their part, everyday citizens, motivated by fear of the Soviet menace and of an awesome technology, abdicated their responsibility to determine the national interest in a time of peace.

This book is a record of what happens when the people in a democratic society cede too much power to the government. Fortunately, it is also a record of what can happen when they demand that that power be returned.

# NUCLEAR LANDSCAPE

EVERYTHING THAT MOVED kicked up more dust that day in 1954, including the boy who ran circles with his dog in the farmyard. While they scuffled in the dirt, a whirlwind blew across the fallow field behind the house. It traced a straight line over the bare ground, making a plume of dust that hung in the air like smoke over a battlefield. The sun stood in a clear blue sky, and the air smelled of fertilizer and sweet hay. The fan blades of an old windmill creaked high above the yard, and the sounds of a radio trickled out of the house.

Ten thousand gently rolling acres—most of it dryland wheat—the Bailie family farm was four miles east of the Columbia River and about ten miles west of the little town of Mesa, in Eastern Washington. In the summer of 1954, seven-year-old Tommy Bailie was happy to while away an afternoon chasing his little brown and white dog named Sandy. A pale, sickly child, Tommy had been in and out of hospitals most of his life, with skin sores, allergies, chronic diarrhea, and asthma. At age five he had almost died from a mysterious paralysis. He had recovered only after spending two harrowing weeks encased in an iron lung, a machine that must have seemed as much torture chamber as medical miracle to a little boy. Rehabilitation had been slow, but Tommy Bailie had regained his health. He had the run of the farm, and he began to grow strong in the summer sun. He was tan, and his blond hair had been bleached white.

It might have been the sunlight glinting off a shovel that caught Tommy Bailie's eye and made him stop playing. While the dog tugged at his pant leg, the boy peered across the field behind the house. Through the veil of dust he could see a dozen ghostly forms.

8

The first to emerge from the haze was a soldier carrying a shovel and wearing green fatigues. He was followed by other soldiers and a couple of men in suits and ties. They carried little boxes connected by wires to what looked like microphones. They waved the microphones at the ground like blind people passing red and white canes over a sidewalk, back and forth, back and forth. One of them stopped and pointed to a spot near his feet. A soldier pierced the soft earth with his shovel, scooped up some soil, and poured it into a sack. Then the group moved on across the field.

Tommy had seen men like these before. They were strangers, but they were always friendly. Sometimes they gave him candy. Once they had even brought him some cowboy boots. Remembering the gifts, he yelled across the field, hoping they would notice him.

The men didn't stop. They just kept walking until they passed on the other side of the house and disappeared from view. Tommy ran around to the front of the house, shouting and waving to the men. They waved back and then crossed the road, wading into the wheat growing in another field. The precious wheat, which held the fortunes of every family in Franklin County, spread like a soft green carpet as far as Tommy Bailie could see. Soon the men crossed a ridge, and it looked, to the boy who stood there watching on tiptoe, as if the wheat had swallowed them up.

Tommy Bailie ran into the house and found his mother in the kitchen.

"I saw some men come through the field out back," Tommy reported. "Some of them were army men, and they took some dirt. Did you see 'em?"

Any sign of life was exciting for a little boy who lived in the isolated farm country of Eastern Washington in the 1950s. But Laura Lee Bailie didn't have much time for looking out her kitchen window. Seven years of hardscrabble farming had taught her to stick to her work. And besides, she was sure it had been just another group from Hanford, across the river. Hanford scientists were always coming around, asking area farmers for samples of soil, water, milk, and vegetables. Sometimes they would even take the remains of dead game—rabbits, ducks, geese. And sometimes they would hold one of those Geiger counters up against the neck of a cow. They always said they would come back to let the farm families know if they ever found anything unusual. And they never came back.

Despite the reassurances, Laura Bailie often wondered what the teams that came out from Hanford were trying to find. But it was clear, considering that Hanford's operations were a military secret, that the less said, the better. So out of respect, and patriotism, Laura Lee didn't ask the questions that were in her mind. Still she could not help wondering why the inspectors came so often and made such a thorough search if, as they said, they never found anything. Was anything harmful ever found in the meat and milk and vegetables they took? The same food she fed her family? Was anything floating over on the wind and settling on the wheatfields? These thoughts flashed through her mind when Tommy reported that the Hanford men had come through the fields again. But as usual, she kept her doubts to herself.

In the summer of 1954, neither the farmers nor the people in the nearby cities of Kennewick, Richland, and Pasco (called the Tri-Cities) worried much about the Hanford Atomic Reservation, as it was called at the time. Indeed, all of Eastern Washington took great pride in the sprawling federal complex that had been built along the Columbia River. Hanford had been a vital part of the famous Manhattan Project, which had made the world's first bomb-grade plutonium, the very plutonium that powered Fat Man, the five-ton atomic bomb that exploded over Nagasaki on August 9, 1945. After the war, the people of the Tri-Cities considered national defense an ongoing responsibility. No one needed to be convinced that the nation was locked in a mortal Cold War with the Soviet Union.

Chilling proof of the seriousness of the Cold War could be found in the newspaper almost every day. The drawn-out spy trial of Julius and Ethel Rosenberg, who were executed in 1953 for passing atomic secrets to the Soviets, convinced most Americans that their country faced a devious enemy. In the same year the Soviet Union shocked the world with the detonation of its first hydrogen bomb.

The ultimate defense against the threat posed by the Soviets was an ever bigger, ever more sophisticated atomic arsenal, a stockpile of weapons so monstrous that no enemy would dare attack. By the mid-1950s the nation was committed to funding and winning the Cold War. The battle was waged in places like the Nevada A-bomb test site and the laboratories and production facilities of Hanford. The nuclear scientists, engineers, and laborers who lived in the Tri-Cities considered themselves front-line soldiers in this struggle. It seemed that world security rested on their shoulders, and they threw themselves into the task of building better reactors and purer bomb-grade isotopes.

Of course, not everyone backed the Cold War buildup. An early "Ban the Bomb" movement developed in the 1950s, attracting intellectuals with a moral argument against weapons of mass destruction. There were also isolated voices of dissent in the scientific community. J. Robert Oppenheimer, who had directed the Manhattan Project, warned that the accumulation of weapons might make their use inevitable. Albert Schweitzer and Linus Pauling argued that radioactive fallout from the testing of bombs powered by Hanford's fuel posed a health hazard. But the critics of America's atomic policies offered no conclusive proof of any health danger, and the Atomic Energy Commission routinely certified that its projects were safe. Besides these assurances, the AEC protected its mission by punishing its critics. It answered Oppenheimer's concerns with a public investigation of his loyalty and former connections with American Communists. Although Oppenheimer was eventually exonerated, his security clearance was revoked, an action that effectively ended his access to the highest levels of nuclear weapons research. Given the government's public statements and its response to the likes of Oppenheimer, it was obvious to all that Cold War patriotism was synonymous with the "American way."

In the Tri-Cities no one seemed to have any doubts about the necessity for atomic weapons or the power and the beauty of nuclear technology. Society life was dominated by the young scientists, who were fast becoming the elite members of a community enthralled by high technology. If their faith in the safety of the nuclear machines they operated ever wavered, they found comfort in the knowledge that—just in case—Hanford experts tested their air and water, even their food, on a regular basis.

Over time, Hanford grew from a local industry into a source of community identity. Without it, this part of the lower Columbia River Basin would be just another sleepy agricultural region. But with Hanford, the Tri-Cities had become the free world's largest center of plutonium production. Richland became a cosmopolitan little city, with its own orchestra and opera company, fine restaurants and country clubs. By 1960, nuclear employment topped ten thousand, and Richland, Kennewick, and Pasco were prosperous.

As one new reactor after another was built and placed in operation on the shores of the Columbia, Hanford became perceived as a citadel from which the inventions and ideas that would power the future would emerge. But the community's obsession with tomorrow also had something to do with the fact that so many of its people came from somewhere else. Thousands of laborers had emigrated from the South. Scientists and technicians had come from both coasts. And it was difficult indeed to find anyone in Richland who even knew what the place had looked like ten years earlier. For this collection of out-of-towners, the Tri-Cities had no discernible past, but only a wonderful, purposeful, fantastic future. There was a distinct sense of romance in this outlook on life. Just like the settlers who had followed the Oregon Trail to the Northwest, these people were pioneers. They were atomic pioneers who pressed forward, building one nuclear facility after another, and never paused to look back.

But of course Hanford did have a past. Before the war it had been a tiny village of about three hundred people, located opposite Mesa, on the western shore of a wide bend in the wild, free-flowing Columbia called the Hanford Reach. Settled at the turn of the century, the village served as a commercial center for farmers who scratched a living out of the vast surrounding plain. They grew apples or winter wheat and let cattle roam the undeveloped range. Most of the area was too dry to farm. In the summer, the irrigated farmland burned in the desert heat. In the winter, sudden swirling storms whipped tons of earth into the air. The powdery soil, rich with nutrients laid down by the meandering river, drifted like snow against fences and barn doors. A single storm could sweep all the topsoil from one farm across a road to a neighbor's land; the next year another storm might move it back again. The blowing dirt would seep under doors and through the cracks in window frames. It ruined farm equipment and killed livestock. But, having endured the dust storms, heat, and lack of rain, the settlers were proud of the steadily increasing crops that their farms produced. They had survived for more than two generations, and considered themselves as much a part of the land as the handful of Wanapum Indians who still scratched out a living by fishing the Columbia. The Indians coexisted with the settlers and with nature, as they had for generations. Indeed, they would cling to traditional ways well into the 1950s, relying on the river, the same river that ran through the Hanford Site, for their daily diet.

In December 1942, Lt. Col. Franklin Matthias gazed down from a small military plane at the gracefully arcing river, the little towns, the farms, and the vast, vacant desert of the Columbia Basin. He had been sent from the East Coast by Gen. Leslie Groves, who oversaw the Manhattan Project for the U.S. Army Corps of Engineers. Matthias, whose previous claim to engineering fame had come in securing the site for the Pentagon building, was to locate a vast territory, somewhere in the western states, for a new government project. He didn't know what would be built, but only that it would be top secret. Matthias carried detailed maps of the region and a plan showing three industrial sites—they would be atomic reactors—spaced three miles apart along a body of water. The best location would fit this plan. It would also be at least twenty miles from the nearest town of one thousand or more residents.

As he flew over the Basin, near the tiny town of Hanford, Matthias placed the template against the map and gazed with delight at what he saw. Here at last was a perfect match. No more than two thousand people inhabited the half-million acres below. Few places in America were so sparsely populated, an important consideration in his search for a top-secret military site. But just as important to Matthias was the river. To the north, the Grand Coulee Dam would turn the river's current into electric power for the federal project.

With a flow of more than five million gallons per minute, the river could provide more than enough water—and hydroelectricity—for whatever Leslie Groves had in mind.

Matthias returned to Washington, D.C., and was met at Union Station by General Groves. The young colonel couldn't help being impressed by the fact that the general had driven himself to the train station to meet a junior officer. The two men drove around the city for an hour as Groves slowly explained to Matthias what would be built on the site he had found. The general also briefed Matthias on the rest of the Manhattan Project, the largest secret military construction project in history.

With the proper site found, the army moved quickly to take control of the area. In March 1943, Hanford area farmers received letters from the government informing them that they had thirty days to vacate so their land could be used for a war-related project. At the same time, federal agents visited with the Indians, informing them that they would no longer be allowed to fish and forage along the Reach. In a matter of a few months, all the area's livestock was sold, and houses were boarded up. With no one to tend them, orchards and crops withered and died. Many of the farmers, who had been paid only for the value of their land, never recouped the cost of the buildings, equipment, and irrigation systems they had added to their properties. But, like the Wanapum, the farm families and villagers dutifully departed, for the good of the war effort.

By the end of the summer of 1943, about 400,000 acres on the west side of the river, from the river bend called the Hanford Reach south to the small town of Richland, had been secured. Comprising approximately 620 square miles, the reservation included an unforested rise in the northeast called Gable Mountain, and another windswept range in the southwest called the Rattlesnake Hills. Between was a desert plain, much of it unchanged from when Lewis and Clark passed through in the fall of 1805.

The construction of the Hanford Engineer Works—which was directed by Franklin Matthias—began with the creation of a sprawling camp that would house, feed, and entertain the laborers. Hanford's birth, recounted in the book *Hanford and the Bomb,* by Steve Sanger, came in a frenzy of construction. Originally a tent city, Hanford Camp would eventually have more than one thousand wooden buildings—barracks, shops, mess halls, taverns, movie houses, even banks. Thousands of workers quickly filled this little city. The newcomers came from around the country, drawn by notices posted in union halls and community centers. The posters, which announced "There's a job for you at Hanford," promised good pay, hard work, and difficult living conditions. Eventually more than fifty thousand people, segregated by sex and race, would occupy Hanford Camp. They brought with them the passions and problems of people everywhere. To control the bootlegging, gambling, and prostitution, Hanford also had its own police force, called the Hanford Patrol.

The army built a second, more permanent settlement in Richland for the managers and scientists who would eventually operate the works. By the end of 1945, Richland's population would grow from two hundred to more than fifteen thousand.

Conditions in Richland and at Hanford were so bad that scores of workers quit each day. When a dust storm hit, resignations would leap into the hundreds. Records of the prime contractor, Du Pont, show that 137,000 laborers came and went before construction was completed. In about three years, these people worked as many hours as the laborers who built the Panama Canal, but the canal workers took thirteen years to complete their task. And unlike the canal workers, the men and women who built Hanford didn't know what they were creating.

It's doubtful that anyone could have guessed that the gray, windowless buildings that rose from the desert floor would house the world's first full-scale nuclear reactors. Placed along the river and spaced roughly six miles apart, they were named 100-B, 100-D, and 100-F, for the sections of land they occupied. On the outside they were concrete blockhouses—factorylike buildings—about seven stories high. Inside each was a reactor, a cube-shaped structure the size of a three-story house, made of precision-milled graphite bricks. Long rods containing uranium would be pushed through holes in the graphite until enough was present to create spontaneous fission. Experimental reactors had shown that as the decaying uranium threw off atomic particles, new elements would be created, including plutonium, which could then be extracted by relatively simple, but hazardous, chemical processes. In order to produce enough plutonium, the Hanford reactors would be large and so high-powered they would generate searing heat. The heat, a product of fission, would pose the first and most immediate hazard at the reactor. Columbia River water, delivered by an intricate system of pipes, would carry off the heat and prevent a steam explosion. Such an explosion was the worst possible accident imagined by the reactor designers, in that it would scatter radioactive particles for miles and endanger the lives of thousands of workers.

Most of the workers would be involved in the thirty-step process by which plutonium would be recovered from the irradiated slugs for use in a bomb. Hundreds of tons of fuel would have to be processed to yield the few pounds of plutonium needed for each bomb. To extract the precious material, workers would dissolve the slugs in acid. The solution would then be treated in three huge chemical factories called the T, U, and B plants. Eight hundred feet long, sixty-five feet wide, and ten stories high, these buildings loomed like battleships on the desert. Designers called them "canyons." The workers affectionately nicknamed them "Queen Marys." The fuel slugs from the reactors would enter the canyons on rail cars at one end, and purified plutonium would leave in minute quantities at the other. The metal—ounce for ounce the most costly substance ever created—would then be loaded into an army ambulance and transported to Los Alamos, New Mexico, where Oppenheimer's bomb builders worked.

Constructing Hanford presented daunting technical challenges; almost every facility in the complex was the first of its kind. Hanford also reflected a profound social change. Here scientists and engineers, who had come to be regarded almost as the guides to America's future greatness, reached new heights. Their invention, the atomic reactor, would unleash the greatest power in the universe. Of course, the nearly mythic nature of this enterprise was not felt consciously by the thousands who were part of the Manhattan Project. But it would be reflected years later in the remorse and ambivalence of many of the scientists who were its leaders. Long after the bomb had been dropped, J. Robert Oppenheimer became almost sorrowful about this turn in human events, remarking that "the physicists have known sin and this was a knowledge which they cannot lose."

Such moral dilemmas were far from the minds of those who constructed Hanford. They were vexed by more practical difficulties, such as the inconvenient fact that all of the machines had to be designed in a way that would protect workers from radiation. A single microscopic particle of plutonium, lodged in the lungs or intestines, would almost certainly cause cancer. But plutonium exposure wasn't the only risk. The facilities would produce huge quantities of chemical waste and many lethal radioactive by-products—thorium, americium, cesium, and others. And then there was the problem of "criticality," which occurs when too much plutonium is concentrated in one place. The result is an instant burst of radiation—not quite an atomic explosion, but a blue flash of heat and radioactivity that could kill anyone nearby.

Plant operators could be protected from radiation exposure with shielding; lead, steel, concrete, and glass three to six feet thick were placed between the workers and the dangerous materials. The workers would then run the plutonium extraction and refining facilities by remote control, secure behind the protective walls. To do this, Hanford would employ experimental television technology. Criticality could be prevented by careful design and rigid rules for operators. Vessels and containers would be made in such a way that they would not hold enough plutonium to produce critical mass. And workers would be forbidden from placing large amounts of plutonium in any one area.

Another unique challenge at Hanford was to protect the environment outside the plants from accidents and radiation. The cooling water that would come out of the reactors would be radioactive. So would the chemical wastes that would be produced by the refining facilities. Some of these substances would remain toxic for tens of thousands of years. Pressed for time, Hanford's engineers decided that mildly radioactive wastes—reactor cooling water or stack gases—could be sent back into the environment, where they would be diluted and become less dangerous. (Engineers refer to this practice as the "dilution is the solution" approach.) The more toxic solids and liquids would be buried or stored in huge steel tanks. A permanent place for these wastes could be found when the war was won. Accidents could be prevented by careful procedures, and their effects would be mitigated by the fact that the areas downwind were so sparsely populated. Save for a few farmers and small towns, there was nothing but grassland between Hanford and Spokane, the nearest big city, and that was 125 miles downwind.

The isolation, the sweeping landscape, and the prevailing sense of urgency all lent an air of excitement to the early days at Hanford. Manhattan Project leaders believed they were competing with German and Japanese A-bomb programs. Losing this race would be catastrophic for the Allies. So the Americans set impossible deadlines. Pipefitters, carpenters, masons, and welders were required to make things work even as drawings and blueprints were being completed and then changed. The craftsmen took pride in their adaptations of designs; they often saved time and money with their impromptu changes. The history of B Reactor, the first to go on line, is an example of this can-do spirit. "B" was completed in fifteen months. But when it was first loaded, it experienced mysterious spontaneous shutdowns. Led by the famous Enrico Fermi, the physicists determined that they needed to add extra fuel to maintain fission. They were able to do this only because Du Pont engineers, guessing that the physicists (they called them "longhairs") had underdesigned the mysterious machine, had added extra loading tubes, just in case they might be needed. The oft-repeated story of the site engineers who saved the reactor with their intuition and common sense reinforced the belief that Hanford's workers could solve any problem, meet any deadline, if only the experts got out of the way.

Off-hours life at the Hanford construction site was rough-edged, with the kind of drunkenness and violence one might expect in a huge mining camp. Hanford was such a tough place that quarters for single men and women were separated by high fences, and the boundaries were patrolled. The strict security measures were intended to maintain order inside the fences and thwart spies who might enter from the outside. To improve security, the government bought up some extra land, on the eastern side of the Columbia, to hide the reactors from the eyes of enemy agents and curious neighbors. Located near Basin City and Mesa, this land rose up from the river to a high ridge. The authorities purchased the ridge and everything beyond it, right up to the fenceline of a sprawling property owned by an old bachelor farmer named Loen Bailie. Bailie, who had come to this area in the 1920s, was one of the biggest landholders in the region. He grew wheat, hay, and other crops with the help of his nephews, Maynard and Wayne.

In the summer of 1945, as Maynard Bailie drove horses for his uncle and Hanford bustled with activity, Laura Lee Small came to Mesa to visit a friend, Lucille Po. A pretty young woman from Walla Walla, Laura Lee had gone to work for the Army Corps of Engineers, which had assigned her to an office in Berkeley, California. She had enjoyed her work and loved exploring San Francisco, but she missed her friends and family and decided to return to Washington. That summer in Mesa, she would meet Maynard Bailie, the man who would be her husband. She would also hear the news of the bombings at Hiroshima and Nagasaki.

In the months preceding the bombings, Hanford had raced to meet the Manhattan Project's demand for "the product," as it was called. Huge quantities of uranium ore were irradiated, and workers rushed to extract the plutonium that was produced. The production timetable was compressed as Colonel Matthias struggled to respond to the goals set by General Groves. Matthias's diary from that period notes the speed-up ordered by Groves. Roughly five kilograms of plutonium were needed to achieve an explosion. Groves wanted the first five kilograms of plutonium by June and another five by July. By the end of July, Hanford had produced more than enough to fuel the Trinity test shot—the first atomic explosion in history—and the bomb dropped on Nagasaki. (The Hiroshima bomb, which was dropped first, was powered by uranium supplied by another Manhattan Project facility, in Oak Ridge, Tennessee.)

Perhaps only those who lived through World War II could fully understand the sense of relief felt by Americans when the atom bomb was dropped and they could at last see the end of the war. While the atomic bomb represented a new kind of terror, its overwhelming force was greeted joyfully by an American public that understood it would mean Japan's surrender. And surrender indeed came eight days after the attack on Hiroshima.

The people who worked at Hanford proudly proclaimed that they had helped end the war, and the entire Tri-Cities indulged in a great celebration. Laura Lee Small, who had heard the news while listening to the radio in Mesa, suddenly realized the truth about her wartime office assignment: she too had been working on the bomb project, as a secretary for a group of government scientists in Berkeley that included J. Robert Oppenheimer. She was disturbed by the knowledge that the pleasant little office where she had worked so diligently for a group of physics professors had contributed to such awful destruction. But, distressed as she was, she told no one in Mesa. She had been instructed to keep her work secret, and she did.

Laura Lee Small and Maynard Bailie were married in 1945. When her first pregnancy ended in a miscarriage, Laura Lee gave it little thought. After all, many other women in the area had miscarriages that year, including her friend Lucille. The second time Laura Lee became pregnant, in 1947, she gave birth to her son Thomas. He was born with some minor deformities—malformed nails, a sunken chest, underdeveloped lungs, and slightly bent limbs—and he developed a long string of illnesses as he grew. But eventually he became a more robust, happy, outgoing child.

As Tommy Bailie grew, so did Hanford and the surrounding community. Under a new contractor, General Electric, more reactors were built—eventually nine would operate at once—along with new refining facilities called PUREX (Plutonium-Uranium Extraction Facility) and PFP (Plutonium Finishing Plant).

The Tri-Cities prospered. Everything in this sunny little community suggested 1950s normalcy: the straight rows of neatly kept homes, the countless women's clubs, and the bustling new schools. The only difference was that people never talked about what they did at work. And while school children in other cities went through "duck and cover" exercises to help them survive a hypothetical Soviet nuclear attack, the children in Richland had "bus drills." Local authorities were so certain Hanford was a Soviet target that they practiced evacuating the children to points in the desert miles away, where they would presumably be safe.

Eventually people stopped giving much thought to the differences between their community and others. The citizens of the Tri-Cities took it for granted that every year the FBI would come to ask questions about their neighbors. They grew accustomed to leaving urine samples on the doorstep for the Hanford health scientists to pick up early in the morning. And they accepted as normal the occasional visits by men with Geiger counters who would check their carpets and furniture for stray bits of radioactive material.

These kinds of experiences became part of everyday life in a community that embraced the atom. In the Tri-Cities, merchants opened businesses named Atomic Bowling, Atomic Foods, even Atomic Lawn Care. In Richland, the high school athletic teams were called the Bombers. The graceful symbol of an atom, with its orbiting electrons, adorned jackets, bumper stickers, a movie theater, even the columns that guarded the entrance to one of Richland's cemeteries. People were so proud of being citizens of America's "atomic city" that when Richland finally became an independent municipality, the town fathers included a mock atomic explosion in the celebration.

If its peculiar industry made the Tri-Cities a unique community, the atom had little apparent effect on those who lived closest to the reservation—the farm families of Mesa and surrounding Franklin County. Hidden as they were behind the ridge, these people couldn't actually see the reactors and plutonium processing factories. In fact, the Bailies and their neighbors wouldn't have been aware of Hanford at all, if it weren't for the occasional visits by scientists and the overflights of airplanes. The airplanes—shiny DC-3s—would lumber overhead, sometimes as low as a few hundred feet. Tom Bailie and other children would run through the fields, waving their arms wildly, hoping the pilots would return their greetings. Though they couldn't know it at the time, some of the airplanes carried special equipment that detected radiation. The pilots, who were chasing hot particles emitted by Hanford, were too busy to wave.

The scientists were much friendlier. Some came to take samples of water, soil, and even the remains of slaughtered animals. Others visited each fall to hunt on Bailie lands. Always friendly, they would never neglect to ask about the condition of the livestock and crops. And they always inquired about the health of the family.

As he grew older, Tommy Bailie's health improved, and his family prospered along with the region. This wealth was created in large part by a series of pumping stations, ditches, and canals that were constructed to bring water to nearly half a million acres, including the Bailie farm. In the late 1950s and early 1960s, this Columbia Basin Irrigation Project turned the area into one of the richest agricultural regions in the world. Using modern machinery, fertilizers, and pesticides, the Basin farmers could produce huge crops of wheat, corn, fruits, and vegetables. As much as the farmers complained about taxes, government interference, and bureaucratic incompetence, they also benefited greatly from the federally financed, low-cost water, crop subsidies, and cheap electric power provided by the government-built Bonneville Power Administration.

BPA power, the irrigation project, and government land sales lured thousands of new families to the small farming communities along the eastern shore of the Columbia. Tommy Bailie's first-grade class in the nearby Eltopia village school had three children; by eighth grade there were nearly ninety in his class. Like all the farm children, young Bailie's life was filled with chores and outdoor activities. A good-natured boy with bushy blond hair and clear blue eyes, he helped with every aspect of farming, even assisting when it was time to birth calves and lambs. Sometimes animals were born deformed or stillborn. Farmers like Tommy Bailie's father would shrug and declare these births to be nature's mistakes; when he was old enough to shoot a .22 rifle, Tommy Bailie reluctantly shared the responsibility for ending their suffering.

Compliant and responsible as a young boy, Bailie developed a wild streak as he grew older. At ten, eleven, and twelve, he became involved in frequent fistfights in the windswept dirt yard outside the three-story Eltopia school. As the smallest boy in his class, he was the first to be challenged by the sons of the newcomers. He always lost, and the humiliation of losing his spot in the playground pecking order burned in his chest.

In high school, Bailie learned to use humor to escape confrontations and get attention. Though he had once been an A student, his grades plummeted as he poured most of his energy into his social life. He began to spend much of his spare time in the bunkhouse on the farm, talking and drinking beer with the hired men. On occasion, some of the old-timers would seem to Bailie to wax paranoid when it came to Hanford. They would make up stories about everything from flying saucers hovering over the reservation to invisible atomic gas that killed and deformed livestock. (This bit of local lore was supported by an incident in 1951, reported in *The New York Times,* in which four air force pilots claimed to have seen a flying saucer over the Hanford Reservation.)

At other times, Bailie and his friends drove back roads, drinking and searching for excitement. They especially enjoyed slipping past the guards and under the fence to ride their motorcycles in the big, wild areas of Franklin County that still belonged to the Atomic Energy Commission. In the vast expanse, Bailie and his buddies would encounter wild deer, foxes, and coyotes. They would break the windows of the old houses still standing on the site, and steal fruit from the few trees that still produced. Eventually an airplane from the Hanford Patrol would buzz overhead. Bailie, who remembered the armed guards who had walked the fenceline when he was a little boy, never stayed around to see the plane land on an old road, but his friends would linger just long enough to feel the rush of adrenaline as the guard emerged from the plane and began to chase them.

Bailie pursued these adventures with an enthusiasm he lacked at school. He was frequently expelled, or forced to transfer between Connell High School, north of Mesa, and Pasco High School, to the south. His girlfriend, Cathy, became pregnant in 1964, before Bailie turned seventeen. They married and soon had a daughter, Jill. After graduating from high school, Bailie attended community college and worked nights for the railroad, which ran both freight and passenger trains through Pasco. He eventually dropped out of college and set about farming on his own. In 1969, at age twenty-two, he talked his way into taking over a foreclosed farm comprising 360 acres off Russell Road in Mesa, with a house, outbuildings, and a substantial loan from the Farmer's Home Administration. But in the same year his marriage fell apart, and his wife took Jill to California.

Through the 1960s and 1970s, while Bailie lived a very active single life and worked hard at becoming a successful farmer, across the river Hanford coped with changing technology and evolving geopolitics. The eight reactors that were built in the 1940s and 1950s were closed, leaving only the newest, N Reactor, operating. In 1972, Richard Nixon and Soviet president Leonid Brezhnev signed the first treaty limiting nuclear weapons. With an era of peace on the horizon, America's need for weapons-grade plutonium waned. While N Reactor continued to operate, generating electric power and a reserve supply of plutonium, the PUREX refinery was placed on "cold standby."

The Nixon-Brezhnev era of detente pushed the world back from the nuclear brink, but the prospect of peace brought worry to the Tri-Cities. Hundreds of workers were laid off and Hanford's future was in doubt. Things got worse in 1976, when a chemical explosion in a laboratory contaminated ten workers. One, Harold McCluskey, received such a heavy dose that he became known as "the atomic man." This was one instance when Hanford fell under the scrutiny of the press, and it was a public-relations nightmare for the Tri-Cities. Another setback occurred at about the same time, when it was discovered that the steel tanks holding millions of gallons of waste had begun to leak. Outside critics used these problems to raise doubts about the safety of the national nuclear weapons program, but the publicity did nothing to dampen support for Hanford in the Tri-Cities region. Civic boosters and the state's political leaders responded to the shutdowns and the bad publicity with a proposal to create an "atomic park" at Hanford, where a huge complex of reactors would be built to produce electricity, develop medical isotopes, and aid research. By the mid-1970s it seemed this atomic center might become a reality. The Department of Energy began construction of an experimental reactor, the Fast Flux Test Facility (FFTF), to produce special isotopes. And the Washington Public Power Supply System, a consortium of utilities known as WPPSS (pronounced "whoops"), proposed to build five or more atomic generating stations, including three at Hanford. WPPSS and FFTF promised a renewed prosperity for the Tri-Cities.

But as the Hanford community celebrated the bounty of the atom, the rest of the nation was growing increasingly wary of this technology. Since Hiroshima and Nagasaki, America had experienced two nuclear buildups. One had involved weapons, the other power plants. In the 1970s—long after the Ban-the-Bomb movement had withered—modern opposition to both programs grew.

Nuclear plants attracted attention first as citizens' groups began to use the licensing process, which required public participation, to slow and eventually block the construction of dozens of reactors on the grounds that they threatened both the environment and public safety. Critics were concerned that the nuclear industry had never found a way to dispose of the waste from power plants. They also worried that natural disasters such as earthquakes, or accidents caused by faulty equipment or worker errors, might lead to radiation releases. The government responded to these concerns with increased regulation and safety requirements, which helped double and even triple the cost of construction, thus making nuclear plants less and less attractive.

Although environmental activists did much to hamper atomic development, the most serious blow to the nuclear power industry was self-inflicted. The near meltdown of a reactor at Three Mile Island near Harrisburg, Pennsylvania, in 1979 all but destroyed public confidence in atomic energy. Matters were not made any easier for the atomic community by the release, at this time, of the hit movie *The China Syndrome,* which followed the fictional malfunction of a reactor in terrifying detail. As public opinion turned against nuclear plants, utilities simply stopped proposing to build them. Several plants were abandoned in the middle of construction, and scores were left on the drawing board.

Everywhere the nuclear industry was on the defensive—except in the Tri-Cities. In 1979 the WPPSS project was already under way, and the utilities found a uniquely welcoming environment. FFTF and WPPSS moved forward, and then a third big atomic project appeared on the horizon. Anticipating a modernization of the nuclear arsenal, officials in the Carter administration decided PUREX would be needed again. Even more workers were hired as the main

contractor, Rockwell Hanford Corporation, began the long process
of refurbishing the twenty-four-year-old plant so that it could once
again turn the plutonium created by the N Reactor into weapons-
grade material.

The WPPSS building boom, FFTF, and the return of PUREX
made the Tri-Cities a nuclear boomtown once more. Thousands of
itinerant construction workers, "atomic cowboys," came seeking
jobs that paid forty thousand dollars a year and more. Housing
developments sprang out of the scrub brush and shopping centers
rose beside newly paved roads. In the early 1980s a new president,
Ronald Reagan, accelerated the nuclear buildup, and communities
with bomb-making industries were flooded with defense dollars.
For a brief time the Tri-Cities could count on WPPSS, FFTF, and
PUREX to provide high-paying jobs. Employment, wages, and
real-estate values soared.

This heady period was short-lived. The legacy of Three Mile
Island, and astounding cost overruns, finally caught up to WPPSS
in early 1983. Four of the project's five reactors were canceled, and
WPPSS declared the largest bond default in U.S. history: $2.5
billion. Fortunately for the Tri-Cities, the weapons buildup softened the effect of losing one of the WPPSS reactors. As long as
America still faced a nuclear threat from the Soviet Union, it
needed PUREX and N Reactor. The atomic cities would survive,
as they had for four decades, as a center for plutonium production
and nuclear research. Civic leaders were confident of the future,
despite distant rumblings of opposition to the atomic buildup. In
Europe, on the East Coast, and in California, protesters massed at
peace rallies. Activists chained themselves to the gates of military
bases and splashed blood on the walls of the Pentagon. These
protests got on television and into the newspaper, but they didn't
seem to affect Hanford. America's policy of maintaining nuclear
superiority over the Soviet Union remained intact. President Reagan declared the Soviet Union an "evil empire" to be countered by
American might. And he proposed a series of new weapons—missiles, bombers, and submarines—that would all be armed with
nuclear devices. "Peaceniks" notwithstanding, Hanford's future as
a center of plutonium production seemed secure.

Through the 1970s and the early 1980s, as Hanford endured cycles of cutbacks and expansion, Tom Bailie's farm grew. He leased extra acreage and got into the beef-cattle business with his cousin Manton Bailie. During this time Bailie also met and married his second wife, Linda Pickett, the daughter of a Hanford worker who had helped run one of the old reactors. A former airline stewardess, Linda was enchanted by both her farmer husband and rural life. She loved animals and children—but she and Tom would never have children of their own. Tom, they discovered, suffered from a progressive kind of sterility; Jill would be his only natural child. Eventually the Bailies would adopt three daughters, Tomalin, Meggin, and Tamson, and a son, Zachary. Their home bustled with children and pets. But Tom would always be bothered that he would never have a child with Linda.

Bailie felt a deep sense of satisfaction as he worked the land and moved among the people of his community. Perhaps more than other local families, the Bailies were part of the landscape. Uncle Loen, who still lived nearby, had helped lead the political fight to get the irrigation project started. He and others in the family were big contributors to local political and charitable causes. But their main civic interest was the Bailie Ranch, a working farm that also served as a shelter for troubled youth. The ranch and their long involvement in community life gave all the Bailies a sense of ownership of the generously fertile region that was their home. They had been here almost as long as anyone. They could remember when there wasn't any water or electricity or roads. And they were deeply proud of the green prosperity that they could see every time they sat in a tractor or drove down a country lane.

Though his family was well known around Franklin County, Tom Bailie was mainly a private person until the BPA proposed to build a power line along a route that took it across several local farmers' lands, including Bailie's. The power-line towers would block the routes Bailie and other farmers normally followed when they plowed. They would also cut down the area that could be covered by the moving irrigation sprinklers that crawled across the fields on five-foot-high metal wheels. In the early 1980s, Bailie led the farmers against the power line. He eventually lost, and the power line was built. But in the process he discovered that he liked

politics. Like his Uncle Loen, he enjoyed participating in the decisions that guided the future of his community. In the summer of
1983, Bailie had some flyers printed and began to campaign for the
state senate. He ran as a Democrat who would stand up for the little
guy, as he had in the power-line case, promising to keep taxes down
and do his best to promote economic development.

The subject of Hanford didn't come up in the campaign until
Bailie was invited to meet with the editorial board of the local
newspaper, the *Tri-City Herald.* Bailie was nervous. An endorse-
ment from the paper, the only daily in the region, could be a
significant boost. A poor showing before the board would damage
his candidacy.

The *Herald* was a tireless booster for all things nuclear. Bailie had
this in mind when one of the editors asked what he thought about
nuclear technology and the future of Hanford. And he considered
offering a diplomatic response. But Bailie and his neighbors had
always harbored suspicions about Hanford.

"Well, me and my family have been here forever and we've
farmed right up to the fenceline of the reservation," Bailie responded. "Nothing ever happens with Hanford, except maybe we
get a few dead and deformed sheep once in awhile."

The *Herald* had once sent reporters to investigate the rumors of
dead and deformed livestock. But all the scientific experts at Hanford had said the plants on the reservation couldn't have harmed
the animals without leaving a trail of radiation behind. And there
wasn't any radiation trail. The editor asked Bailie if he had any new
evidence connecting Hanford to the problem.

"Well, no, I can't tell much more than what I said," Bailie
answered. Bailie couldn't even explain why he had said it. "It was
really just a joke. I don't have anything against Hanford personally.
I support nuclear power, and I figure we got to have nuclear
weapons.

"Don't get me wrong," Bailie added nervously. "It's just something some of us out in Mesa have always heard. It's a joke, really.
Let's talk about something else."

Bailie tried to steer the conversation toward economic development and agricultural policy. But the interview was soon finished,
and the main impression he had left was that of a loose cannon. He

departed the paper convinced the editors would endorse his opponent, which they did. Through the fall, Bailie campaigned door to
door, but it was little use. He was overwhelmed in the election.
When it was over, all he had left was a bruised ego and a gnawing
curiosity about Hanford. The stories about dead and deformed
livestock had always fascinated Tom Bailie. As the year ended and
a cold wind blew in from Canada, covering his winter wheat with
snow, he couldn't get the mystery out of his mind.

# THE ACTIVISTS

IN THE SPRING of 1984, thirty years after he saw the soldiers marching through the dust at his father's farm, Tom Bailie climbed into a huge green John Deere tractor and rode out to one of his fields to plant silage corn. As he sat about ten feet off the ground and steered along perfectly straight rows, Bailie was enveloped by the constant, numbing roar and whine of the machinery. Beneath him the tractor and its attachments made the furrows, spit the seeds into the ground, applied fertilizer, and covered them. Bailie could plant acre after acre and not even touch the soil.

In the solitude of the tractor's cab, Bailie's mind drifted across the river, to Hanford. Since the meeting at the *Tri-City Herald,* an old high school buddy of his, who worked at the site, had stoked Bailie's curiosity with stories about excess radiation sent up the smokestacks at various facilities. He had even given him a few documents that seemed to show radiation measurements made throughout Franklin County. Bailie couldn't make sense of the numbers. But they made him worry.

About 125 miles north of Mesa, a preacher who lived and worked in Spokane was also preoccupied with the nuclear reservation. A balding man with a gray beard and a middle-aged paunch, the Reverend William Harper Houff did not look like a wild-eyed political radical. Indeed, he was reluctant to get involved. He had assumed that his time of fiery social activism had ended long ago. But now the senior minister of the Unitarian church of Spokane was troubled by a familiar feeling. He had felt it in the early 1960s, before he delivered a sermon titled "Tragic Mistake in Vietnam." The good Baptists of the Shenandoah Valley, where Houff had been raised on a small farm, would have called this feeling "the burden of conscience."

The preacher had begun to sense this particular burden in January, when a Seattle newspaper reported that Hanford's Plutonium-Uranium Extraction plant—PUREX—had puffed excess radiation from its two-hundred-foot smokestack, and that officials had decided against notifying the public. The story got out when a whistle-blower working at PUREX placed an anonymous call to the paper. Months later, Hanford managers were still trying to explain which radioactive isotopes—plutonium or the less dangerous thoron—had gone up the stack, and why they had kept the release secret.

Houff had been further alarmed by a speaker at a recent meeting of area ministers. Joan Mootry, a local antinuclear activist, had talked about the potential hazard posed by the restarting of PUREX and warned of a government plan to create a permanent nuclear waste dump at Hanford. Called the Basalt Waste Isolation Project, the dump would be a final resting place for nearly all of the nation's high-level radioactive waste. If it was built, thousands of shipments of nuclear wastes would likely pass through the center of Spokane on their way to Hanford, where they would lie in a poisonous state for thousands of years.

In the weeks following the pastors' meeting, Houff read several books and articles on radiation and nuclear technology. He held a Ph.D. in chemistry, and though he hadn't worked in the field since he became a minister in 1964, he considered himself well qualified to judge what he read. He was most disturbed by *Killing Our Own,* a primer for the antinuclear movement that traces nearly a century of accidents, mishaps, and fatal misconceptions about the atom. It describes the lung cancers suffered by uranium miners, the quiet damage done by X rays, and the dangers posed by atom bomb tests and nuclear wastes. It even refers to the deaths of young factory women who had licked their brushes while decorating watch dials with radium paint in the 1920s. In Ottawa, Illinois, where one watch factory was located, the bodies of some of these women buried in a local cemetery, remain radioactive. In all, the book's authors claim, tens of thousands of people have been killed silently by radiation's slow-working effects.

Of course, those on the other side of the nuclear debate would

argue that atomic energy, nuclear medicine such as radiation treat-
ments for cancer, and even nuclear weapons have made an im-
measurable contribution to society. They might admit that honest
mistakes have been made by those charged with safeguarding people and the environment. But atomic advocates also insist that
modern science knows enough about the effects of radiation to
ensure that it is handled safely, and that, besides, no large-scale
study has been done that definitively proves, or disproves, the
connection between low-level radiation and cancer.

None of the atomic industry's arguments mattered on the Sunday morning in May when Houff stood, trembling slightly, before
his congregation. He hadn't checked any of the pro-nuclear
sources, and he wouldn't have trusted them if he had. For more
than twenty years his main interest in science had been moral. He
was particularly concerned about the responsibilities that accom-
pany the benefits of new technology. He was convinced that sometimes humankind was unable to handle the moral burden that came
with unlocking Nature's secrets. In the case of nuclear technology,
Houff concluded that a Frankenstein's monster had been un-
leashed. He was certain that Hanford threatened the environment
of the Pacific Northwest and the health of its people. He had never
intended to make an unbiased study of the issue. The danger was
real, and time was short. He felt compelled to warn his congregation at a Sunday service.

"Today the word holocaust is most frequently associated with
nuclear war, as in nuclear holocaust," Houff began. "But the holocaust I'm looking at is not presaged by the mushroom cloud.
Rather, it is silent. Not only is it silent, but except through certain
kinds of scientific instruments and the broken health of living creatures, atomic radiation is not detectable at all. Its silence is also
manifested in the fact that despite massive evidence, American
officials have uttered almost no words of alarm."

Years of study and travel had erased all evidence of the South
from Houff's speech. Now he possessed an almost professional
speaking voice, one that made him sound more like a TV newscaster than like the Bible-thumping preachers he had heard as a
child. Houff hoped to inspire with reason rather than theatrics. But
this subject, and his convictions, had moved him to write a text that

was both impassioned and dramatic. And he was flushed by emotion as he spoke. Hanford had made him both angry and afraid. These feelings were in the tremor of his voice and the words he chose.

"*Holocaust* may seem too strong a word to apply to this situation. But I doubt that it is. Not only have hundreds of thousands—and probably millions—of persons died because of such radiation, but many more millions will almost surely die in the future. It may well be that through ignorance and deceit we have already set in motion the processes and forces which will annihilate the human species at least as effectively as would an all-out nuclear war."

Houff preached for more than an hour to a congregation that sat in shocked silence. Many of those listening knew nothing about Hanford's nuclear weapons production. Indeed, few people in the entire Northwest gave much thought at all to the mysterious atomic facilities that were scattered on the desert floor near Richland. Hanford was in an out-of-the-way spot, far from the major highways that ran east-west or north-south. Few would even think of visiting the area. Isolated and shrouded in official silence, Hanford was almost invisible. But as Houff recited a litany of atomic projects once thought to be safe but later discovered to be deadly, Hanford came into frightening focus. He mentioned the watch-dial painters who had died of cancer of the esophagus, and the soldiers and sailors who had witnessed atom bomb tests and later developed deadly tumors. But more frightening than the deaths that were caused by radiation was the silence of those who understood the hazard but said nothing.

"One of the most heartless results of official policy is that, through silence, it has allowed thousands to delay treatment for what are probably radiation-induced illnesses until it is too late," Houff declared.

The main scientific source for Houff's arguments was a group of researchers who had made careers out of challenging the nuclear establishment. One of the most outspoken of these was Ernest Sternglass, a professor of radiology at the University of Pittsburgh Medical School, who claimed that fallout from aboveground nuclear bomb tests had caused widespread cancers and other health problems. Sternglass and his allies represented a minority view, and their science was routinely attacked. But Houff believed their criticism of the scientific establishment was a warning sign, a red flag that should rouse public concern. A case in point was the dispute raging between the two camps over the effects of the Three Mile Island accident. Sternglass insisted that the TMI accident had caused an increase in infant mortality. Others said no health effects could be proved. Houff believed Sternglass and those who said that years before the accident there were signs that all was not well in the community nearest the reactor.

"Long before Three Mile Island melted down, the farmers in the area were complaining about strange things happening to their animals. Miscarriages were occurring, eggs were not hatching, animals were falling down and not getting up, calves were being born deformed, cats gave birth to entire litters stillborn, heifers were unable to conceive, and animals lost their hair in splotches." All of this anecdotal evidence was in dispute, but Houff charged that officials had never made a sincere effort to check the facts. Here was more evidence, he suggested, of how the nuclear establishment had violated the public trust. Even if one believed the technology was safe, Houff said, there was no reason to trust those in charge. "If you do," he concluded, "you are living in a fool's paradise."

The preacher went on to sound an alarm about resumed plutonium production at the Plutonium-Uranium Extraction Facility, and the government plan to use Hanford as a permanent repository for highly radioactive nuclear wastes. "Hanford . . . has already served as one of the major dumping grounds for these materials," he noted. Joan Mootry and others had stumbled upon the fact that enough radioactive liquid wastes had been poured into the soil at Hanford to fill a forty-foot-deep lake as big as the island of Manhattan. At the same time, untold quantities of fission by-products—flakes and particles of radioactive elements—had been released into the atmosphere around the plant. Of course, no one outside the government knew how much radiation might have leaked out of Hanford, or how many mishaps and near accidents had occurred there. Houff knew enough, however, to be afraid of the disposal project. But in the proposal, Houff also saw an opening. The legislation authorizing the creation of a repository had required the Department of Energy, which ran all of the government's atomic facilities and would develop the dump, to involve the general public in the process. Many in the energy department considered Hanford, with its seemingly stable geology, arid climate, and thousands of empty acres, an ideal place to entomb nuclear wastes for eons. But wherever they chose to place the dump—Hanford was one of nine potential sites—the Department of Energy would have to disclose information about the condition of the property and the potential environmental impact of a repository. This meant it would have to reveal Hanford's mysterious past. Houff called on his congregation to use this opening to demand information and confront "politicians, bureaucrats, and technicians who offer us platitudes and lies while inexorably killing us and our unborn children. We need to become more humble and demand more honesty in ourselves and our public officials." He lowered his voice at this point, and spoke slowly, pleadingly. "We need to admit that we don't know what we are doing . . . especially we need to stop trusting scientists and officials with vested interests in the nuclear industry."

On a religious level, this pastor just didn't trust mankind with the power that came with creating new forms of matter. He feared that human attempts to harness atomic energy amounted to sinful hubris. "It may be," he concluded, "that we as creatures are constitutionally and morally incapable of managing the responsibilities we have so blindly assumed."

At the end of his sermon, the preacher invited people to gather after the service to talk about the issues he had raised. About forty members of the congregation stayed, pulling chairs into a circle in the church sanctuary. Stunned by what they had heard and almost entirely ignorant about Hanford and the whole process of making nuclear weapons, they talked for more than an hour. When there seemed to be no end in sight, Houff suggested they meet again after services the following Sunday. About two dozen of these people continued to meet through the summer, exchanging ideas and concerns about nuclear technology in general, and Hanford in particular. At the time they had no purpose, Houff would recall later, other than "therapeutic talking."

One curious member of the congregation did not join the after-church discussion group, even though she was fascinated by the subject. A youthful woman with shoulder-length blond hair, clear blue eyes, and a softly chiseled face, forty-one-year-old Karen Dorn Steele had listened and then left. She was concerned about what Houff had said. She was also impressed by his courage. After all, Spokane was a politically conservative place, where patriotism, respect for authority, and support for the government ran high. Defense industries and a local air force base that was home to a wing of nuclear-armed B-52 bombers were vital to the local economy. Anyone who spoke against the government and the defense establishment was inviting attack. But as a reporter for the local paper, the *Spokesman-Review,* Steele also knew that Houff and the Unitarian Church were about to make news. She had written of the plans to establish the atomic landfill, and she knew the issue would be an important story for years to come. She also knew that any reporter who wanted to cover it should be careful to avoid even the appearance of choosing sides.

Steele had an instinctive sense of how a reporter operates. Her father, Ronald Moxness, had been an award-winning writer for the Portland *Oregonian,* and she had grown up listening to journalistic war stories. In 1952, Moxness had left the paper to work for a Marshall Plan agency helping to rebuild Europe and Africa after World War II. Then nine years old, Karen went along, to postings in Brussels, Paris, and eventually Morocco. It was in Morocco that Karen developed the sensibilities of an outsider. She felt more isolated than she had in Europe, and she spent much of her time quietly observing both Arab culture and the behavior of her fellow Americans, whom she considered condescending to others. In Morocco she first felt the courage to question accepted wisdom and stand against a dominant group.

Steele returned to the United States to attend college at Stanford and earn a master's degree in history at Berkeley. Along the way she met and married a young lawyer named Charles Dorn. The couple moved to Spokane, and through the late 1960s and early 1970s the Dorns put down roots. Karen produced a weekly news program for children for the local public TV station. Her husband won election as a local judge, and they had two daughters, Trilby and Blythe. But despite a comfortable, outwardly successful life, the Dorns' marriage did not endure. In 1981 they were divorced. Suddenly single, Karen Dorn realized she might not make it on the tiny salary paid by the public TV station. When the Spokane paper offered her a raise in pay to be a reporter, she grabbed at the chance. And she discovered that, like her father, she loved the challenge and excitement of journalism. Her first important stories, about financial scandals in the local utility and problems with the WPPSS project at Hanford, earned her a reputation as ambitious and aggressive. But as she had done in Morocco, she could look at her community with the eye of the outsider. She believed she understood the world in a way others did not. She found a kindred spirit in Richard Steele, an old friend, whom she began dating and then married in the summer of 1983. Steele had an undergraduate degree in physics, which meant he could answer some of the technical questions his wife posed. But, more important, he supported her reflexive skepticism about government and politicians.

When she left church that Sunday in May, Karen Dorn Steele believed that Reverend Houff had issued a credible challenge to Hanford and the nuclear establishment, and she was intrigued. She went home and discussed what she had heard with her husband. He told her there was something to Houff's warnings. The critics of atomic technology were not all crackpots, he said. Atomic weapons and power plants did pose a potential threat to public health and the environment. He also predicted that the story of Hanford would become bigger than anyone imagined.

During the next few months, Steele threw herself into the task of understanding the history of atomic science and the politics of nuclear technology. She spent long hours in the newspaper's morgue and local libraries, foraging for articles, books, and papers on nuclear issues. Steele was already the paper's "energy and environment" reporter, and she had gained some understanding of the issues when writing about WPPSS and the dump proposal. But she sensed that Hanford would be more challenging than anything she had ever covered, and she wanted to use this time to learn as much as possible.

Steele also believed that she needed to arm herself for battle with some of the paper's editors. She was still relatively new to the staff, and unlike many of the male reporters, she had no mentor. Worse, some colleagues considered Steele a pushy, liberal-minded crusader. Like Spokane itself, the paper was conservative, and resistant to renegades who would question the status quo. In an ideal world, Steele thought, her editors would share her suspicions and turn her loose on Hanford, letting her dig into the story until she got results. She didn't expect this to happen. But she hoped that if she had enough facts, and solid leads for stories, they might let her pursue it further.

As she pored over background materials, Steele tried to understand the evolution of both scientific and popular attitudes about atomic hazards. The history books showed that by the 1940s, experts were well aware of the connection between radiation and certain cancers. They were absolutely certain that a sudden dose of intense radiation could be lethal. But there was a wide range of scientific opinion about how much low-level radiation a body could absorb without harm. This debate became a matter of public concern in the 1950s, as studies of the dispersal of fallout—radioactive particles from A-bomb tests—suggested that people far from the test sites were vulnerable. Several of the articles Steele found referred to a startling "washout" of radiation recorded during a storm in Troy, New York, in 1953, two days after a forty-three-kiloton explosion at the federal atomic test site in Nevada. Old Atomic Energy Commission records show that while some experts expressed concern, testing continued. Then, in 1956, a small group of Utah farmers living downwind from the test site sued the government, alleging that their sheep, lambs, and lamb fetuses had been injured and killed by fallout. The Atomic Energy Commission submitted studies proving that the sheep could not have been affected by radioactivity, and U.S. District Court Judge Sherman Christensen ruled against the ranchers.

While the courts, government agencies, and many scientists offered repeated public reassurances about radiation and fallout, the matter was by no means settled. In 1962, researchers proved conclusively that radioactive iodine 131 from fallout had been concentrated in milk. Iodine 131 has a tendency to settle in the thyroid, and causes both benign and cancerous tumors. Children, the main consumers of milk, were found to be especially vulnerable to this type of radiation.

Even after the danger posed by fallout became clear, great efforts were made to calm public apprehensions. In 1963, Edward Teller, the physicist known as "the father of the hydrogen bomb," appeared before Congress to declare that Americans needn't be concerned about fallout. "The real danger," Teller concluded, "is that you will frighten mothers from giving milk to their babies."

The fallout debate took place against the backdrop of the Cold War, and government officials often raised the specter of the Soviet menace to defuse concern about radiation from bomb tests. But concern about test-shot fallout persisted, and aboveground testing was finally stopped by the Limited Test Ban Treaty of 1963. The scientific dispute over the effects of fallout continued, however. It reached a high point in 1969 when, more than a decade after the washout over Troy, Ernest Sternglass published a paper connecting dramatic increases in infant deaths and childhood leukemia in upstate New York to radiation from nuclear tests. Using data from the New York Health Department, Sternglass estimated that 375,-000 American babies had been killed by fallout radiation in the years 1951 to 1966. He was challenged by other experts, but his paper, published in the *Bulletin of the Atomic Scientist,* attracted national media attention. The Sternglass report, and the wide circulation it received, foreshadowed a period when the scientific conflict over radiation and health would tumble out into the political arena.

As Karen Steele worked her way through the more recent history of America's experience with the atom, she noticed a gradual but dramatic change in public attitudes. Perhaps it was detente, or the general skepticism bred by the Vietnam War, but in the early 1970s greater numbers of critics raised their voices against nuclear technology. And it was not just atomic power plants that received scrutiny. Concerns were also raised about the safety of medical X rays and the possible health effects of the electromagnetic fields generated by everything from high-tension power lines to appliances.

It was comparatively easy for everyday citizens to gather information about power plants or medical X rays and voice their fears. But as Steele's struggle to investigate it showed, the nation's atomic bomb complex was another matter. The federal government's weapons laboratories and production facilities operated in utter secrecy. Even the people working inside these plants—in places such as Richland, Denver, Amarillo, and rural South Carolina— knew little about what occurred outside their small work areas. Outsiders understood only that the reactors, refineries, and assembly plants scattered across the country produced the nation's atomic arsenal. And it was the fear of these weapons, not concerns about the bomb factories themselves, that led to the growth of a large-scale American campaign against the arms-making industry in the 1980s.

The modern anti-nuclear-weapons movement arose as a reaction to Ronald Reagan's massive rearming of America. Supported by an overwhelming voter mandate, Reagan embarked on the largest peacetime arms program in history. He also adopted a new outlook on nuclear weapons. For almost forty years, presidents of both parties had subscribed to a doctrine called MAD, for "mutual assured destruction." This philosophy held that nuclear war would be averted by the fear that once begun, such a conflict would escalate, guaranteeing the destruction of all parties. Peace was achieved through a balance of terror. The Reagan administration was the first to suggest that a nuclear war might be won by one side or the other. One top official even said that "with enough shovels" Americans could hope to survive a Russian nuclear strike by hiding in hastily dug holes covered by wooden doors. The United States could then win a nuclear war by retaliating with its own missiles.

The Reagan buildup and abandonment of MAD frightened many people. In Europe, where citizens lived at the flashpoint of a superpower conflict, anti-nuclear-weapons activists portrayed America as bellicose and dangerous. Their movement spread quickly to the United States, where critics argued that the president's policies would tip the balance of power and invite a preemptive Soviet attack. Thousands of people were arrested during protests at military bases and weapons contractors' factories. Hundreds of American cities and towns declared themselves "nuclear-free zones," where nuclear weapons and power plants would be banned. While this movement may have been dismissed by nuclear workers in the Tri-Cities, it represented a historic change in public attitudes about nuclear arms. For the first time a substantial percentage of the Western world no longer accepted atomic arsenals as a necessary evil. The fervor of the antinuclear crusade was increased by a new ecological theory developed by prominent scientists, most notably the physicist and popular writer and TV documentary narrator Carl Sagan. Sagan and the others believed that an atomic war would produce so much smoke and hurl so much dust into the atmosphere that the world's climate would be changed. Even if one side appeared to win a nuclear battle, a cold, dark "nuclear winter" would settle on the land, destroying most living things.

The anti-nuke crusade was further helped from an unlikely quarter—network television. In November 1983, ABC broadcast *The Day After,* a disturbingly effective drama about nuclear war and its aftermath. The program was so upsetting to children that many schools developed special lessons to reassure them that efforts were being made to prevent nuclear war. The film became the subject of an intense political debate that lasted into the 1984 presidential campaign. Antinuclear activists showed videotapes of *The Day After* to raise emotions at rallies and public meetings. Those who supported the American arms buildup dismissed the program as the fantasy of left-leaning Hollywood propagandists. But its effect could not be denied. It alarmed millions.

With her background in history, Karen Dorn Steele understood the larger currents of change that allowed the peace movement to flower and created an audience for *The Day After.* Public attitudes toward government, science, and technology had undergone a profound transformation with Vietnam and Watergate. The expansive confidence of the postwar era had faded. Great numbers of people had lost faith. They no longer trusted federal officials. They no longer believed that science and technology would yield an endlessly brighter future. They no longer believed in progress for the sake of progress.

Steele's research also showed that the atomic bomb complex, and Hanford in particular, was rarely the subject of public scrutiny, and it had operated with virtually the same top-secret status since World War II. Early historical materials referred to the "Hanford Works" and its vital role in the Manhattan Project and continued plutonium production. But what little she found on Hanford's effect on the surrounding environment was inconclusive. Highly technical reports, published for the benefit of scientists, suggested that Hanford had done no damage. But then there were the leaking waste tanks, the "atomic man" explosion, and the whistle-blower's report on the January 1984 PUREX releases. Finally, she had to consider the pattern of government secrecy and coverups in the long history of nuclear technology. Keeping this pattern of deception in mind, she couldn't believe that Hanford was as safe as the record suggested. She was sure that the fences that protected PUREX, N Reactor, and the other facilities also protected secrets that would have a direct bearing on the proposed nuclear waste site, PUREX, and the future of the reservation. But as a citadel of the Cold War, Hanford was hidden behind a wall of national security concerns. Everything having to do with plutonium was secret. She could only guess what was contained in the thousands of classified reports Hanford had produced. And like every other skeptical outsider who tried to get past the official history of Hanford, Steele made little headway.

Through the summer, as Steele labored in the library, the discussion group at the Unitarian church experienced similar frustrations. Some of the church members spent hours with computer data bases and scientific indexes, searching for information to share at the Sunday meetings. Others went to Richland to look for materials in the Department of Energy's public reading room, which held a small number of unclassified reports. There was little in these documents suggesting any controversy. But they were not satisfied. If what Houff had said in his sermon was true, if the atomic industry was beset by technical problems and arrogance, there should be some evidence of Hanford's effect on the region's environment and public health. Frustrated as they may have been, they also became obsessed with finding out more.

This obsession was fed by their fear of both the waste-isolation project and the nuclear arms buildup. Many in the church group found themselves sympathizing with the peace activists who mounted protests around the country at arms depots, weapons factories, and federal buildings. These protests were often organized by churches and inspired by an antinuclear document adopted by America's Catholic bishops. The document questioned the morality of nuclear weapons and called for both sides to stop the arms race. Some individual bishops went further, denouncing the very existence of nuclear weapons as evil and calling on Catholics to work for their elimination. Other denominations followed the lead of the Catholics, making antinuclear work a matter of religious conviction.

The Spokane church group concluded that their community was on the front lines of the worldwide nuclear controversy. By summer's end they had founded HEAL, the Hanford Education Action League, as a base for action. At first some members advocated direct protest: sit-ins on the roads leading to Hanford, vigils, and mass protests. But there were others who wanted to take a more sophisticated political approach. Gradually this side won out, and it was decided that HEAL's official purpose would be to promote public involvement in the decision on the waste repository. HEAL's activists would avoid discussing nuclear weapons policy and national defense, and would focus only on the environmental and health issues associated with the nuclear dump and PUREX.

HEAL was to be a grassroots organization. Its founders believed that everyday citizens—taxpayers—owned the nuclear weapons complex, and they believed that in a democratic society they should play an active role in deciding its fate. Houff argued that no matter how complex an issue became, citizens should be trusted to make the ultimate decisions. And he said that HEAL's citizen activists didn't have to know everything about Hanford to start fighting. All they had to do was raise enough doubts to tap the public's latent skepticism about nuclear technology and big government.

As the months went by, HEAL's members became remarkably well informed on the general problems affecting the nuclear industries. They got background materials from longtime activists such as Joan Mootry, and learned research techniques from a free-lance journalist named Larry Shook, who became a member of HEAL after writing several articles about Hanford. Shook enjoyed jousting with bureaucracies over information. But the Hanford issue had pushed him out of the role of journalist and into that of activist. He was motivated by fear—not the fear of what he knew about Hanford, but the fear of what he didn't know.

Years after his work with HEAL ended, Shook recalled one of the encounters that made him afraid of Hanford. He had gone to Richland to interview some scientists about PUREX stack releases. "When they said that plutonium had not been released, I asked them to prove it," he remembered. "They were stunned by this, hurt actually. They said, 'Larry, why don't you wish to believe us?'

"I said, 'It doesn't have anything to do with what I wish. This is about science. Numbers. You can't just believe what someone says.'

"This is when they got very excited. One of the women was really upset. She told me, 'I have children and grandchildren living near here. Do you think I would do anything to hurt them?'

"I didn't think she would. But that wasn't good enough. We had to ask them to show us the documentation that says it's safe. They couldn't, and that worried me, a lot."

During his first months with HEAL, Larry Shook guided the group's effort to use the Freedom of Information Act to pry more information about Hanford out of the government. Adopted in the Watergate era, the act (known by the acronym FOIA) established a procedure for citizens to receive government documents. But it also allowed agencies to hold on to information deemed sensitive to national security. The Department of Energy had hidden Hanford behind this shield for years, and HEAL's members did not expect that their request would produce much meaningful information. Still, Shook wrote several requests for information, making them as broad and inclusive as possible. He asked for all documents relating to radiation mishaps—"unusual occurrences," in the language of Hanford—and for environmental monitoring reports.

While Shook could help the group with research, HEAL relied on Allen Benson, Ph.D., a chemistry professor at Spokane Falls Community College, to analyze the materials they collected. Then forty-eight years old, Benson believed that mainstream scientists, especially those paid by the government, had no monopoly on truth. He advised the members of HEAL to study what they could find on the effects of radiation and the history of nuclear science. "Don't let them get away with making statements without backing them up," he advised. "Make them prove it."

Allen Benson was the child of a poor Montana farmer who had taught his son to question authority and think for himself. (In seventh grade, young Benson got into serious trouble when he opposed a plan to name his junior high after the superintendent of schools. He told his teacher the superintendent was a mediocre man undeserving of the honor.) As an adult, Benson had worked as a miner and laborer for the railroad before earning degrees in teaching and physics. A voracious reader with eclectic taste, Benson was fascinated by the relationship between scientists and the larger society. He first became interested in Hanford when one of his classes examined how nuclear discoveries had been quickly put to practical use. He concluded that the experts had rushed to reap the benefits of nuclear technology without fully considering its potential for harm. From this study, Benson went on to become a prominent critic of nuclear technology. When voters were asked to authorize the WPPSS construction program in 1976, Benson appeared at public forums and in the media, pointing out the economic and environmental problems. His side lost, but Benson became a well-known watchdog of the local nuclear industry who, considering the WPPSS fiasco, might be viewed as rather prescient. From time to time disgruntled insiders would anonymously send Benson reports on problems at nuclear facilities, including commercial power plants in the region and Hanford.

Over the years, Benson amassed a small library of documents about Hanford. He had reports on leaking waste tanks, and others on the problems of "crib" systems, which were little more than great holes in the ground into which liquid wastes were dumped. He had old studies on the radioactive contamination of the groundwater beneath the reservation, and he possessed a large amount of information on problems at other nuclear facilities. He would use this information to help HEAL challenge the credibility of Hanford's science and the nuclear dump proposal. Benson was determined to emphasize scientific debate rather than politics. He did not share the others' fear of nuclear weapons, and he wouldn't engage in a moral debate about their existence. He was more concerned with the scientific integrity of the nuclear establishment and about the pollution and health effects that were hidden from public view. Benson supported the idea to make the word *education* part of the group's name and one of its primary functions. He believed that if the public could be educated on the scientific issues, the right decisions would be made when it was time to set production goals, establish safety standards, or choose the right site for an atomic dump.

Led mainly by Houff, Shook, and Benson, HEAL's amateur scientific sleuths searched for any evidence that would discredit Hanford's operators. One of their first valuable finds was a critique of the nuclear waste dump proposal done by the United States Geological Survey in 1983 and 1984. The geologists had checked research done by scientists working for Rockwell International— one of the contractors DOE had chosen to run Hanford—who had concluded that the basalt beneath the sands of the reservation would be a suitable place for a nuclear repository. The Rockwell report noted that it would likely take more than ten thousand years for groundwater to migrate from the dump site to the Columbia River. (Energy officials had determined that a ten-thousand-year flow rate was necessary to protect the river.) The geological survey experts believed this was unreasonably optimistic. In fact, the agency concluded, "it is possible to make rough travel-time calculations that are less than one thousand years." If this was true, Hanford would be disqualified as a nuclear waste repository.

Benson also helped focus HEAL's attention on a controversial health study done on Hanford workers by Dr. Thomas Mancuso, one of Ernest Sternglass's colleagues at the University of Pittsburgh. Mancuso was originally hired by the Atomic Energy Commission in 1964 to do the largest survey ever of workers exposed to low-level radiation. This work had the potential to settle, once and for all, the controversy over low-level doses. Mancuso had published a paper in 1977 that suggested that Hanford workers suffered excess bone marrow and pancreatic cancers, even when they had been exposed to radiation levels that were believed to be safe. Mancuso's work was roundly attacked, even by his former project manager, who said the cancers were likely caused by common environmental carcinogens, not radiation. Shortly after this exchange, federal officials terminated Mancuso's contract and handed his data to a Hanford-based researcher who concluded there were no excess cancers in the work force.

With these and other bits of information, HEAL's members started formulating serious questions about Hanford. Was the January 1984 release of extra radiation from PUREX a unique incident, or part of a pattern of problems? Was Mancuso's work on radiation and health stopped for political reasons? Why was the Department of Energy pressing ahead with the dump if the U.S. Geological Survey had found so many problems with the site? Armed with these concerns and others, they invited Michael Lawrence, DOE's recently appointed manager of Hanford, to provide some answers. At age thirty-six, Lawrence was among the brightest of the department's rising young stars. Before coming to Hanford, he had been the head of the Office of Civilian Waste Management, the very agency responsible for finding and licensing nuclear dump sites. A few months earlier Lawrence had appeared before Congress to defend the Reagan administration's waste-disposal program, which at the time had identified only Hanford and two other locations as candidate sites. By midsummer he was working in Richland as the federal government's manager of operations. Though he denied it, many in HEAL believed that Lawrence had been sent to ensure that Hanford would ultimately be chosen as the atomic dump site.

On a cool autumn night in 1984, Michael Lawrence, accompanied by his wife, Cindy, came to the Spokane Unitarian church with a slide projector in hand. A wiry, athletic-looking man, he kept his brown hair trimmed short to reflect a no-nonsense, confident manner. This was a self-consciously created image. Shy and fat as a child, Lawrence had learned the skills of debating in high school and had become an adept communicator. He took up running and adopted a careful diet. In his determination to overcome his ugly-duckling beginnings, Lawrence had become a self-described over-achiever. As one of a new breed of politically sensitive energy department managers, he believed that in the era following Three Mile Island, the department's most important challenge was public relations. At Hanford the flap over the PUREX release, and the waste repository controversy, had made this challenge even more difficult. But he was convinced that PUREX, the Plutonium-Uranium Extraction Facility—could be operated safely, and he knew that somebody had to find a solution to the country's nuclear-waste problem. Thousands of tons of high-level waste—the blue-green glowing by-product of commercial nuclear reactors—waited in temporary holding tanks. Someone had to take responsibility for getting rid of it.

Determined to improve the image of the Department of Energy and Hanford, Lawrence was eager to talk to HEAL. Though he held a bachelor's degree in physics, he considered himself a "people person" as much as a scientist. The department had begun a campaign to burnish its image. The entire nuclear industry was concerned about public-opinion polls showing that a majority of Americans believed a nuclear power plant could actually explode like an atom bomb. The Department of Energy had gone so far as to hire consultants to craft an extensive program for disseminating pro-nuclear arguments to influence public opinion in favor of atomic projects. All of this was done by officials like Mike Lawrence, who believed the nuclear community was under siege and needed to be defended with reassuring facts.

In this spirit, Lawrence arrived determined to defuse the emotional aspects of the nuclear debate. On the drive to Spokane, Cindy had reminded him that HEAL's members probably didn't trust anyone connected with the federal establishment. So he had decided that the best he could hope for was to begin a process of winning their trust. To do that, he would marshal the facts and present himself as a person of integrity and honesty. He had this in mind as he stood in the front of the sanctuary, next to a portable movie screen, facing about one hundred people arranged in orderly rows of plastic chairs. Before be began to talk, Lawrence paused for a moment and glanced at Cindy, who sat in the middle of the audience.

"I'm sure that there may be some differences of opinion tonight, but hopefully those differences will lead to a better understanding of the problems," Lawrence said as an assistant set up the slide projector. "So I really do appreciate opportunities like this to get out and talk to people about our operations. Okay, let's go to the projector."

The lights were turned down and Lawrence commenced with a fifteen-minute "This Is Hanford" presentation. As maps, pictures, and diagrams were flashed on a screen, he slipped comfortably into a monologue. The slide projector clicked one picture after another into place. Lawrence described the images on the screen.

Click.

"The Hanford site is located in central Washington along the Columbia River, and is 570 square miles."

Click.

"There are $5 billion worth of facilities, and those facilities range from nuclear power reactors to the common type of support facilities for any industrial activity including fire departments. . . . The budget for this year for Hanford is $937 million. . . . There are 13,350 employees on site. The 350 are federal employees. The other 13,000 are among the eight contractors. . . . Our missions at Hanford are of national significance. The largest is defense material production and the management of wastes resulting from it. . . . This is a picture of the N Reactor, which is located on the Columbia River. It is the only dual-purpose reactor in the free world. It produces plutonium for the defense program, but it also generates 850 megawatts of electrical energy which goes into the supply grid for the state and the region."

Though most of his comments were brief, Lawrence gave extra attention to the leaking waste tanks, one of the few problems at Hanford that had received public attention. "Those tanks did experience leaks," he said, without referring to the toxic nature of the wastes. "Unless we stabilized them, they would continue to leak. Therefore, we put a program into effect to fix them. What you see on the bottom of that slide are the tanks we assume to be leakers. By the late 1980s, all of these tanks will be stabilized and no longer in active service."

Along with pictures of N Reactor and waste tanks, Lawrence showed photographs of a grassland preserve that covered about one-quarter of the site, and drawings suggesting what the nuclear dump would look like. He reassured his audience that Hanford was only a potential site, that no decision had been made. He wanted them to trust in the site-selection process. He wanted them to trust him. "My job is not to get Hanford that repository program. It is to make sure that the data on which selections are made is good, sound technical data that can withstand scrutiny. And if that data says we should not look at it, then so be it. We'll walk away from the site."

It was a sincere pledge. But it didn't matter. The members of HEAL were not ready to trust Mike Lawrence or anyone else from the Department of Energy. Some in the crowd began to grow restless and impatient. Lawrence could hear the faint murmur of disagreement. Anticipating a skirmish on the issue of the health effects of radiation, Lawrence tried to stake out what he believed was a middle-ground position. "With any subject, you can have one scientist saying this and another saying that," he said. "But the observed incidence of cancer in Hanford workers is less than would be expected. If you break the cancers down into fine points, there are going to be variations. But, overall, the message I want you to take away is that we do study the health effects."

"Is the Mancuso data included in your report?" a woman in the audience shot back. "I'm talking about the Mancuso whose grant money was removed because of politics."

"Dr. Mancuso's findings have been reviewed by a number of bodies and found not to be valid," Lawrence replied. "There have been studies by the National Academy of Sciences and others that did not support his data, and that's why we do not use that data."

Although Lawrence considered the National Academy of Sciences a most credible judge, it was part of a scientific establishment that the HEAL members did not trust. Another questioner wanted to know how Lawrence could be certain that there were no excess cancers. "Were these observations made in the same year that the workers were exposed to radiation, or was the latency taken into account?"

"It was over a period of time," Lawrence answered. "It is not just what happened one year."

"Well, it seems to me the only good sample would be Hanford workers who were there at least twenty years ago," replied the questioner. "I think your figures might be treated with some skepticism."

As the night wore on, the HEAL group treated everything Lawrence had to say with some skepticism. Standing alone at the front of the room, Lawrence felt besieged. But he persevered, glancing occasionally at his wife, who smiled reassuringly as the meeting devolved into a series of confrontations. When Lawrence explained that the nuclear-waste-depository idea would be subjected to fair scientific scrutiny, several members of HEAL rose to challenge him.

"I have a report by the USGS, which reviewed the study done by DOE and Hanford," said one woman. "The USGS really refuted that study, saying that a lot of the data was inadequate and inaccurate. I am under the impression that this was more or less ignored by DOE."

Lawrence tried to reassure her that the USGS review would be considered. But he also wanted to defend his own people. "I said earlier this evening that you can always get one scientific body saying this and another saying that. The National Academy of Sciences looked at it and found some very beneficial aspects about Hanford. But the USGS report will also be taken into consideration if Hanford is one of the three sites characterized. Then we'll get the data to resolve the USGS questions about the basalt."

Others in the audience were worried about shipments of nuclear waste that might go through Spokane. They also brought up the matter of the January PUREX release, which had led the Department of Energy to halt operations for a time. "You stated several times that there was no plutonium released in January," said a young woman questioner. "But scientists from Hanford met with Allen Benson and they acknowledged that there had been significant quantities of plutonium released."

"I said the concentrations were first thought to be plutonium," answered Lawrence. "But on further analysis, the concentrations that led to the shutdown were thoron. I later said plutonium in small quantities was released to the environment, and the quantities were not of a significant level." (The thoron isotopes Lawrence referred to are less dangerous than plutonium.)

So it went for another hour, as HEAL members, well versed in antinuclear positions, peppered Lawrence with questions about PUREX and the atomic dump. There were some lighter moments during this long debate. At one point a crusty old man stood up and suggested that nuclear power be done away with entirely. "When you consider that the gambling houses and whorehouses in Las Vegas and Reno consume all the power of one nuclear plant, you can see a way to do it, too. Just shut 'em down. Besides, at least half of what they do down there would be performed better in the dark!"

Unfortunately for Lawrence, there were few such flashes of comic relief on this evening. Nevertheless, he thought he performed well. His main goal had been to put a human face on Hanford, to show the people of HEAL that they weren't dealing with a cold technological bureaucracy, but rather with reasonable, flesh-and-blood people. As the meeting wound down, he felt confident he had achieved this goal. He glanced knowingly at his wife and then called for one last question. A man who was sitting next to her stood to talk.

"Have you considered," he said in a slow, deliberate voice, "that what you are doing is analogous to the people who built gas chambers for Nazi Germany?"

Lawrence was immobilized for a moment. Then he gathered himself and offered a succinct answer.

"No, sir, I haven't. But I have thought very seriously about what I am doing, and I would not be doing it if I personally did not feel that what I was doing was contributing to peace."

In a moment the HEAL moderator who had introduced Lawrence rushed to the microphone. She pleasantly thanked him for coming, and announced that the meeting was over. Lawrence collected his slides, found his wife, and left.

When they got into the car, Cindy Lawrence was flushed with anger. The comment about Nazis had been too much for her to stomach. But though he appreciated his wife's anger, Mike Lawrence wasn't as much upset as he was intrigued. He had come to Spokane expecting an emotional encounter. But he hadn't understood the depth of the feelings held by some HEAL members. Now he knew.

Back inside the church, Larry Shook and Reverend Houff stood in the rear of the sanctuary, chatting as others put away the plastic chairs. Both men were chastened by what they had seen. Shook had not expected that Lawrence would be so relaxed, so convincing, so human. "This is going to be a lot harder than we thought," he sighed. Houff was more philosophical. "Down on the farm, we had these bugs that used to roll cow manure into little balls. Doodle-bugs. I used to think these bugs were the lowest form of life on earth. Well, when I grew up I found out these beetles were the sacred scarabs of the Egyptians. They symbolized immortality and resurrection, and the manure ball was a symbol for the world. Sometimes, Larry, when I start taking things too seriously, I try to remember that we aren't much different from the doodlebugs. We might roll our balls around bigger pastures, but in the end it's all still just cow shit."

At the time of the confrontation at the Spokane church, the national argument over atomic policy was reaching a noisy crescendo. In the 1984 presidential race, Democrats depicted Ronald Reagan as a warmonger whose fundamentalist Christian beliefs included the expectation of a world-ending, nuclear Battle of Armageddon. In his overwhelmingly successful campaign, Reagan painted the Democrats as weak on defense, and ignorant of how a "stand-tall" strategy would discourage Soviet aggression. Reagan prevailed in the election with one of the largest victory margins in modern times. But among a significant minority of citizens, fear and concern about nuclear weapons would continue to smolder.

In Washington State, politicians were more concerned by the problems of the WPPSS nuclear program. The largest nonmilitary atomic project in history, the series of five generating stations the Washington Public Power Supply System planned to build had suffered enormous cost overruns. After the 1983 bond default it was clear that only one of the consortium's reactors, Unit Number Two at Hanford, would ever operate. The debt associated with this debacle threatened to inflate consumers' bills and bankrupt the Northwest utilities that had backed construction of the five plants.

Together, the peace movement, the WPPSS fiasco, and the comprehensive press coverage of the whole nuclear debate drove public confidence in atomic technology to an all-time low. At this moment in history, a great many Americans worried that their country had made a Faustian bargain with the atom, trading potential environmental disaster for its secrets.

# THE REPORTER

IN THE FALL of 1984, at about the time when Mike Lawrence spoke at the Unitarian church, reporter Karen Dorn Steele attended a political fund-raising party for Spokane's Democratic congressman, Thomas Foley. She arrived at about eight o'clock, mingled with political sources, and inspected the Victorian-era house-turned-restaurant where the party took place. A landmark in the city's historic district, Patsy Clark's Mansion is a rambling yellow brick building with tall windows, enormous rooms, and opulent wood paneling. Steele drifted through the stately rooms until she found herself in one of the parlors, chatting with the congressman's wife, Heather Foley. She was about to ask about the congressional race when she heard what sounded like a fight breaking out across the room.

"You bastard! How could you let those sons of bitches testify against us?"

Steele turned to see a strongly built man in a blue blazer jabbing his index finger into the chest of the dean of the Washington State University School of Agriculture. The dean backed up, almost falling into a fireplace. As he did, the pipe he held in his hand fell to the floor and broke.

"We may be a buncha farmers, but it's our livelihood, damn it!" The accuser's face turned red with anger. "Don't you ever let that happen again. And don't think the Bailie family will ever support WSU."

By this time the other guests had stopped talking and were staring at the drama beside the fireplace. Heather Foley moved in to rescue the dean. In a matter of seconds she was asking Steele to escort his attacker away from the other guests.

Steele grabbed Tom Bailie by the arm and firmly invited him to join her for a drink. She thought she would take Bailie to look at the stained-glass window she had noticed on the landing of the mansion's front stairs. Holding his arm, she wove through the other guests, ignoring their stares and laughter. Bailie half resisted, but then lurched along behind her. As they passed the bar he grabbed a bottle of wine and two glasses.

Along the way, Steele reminded Bailie that they had met a few years before, when she covered the Mesa power-line controversy for the *Spokesman-Review*. "That was what I was yelling about," Bailie responded. He explained that the WSU dean had promised to help the farmers fight the Bonneville Power Administration at a judicial hearing. Instead, several WSU professors had testified that the power line wouldn't hurt the farmers. "They double-crossed us, you know, and I'm still pretty damn pissed off about it."

The two climbed the stairs, admired the window for a moment, and then sat on the landing. Steele was careful to keep some distance between herself and the drunken farmer. Alcohol can loosen inhibitions, and she wanted to be sure that Bailie remained as inhibited as possible. After establishing some physical distance, she poured herself a drink and asked Bailie about life in Mesa.

"Oh, jeez, it's the same old deal. Everybody's going broke. The Russian grain embargo broke everybody, and there's suicides. It's the same old stuff in agriculture." Bailie employed his best flat, ironic country accent and his most fatalistic attitude. It was a pose that allowed him to hint at serious problems, but not appear to be a complainer. He would look at his feet, shrug his shoulders, and claim to be a simple farmer. But whoever listened knew Bailie was smarter than he let on.

"You live next to Hanford, don't you?" Steele asked.

Bailie asked if Steele was "one of those radical anti-nukers," but didn't wait for her answer. Instead he told her that nuclear weapons were a necessary evil, the price of keeping the Communists at bay. When Steele asked if Bailie had ever noticed anything strange related to Hanford, the farmer fell back on the same line he had used during his disastrous meeting with the editorial board at the *Tri-City Herald*.

"Nah, hell, all Hanford ever does is kill and deform a few sheep once in a while."

"Deform sheep?"

Bailie went on to explain that in the early 1960s, farmers around Mesa had noticed an unusual number of deformities in their spring lambs. This reminded Steele of the Utah sheep kill that had occurred after bomb tests in the 1950s. She asked Bailie if he thought there might be a connection. He was sure there wasn't.

"That Utah thing was just a bunch of Mormons trying to cheat the government out of some money. They were lying about their sheep. They weren't feeding them right. It was a selenium deficiency or something. I know all about it."

Steele dropped this line of questioning, in part to cover her fascination. She couldn't understand why Bailie was telling her all this, and she didn't want to come on too strong and frighten him away.

The truth was that Bailie was trying to impress her. There was still a lonely farm boy inside of him, a boy who craved attention. The Hanford mystery was certain to catch Steele's attention. But Bailie was also baiting her, hoping she would do the work to confirm or disprove his fears about Hanford. Before the night was over, she took the bait, asking Bailie if he would introduce her to other farmers, if she ever got the chance to visit Mesa. In a somewhat slurred voice, he said he'd be happy to show her around Franklin County any time.

The farmer and the reporter talked and drank for at least an hour more, rehashing Bailie's failed state senate race and discussing Foley's reelection campaign. After the wine ran out, they went their separate ways. She left for home. He wandered about the party and eventually departed, driving the 120 miles south to Mesa.

The next morning, as Bailie drank coffee with a crowd of farmers at the Country Kitchen Cafe in Mesa, Karen Steele drove to work and thought about what he had said and how she would explain it to her editors. She parked her car in a company lot and walked up to the ornate brick building that had housed the paper since the turn of the century.

An almost arrogant structure, with turrets and elaborate brick-work, the *Spokesman-Review* building reflected the paper's position of influence and responsibility. For years it had been a middle-of-the-road kind of daily, where investigations took second place to basic reporting of community news. The *Spokesman-Review* moved cautiously when it came to controversy. Steele had this in mind as she tried to explain Bailie's story to assistant city editor Brenda Tabor. Tabor was skeptical. Bailie was a small-time politician, and she wondered aloud if he wasn't hoping to gain something by spreading rumors. She also believed that Steele had more than enough work to keep her busy. "And this isn't a very solid lead, is it?" she asked rhetorically.

The two women did not get along well. In a newsroom still dominated by male prerogative, they should have been natural allies. But Tabor, who was just thirty years old, worried that Steele's strong political views influenced her judgment. Steele seemed always to skate on the edge of biased advocacy, and Tabor believed it was her job to make sure her reporters obeyed the rules of conservative reporting. For her part, Steele saw Tabor as an overly cautious corporate climber who refused to take even modest risks. Steele was part of the post-Watergate generation of reporters who saw journalism as a sacred calling. She thought that Tabor was part of a younger crowd of newspeople who saw journalism as not much different from insurance or accounting. Rather than making a difference, they wanted to make more money, collect higher titles.

These personal differences were not the only reasons why Tabor didn't offer Steele the kind of wholehearted support she had hoped to get from her editor. Tabor also had to consider the time Steele might waste chasing the legend of the dead sheep. The paper didn't have enough reporters to follow every lead. Something would have to be neglected if Steele took up this story. All of this was in her mind as she thought about what Steele had laid out. But it wasn't quite enough to make her tell the reporter to drop it. Maybe it was the fact that Tabor knew good reporters followed even the most ridiculous leads, just in case. Maybe it was the fact that she had gone swimming in the Columbia downriver from Hanford when she was a little girl. Whatever the reason, she told Steele she could stick with the Bailie story, if only part-time. "Go ahead. Try to get some confirmation, something on the record," she said. "But try to do it in your spare time."

Through the winter of 1984–85, Karen Dorn Steele spent her evenings and weekends researching articles on Hanford and the proposed nuclear dump. Though the Department of Energy had named nine potential locations for the repository, Hanford was a favorite for a number of reasons: it was a vast, secluded territory; it was owned by the federal government; it had already served as a holding area for radioactive waste; and, best of all, the Tri-Cities—unlike most other communities—wanted it. So no one was surprised when Hanford was on the list of three final candidate sites announced by the Department of Energy in December 1984.

In the Tri-Cities, civic leaders celebrated the news that Hanford had made it to the final stage of the site-selection process. The Basalt Waste Isolation Project would create hundreds of high-paying jobs and ensure Hanford's future as an atomic center. But in other areas of Washington State, opposition to the repository was strong. The Spokane city council listened to a forty-five-minute presentation from HEAL and promptly passed a resolution opposing the nuclear-dump idea and the shipping of nuclear wastes through the city. At public meetings the State of Washington's Nuclear Waste Board heard endless complaints about the Department of Energy's plans. In a matter of weeks it became plain that the entire Northwest was against Hanford becoming a nuclear waste repository, except the Tri-Cities.

As she wrote about the public debate over the repository, Steele snatched time whenever she could to chase Tom Bailie's rumor. She read everything she could find on nuclear facilities in general and their effects on workers, nearby residents, and the environment. Through the Freedom of Information Act, she also requested reports on Hanford emissions. Although she hoped that she might stumble across something about Hanford, she was not optimistic. The Department of Energy could withhold almost anything by claiming its release would compromise national security. This had been standard procedure for decades, and there was no reason to hope that officials would do anything but drag their feet and then say no. At best, Steele believed, she might be able to put together enough information from outside experts to show that Bailie's fears had some foundation, that they were not simply a minor politician's self-serving grasp for publicity.

Much of her work was done in the newspaper's library and at college libraries around Spokane. Steele spent hours peering at computer screens, searching scientific data bases for references to Hanford. She copied scores of documents and brought armloads of books and articles home to read. The cedar-paneled living room of her home, a modern house overlooking a beautiful ravine on the west side of Spokane, was gradually filled with Hanford materials. Each night, after her daughters went to bed, Steele would sit on a sofa with stacks of papers and books spread out on the coffee table. The sofa faced a window, and as the evening wore on she could see the lights in the houses across the ravine go out, one by one. Steele was able to pour her nights into her work because she and her husband, Richard, had a long-distance marriage. He worked in Palo Alto, California, and lived there weekdays. This separation allowed each of them to be immersed in work without guilt.

As the winter of 1985 wore on, Steele gathered bits of information that fed her suspicions. Insiders at the U.S. Geological Survey told her they had serious doubts about the scientific integrity of some of the people at Hanford. They showed her internal memos from Rockwell International that suggested the contractor's feasibility study on the nuclear repository, which was supposed to be an unbiased investigation of the plan to bury waste in deep tunnels, was far from objective. In the memos, Rockwell officials noted that they intended to prove that the dump belonged at Hanford. But the scientific facts, according to USGS geologist Donald E. White, did not favor the project. The basalt where the wastes would be buried, in tunnels thousands of feet deep, presented serious problems. Core samples showed that the basalt was subject to frequent shifts, minor tremors that could cause rocks to burst, destroying tunnels or flooding them with water. And the rock formations under Hanford were so hot that the repository would have to be built with special air-conditioned sections to provide workers with some relief. "It would require refrigeration on a scale not yet attempted anywhere in the world," White said in an article Steele wrote. "I was very

disappointed when I saw that the Department of Energy had chosen Hanford as a finalist. They obviously hadn't paid attention to
my report."

The USGS experts also disagreed with the Department of Energy
and Rockwell when it came to the groundwater under Hanford.
Rockwell said it flowed under, not into, the Columbia River, and
that it would take ten thousand years for water contaminated by
nuclear waste to migrate off the site. The USGS found that the
underground water flowed directly into the Columbia River, at a
rate much faster than ten thousand years. Steele also came across
another critical assessment of the Hanford proposal, this one issued
by the Nuclear Regulatory Commission. Steele would eventually
report that the NRC, which would have to license the atomic dump,
found that the Department of Energy had displayed "too much
optimism" about the Hanford site. Indeed, even after paying
Rockwell $300 million to study burying nuclear waste at Hanford,
energy officials still could not answer basic questions about groundwater flow.

None of the information about the dump-site proposal proved
that Hanford had harmed any people. But it suggested that the
government was willing to overlook problems, even ignore vital
information, in order to keep an important program going. Steele
came across this same tendency in a book on the Utah sheepherders
case that contained startling parallels to Tom Bailie's stories of
deformed and aborted lambs. *The Day We Bombed Utah,* by John
G. Fuller, provided a detailed description of the original trial and
new evidence unearthed years later by the sheepherders' lawyer,
Daniel Bushnell. The evidence included a study by a Hanford veter-
inary researcher named Leo Bustad, whose work had been part of
the government's original defense. In 1956 the government had
reported that Bustad had fed a test flock of sheep some radiation-
laced grains and vegetation. The federal lawyers said that these
sheep did not suffer the same injuries that appeared in the Utah
farmers' livestock. The government offered this fact as conclusive
proof that fallout could not be blamed for the sheepherders' losses.
But years later Bushnell discovered another of Bustad's experiments, which had produced the same kind of fetal anomalies—

underweight and stillborn fetuses—reported by the farmers. Both groups of animals had been exposed to heavy doses of airborne iodine 131, one of the radionuclides found in fallout. But the Bustad study that would have confirmed the claims of the sheepherders was never revealed by the government's lawyers.

The government omissions in the Utah case went beyond Bustad's study. The Atomic Energy Commission had apparently lied in response to questions about whether any government scientists had supported the farmers' claims, and had lied again when asked if any of the farmers' sheep were known to have been contaminated. Years later these revelations did not persuade an appeals court to allow a new trial for the Utah sheepmen. But they did give new urgency to Steele's investigation of the Mesa sheep-kill mystery. And they supported the near paranoia expressed in Reverend Houff's sermon. Indeed, the Utah story, as recounted in *The Day We Bombed Utah,* confirmed many of Reverend Houff's claims. The government had been aware of high cancer rates in the rural communities downwind from the bomb-test sites, but this information had been suppressed. Federal officials had even restrained health officers who wanted to warn downwinders to stay indoors when it was known that a particular test—including an atomic explosion—would blow radiation into populated areas.

With the new information on the Utah case, and her growing files on other radiation incidents, Steele developed a list of key sources that included Hanford managers, scientists, nuclear watchdog organizations, and local officials dealing with a host of long-running radiation mysteries. Her initial impulse was to follow the lead that was closest to home: Leo Bustad. A quick check of the state's telephone directories turned up a Leo Bustad in Pullman, the home of Washington State University. Steele dialed. When Bustad answered, she quickly blurted out something about the Utah sheep case and Hanford. Just as quickly, Bustad refused to talk, and hung up the phone.

Moving down her list of sources, Steele next contacted Thomas Mancuso, the old University of Pittsburgh radiation expert who had lost his funding when it looked as though his study would show increased cancer among Hanford workers. Mancuso's opponents had tried to discredit his work and portrayed him as an outsider in his own profession; Steele respected people who stubbornly stood against the tide more than those who clung to established ideas.

When the reporter telephoned, Mancuso explained that during the early stages of his work, in the 1960s, the AEC had pressured him to quickly publish initial findings because they confirmed a low cancer rate in the work force. But he had resisted, arguing that the latency period for many cancers was greater than twenty-five years. He had prevailed, and, continuing to update his figures on Hanford workers, he had seen a small increase—five percent—over the cancer rate in the general population. As Mancuso had prepared to report this, the government had cut off his funding and handed responsibility for continued health monitoring to Battelle Northwest Laboratories in Richland, which has been a major Hanford contractor since the 1960s.

"Isn't it ironic," Mancuso asked Steele, "that they badly wanted me to go public when my early data was showing negative results, and then they defunded us after the analysis showed positive results?" Mancuso's questions would be later published in one of Steele's articles.

Mancuso also told Steele about a doctor with the State of Washington Health Department who had discovered that Hanford workers suffered a cancer rate higher than other industrial workers. Dr. Sam Milham's work had never been published, but when Steele called him, he confirmed the results. He added that he had continued to follow Hanford workers and he continued to see excess cancers. But Milham wasn't interested in challenging the atomic establishment. In fact, he said wasn't sure what his data meant. So he had simply sent it along to the Battelle team, assuming it would be incorporated in their larger, long-term analysis.

Steele went on to contact others who had joined the controversy around radiation and health, including British researcher Alice Stewart and John Gofman, a physicist and medical doctor, who had founded the government's Lawrence Livermore Laboratory's biomedical division. Gofman had worked deep inside the weapons industry. He had been a member of the scientific team that isolated the first milligram of plutonium, and he had been an enthusiastic supporter of nuclear technology. But Gofman had experienced a change of heart in the 1960s, when he traced genetic damage in Livermore lab workers to radiation exposure and gradually came to believe that the silence of medical experts in the nuclear field was the moral equivalent of murder. Over the telephone he warned Steele not to trust federal agencies or their scientists. Most of them, he said, were willing to lie for the sake of national security. Alice Stewart, whose research had shown that X rays once considered harmless actually damaged fetuses, predicted that the cancer death rate at Hanford would climb as time passed. "The worst is yet to come," she told Steele in a clipped British accent.

Officials at Hanford disputed any suggestion that workers there were exposed to any significant risk of excess cancer. Dr. Bryce Breitenstein of the Hanford Environmental Health Foundation—the agency responsible for monitoring workers—told Steele there was no good evidence to support Mancuso's cancer claims. Instead, he said, "Our overall cancer rates, when compared with national statistics, are lower." Stanley Marks, the Battelle researcher who had actually taken over Mancuso's work, was less certain but nevertheless insisted that Hanford's workers were not significantly sicker than anyone else. "We will accept the fact that there may be a few deaths that relate to radiation here," said Marks. "As time goes on, there'll be more deaths and you'll get a more complete follow-up. But I wouldn't look for anything striking in this population."

The two sides in the debate over the Hanford workers based their claims in part on the same statistics. The difference came in their interpretation. The Hanford experts counted cancer deaths in the work force, compared them with the general population, and found only a small excess in a certain kind of bone cancer, which had not been linked to radiation. Mancuso and his supporters used the same numbers, but interpreted them with a formula that took into account the fact that the Hanford workers were younger and healthier than the general public. They also considered that some workers would develop cancer but not die from their disease. Both methods were considered valid by health researchers, but in the case of Hanford they produced quite different results.

In early 1985, after scores of telephone interviews with various experts, Steele finally drove the 150 miles to the Tri-Cities to see Hanford up close. Inside the gates she found workers who were unconcerned about the academic debate over radiation and health and unafraid of the "product" they produced.

On a tour guided by public-relations officials, Steele and several other local reporters and concerned citizens were taken to the massive Plutonium-Uranium Extraction Facility, which looked like nothing so much as an enormous concrete bunker squatting in the desert sand. The guide escorted the group through a series of steel doors—some resembling the hatches on a ship—and then walked them down the production line. The line was really a series of work stations, each with dials, gauges, and controls. At a station called "N Cell," Steele met Karen Moore, a twenty-eight-year-old woman who was already a seven-year veteran at Hanford. A steel and glass wall separated Moore from the "product." She could stick her hands through two portals and wiggle them into a special pair of gloves. Peering through the thick protective glass, she then worked on the other side of the wall, packing loose plutonium oxide powder into metal containers the size of the vegetable cans found on supermarket shelves. Steele would later write about what she learned in a brief conversation with this worker.

"Are you worried about the health risk here?" Steele asked.

"No," Moore replied bluntly. "We respect the product, and we follow procedures. If you do, it's safe."

Steele got the same view from everyone she met. Gerry Cline, a steward for the Oil, Chemical and Atomic Workers Union local, told her that Hanford was so safe that he felt comfortable having his own son join him on the job. Even Harold McCluskey, the "atomic man" who had been sterilized and temporarily blinded by an explosion of radiation-laced chemicals at Hanford in 1976, refused to discuss the inherent dangers in radiation work. McCluskey spoke proudly of being the only man to receive so much radiation "and live to tell about it." Even though he had endured three heart attacks, repeated infections, and other mysterious symptoms since the accident, McCluskey wouldn't say anything to suggest there might be something dangerous about Hanford. He obviously believed in Hanford's mission and its commitment to safety. And he was an example of how Hanford, which continued to provide him with medical care, could shelter its loyal workers.

It seemed that everyone Steele met at PUREX believed that Hanford was entirely safe, everyone except the Doyles, who asked Steele to speak with them off site. Thomas Doyle, a Hanford old-timer, had led a strike in the 1950s to lower the level of acceptable radiation exposure on the site. His son Bob had worked at Hanford from 1980 until 1983, when he left to study law in Los Angeles. Steele hoped that because he was outside the Hanford system, young Doyle might speak candidly. He did. He told her that workers were trained to avoid exposure, but when alarms sounded a warning of excess levels of radiation, they laughed at those who ran. Worse, in a radiation safety lecture presented in Battelle's auditorium, in which a visiting expert told workers that a little radiation was good for a body, "the speaker told us that radiation can improve your sex life, and ward off the common cold," Steele would quote Doyle in an article.

Bob Doyle had other complaints, most of which had to do with the general attitude of workers toward radiation and health. He recalled that workers would often cheat when reporting the radiation exposures indicated by dosimeters—small devices that measure some kinds of radiation exposures—so that they would be eligible for lucrative overtime pay in "hot" areas. (When workers reached a maximum weekly dose, they were barred from radiation areas.) Doyle also complained that women felt pressured to work in radiation zones even when they thought they might be pregnant.

After talking with the Hanford workers, Steele began to look for evidence that might connect the nuclear reservation with health problems in surrounding communities. If Tom Bailie was right about the sheep, then it stood to reason that Hanford would be affecting people, too.

In a small office in the shadow of the Department of Energy's headquarters in Richland, Dr. Herbert Cahn, the county health officer, told Steele he had no proof that Hanford was harming the people who lived nearby. But he was disturbed by the attitudes of federal managers and local politicians. He told her how he had almost lost his job a few years earlier, when he suggested handing out potassium-iodine pills that would protect the public from an

accidental release of radioactive iodine. British authorities distrib-
ute the antidote to people living near nuclear plants in their country, and after the Three Mile Island incident, Cahn thought it would
be a good idea to give the same pills to people living near Hanford.
A white-haired man with a deeply creased face, Dr. Cahn recalled
the reaction from the Department of Energy. The department had
insisted he not move forward with his idea, and local political
leaders apparently felt the same way. Cahn said that a member of
the board of health instructed him to drop the idea or face being
fired. He did what he was told. "People here don't want to admit
that an accident could happen," he told Steele.

Cahn also helped Steele find an old study done by Ernest Sternglass that showed startling increases in infant mortality in the areas
around the plant during its first years of Hanford's operation.
Sternglass had looked at infant mortality in 1943 and 1945, the
years just before and just following Hanford's start-up. In Franklin
County he found a 50-percent increase. Benton County, where
Hanford, Richland, and Kennewick were located, had a 160-per-
cent rise. And in Umatilla County, to the south, the increase was 60
percent. These dramatic increases took place in a year when infant
mortality declined in the rest of Washington and Oregon.

As she collected critical studies and reports—and the arguments
against them issued by federal energy officials—Steele looked for
experts to interpret them. She came to rely on two in particular,
Robert Alvarez and Carl Johnson, M.D. Dr. Johnson was the
former health officer for Jefferson County, Colorado, where the
Rocky Flats nuclear reservation is located. He had first gained
prominence in the late 1970s when he found high cancer rates
downwind of Rocky Flats, which milled Hanford-made plutonium
into munitions for warheads. Johnson had developed a method for
calculating excess radiation in the environment by subtracting
known levels of naturally occurring "background" radiation and
depositions from fallout. Near Rocky Flats he used this method,
combined with an exhaustive house-by-house medical survey, to
show how increases in cancer—over and above the number of
expected cases—corresponded with radiation pollution from the
nuclear facility. He estimated that over the course of thirty years

Rocky Flats could cause as many as twelve thousand excess cancers and fourteen thousand birth defects in the neighboring population. Of course, Johnson's work was controversial, and many in the nuclear field dismissed it as scientifically flawed and biased against the industry.

Like Reverend Houff, Johnson, a bespectacled, soft-spoken man with a round face and only a wisp of hair, didn't look anything like a radical. As an army reserve officer, he had supported a strong national defense, including nuclear weapons development. But he had been outraged by what he believed was government negligence at Rocky Flats, and he no longer trusted the Department of Energy's science. He encouraged Steele to press her investigation because he suspected that Hanford posed a health risk similar to that of Rocky Flats.

"It's my experience that the communities that most need good epidemiological studies are ignored on purpose by the Department of Energy," Johnson told Steele over the phone. "The people at Hanford will tell you they've never found anything wrong with the community. But the truth is, no one has ever really looked, because they don't really want to know."

Besides Dr. Johnson, Steele often turned for help to Robert Alvarez, who, at the time, worked for a Washington-based research group called the Environmental Policy Institute. Alvarez was an even more vocal critic of the government and the nuclear industry. He didn't trust scientific reports issued by the Department of Energy, especially those that had anything to do with health or the environment. As far as he was concerned, asking the department to monitor its own effects on the environment, its workers, and public health was like asking a baseball batter to call his own balls and strikes. The batter might do it fairly, but that wasn't very likely. He told Steele about yet unpublished reports on excess cancers among the workers at several atomic weapons facilities, including Rocky Flats, Savannah River in South Carolina, Los Alamos in New Mexico, and Oak Ridge in Tennessee.

As a coauthor of *Killing Our Own,* Alvarez was a widely known critic of nuclear interests, a role he took quite seriously. In one casual conversation with Steele he informed her that she too would soon join the industry's enemies list. He reminded her of Karen

Silkwood, a nuclear worker who had been killed in a mysterious one-car accident while on her way to meet an investigative reporter for *The New York Times.* In the sometimes paranoid world of antinuclear activists, Silkwood was considered a martyr to the cause. He told Steele to be careful and to keep in touch with friends and family, informing them of her movements whenever she went to the Tri-Cities.

Though Steele was hardly so concerned about her own safety, she did follow Alvarez's advice. She did this in part to reassure her daughters, who had been frightened once before when their mother received threatening phone calls after doing a series of articles about financial wrongdoing in a local utility. Her daughter Blythe remembered one call in particular, in which a male voice had asked, "Do you want your mother to die?" The caller had said that the little girl's mother should back away from the story, and then hung up.

None of the threats turned out to be anything more, and Steele was confident that it would be no different with Hanford. Still, her daughters knew she was working on something controversial, and they worried. She eased their fears by telephoning often whenever she went to Richland, and by avoiding overnight trips. This caution was neither strange nor unique. Almost any outsider who went to the Tri-Cities to investigate Hanford would feel slightly anxious. A high-security facility, Hanford was protected by a substantial force of uniformed guards and undercover detectives. The Hanford Patrol was as well equipped as a small army, and was an obvious and ominous presence on the reservation. But even more than the security force, the aura of secrecy that surrounded Hanford made people feel uneasy. Hanford workers were under strict orders not to discuss their jobs and to report inquiries by reporters as if they were contacts with Soviet spies.

When her research was done, Steele published in the *Spokesman-Review* a series of articles that challenged both the waste-isolation project and Hanford's claim that it had always operated without injuring workers or local residents. As with virtually every piece of objective reporting on the nuclear debate, the articles reached no firm conclusions. Instead, Steele used each piece to pose questions about the Department of Energy's plans, reports, and proposals. Indeed, the entire series was titled "Hanford: The Unanswered Questions." In her articles Steele presented the statements of Sternglass and Mancuso and geologist Donald White along with those of Robert Alvarez, Carl Johnson, and the Doyles. But she also published the views of the other side. Production worker Karen Moore was on the front page one day; Hanford health expert Bryce Breitenstein got his chance on another. But despite this balance, the series was a showcase for nuclear critics. Steele had begun her investigation with the assumption that the secrecy that shrouded Hanford from foreign spies also hid its sins from the American people. At the end of the series, an unbiased reader would likely have agreed and concluded that Hanford was a threat to its workers and neighbors, and that creating a nuclear waste dump at Hanford would be foolhardy.

In the Tri-Cities, where the *Spokesman-Review* sold few papers, the articles had little effect. The waste project's supporters dismissed it as an unfair attack on a sensible plan that would resolve the serious matter of dealing with accumulating nuclear waste. In Spokane, Steele's reports fed growing public opposition to the repository. The reporter and her newspaper won several regional awards for the series and, most important to Steele, she earned her editors' support for continued, aggressive coverage of Hanford. She was freed to pursue Hanford full-time. And a convenient bit of assistance, provided by HEAL, immediately allowed her to turn her attention to Tom Bailie and the most dramatic human aspect of the controversy.

In early April 1985, HEAL provided Steele and the public with a concise white paper containing excerpts from key Hanford documents that had been leaked to Spokane college professor Allen Benson over the years. Titled "Blowing in the Wind," the paper revealed that the land just outside the boundaries of Hanford harbored an average of 84 micrograms of radiation per acre, much of it traceable to Hanford. (Inside the fence, contamination reached as much as 1,200 micrograms per acre.) It also disclosed that 12 million cubic meters of soil on the Hanford site were so contaminated that the area had become the nation's largest deposit of transuranic nuclear waste. (This problem had been solved in the early

1980s, when officials changed the definition of this waste in a way that excluded much of the Hanford soil.) The paper further revealed that in one year, 1959, Hanford had released more radioactive iodine during every day of operations—20 curies—than the Three Mile Island accident had released in total.

In dry, carefully footnoted detail, Benson and coauthor Larry Shook used the government's own data to detail the harm that may have been done by airborne plutonium particles, and the process by which plants—such as Tom Bailie's crops—could absorb and concentrate radionuclides. It was clear that the government had long been aware of Hanford's threat to the surrounding farm families. And the Department of Energy's own documents suggested a series of sobering questions. How seriously had Hanford irradiated the people and lands surrounding the reservation? Were people, animals, and crops affected? Why was no one told of the danger? Was radiation still emanating from the site?

Karen Dorn Steele didn't have to review these questions with Brenda Tabor. With the release of the white paper, it was obvious that it was time for the reporter to visit Tom Bailie and the farmers of Franklin County. When she came to ask Tabor's permission, the editor answered with a single word: "Go."

# THE DOWNWINDERS

By the end of April 1985, Tom Bailie's wheat was a foot high, and his newly planted cornfields smelled of warm earth and spring growth. He started a typical day out in the shed beside his house, reviewing the work schedule with his hired man, a Japanese exchange student named Sabro Morita. Sabro, who was thirty years old, had been assigned to Bailie's farm as an intern when he was an agriculture student at WSU. He had stayed on after graduation, rather than return to Japan where land was so expensive he could never expect to have his own farm. He was saving much of what he earned in the hope of one day buying a place somewhere in Eastern Washington.

Sabro and Bailie were walking toward the house when Linda Bailie stuck her head out the front door. Linda was a no-nonsense person who was jealous of the time her husband poured into politics. She expected him to dedicate himself to the farm, the family, and little else. So when an unfamiliar woman's voice on the phone had asked for Tom Bailie, she felt a little annoyed.

Bailie hustled inside and took the phone from his wife. On the other end, Karen Dorn Steele got right to the point. "Are there any of those people who had deformed sheep left around there?" Bailie said he was sure there were plenty of farmers who remembered the deformed lambs. He invited Steele to drive down the next day to meet some of them. Bailie was glad to give Steele as much time as she wanted. Her stories about Hanford's current operations had renewed his curiosity about what had happened in the past. He wanted to know if the suspicions he harbored about Hanford's effect on the environment off the site had any basis in fact. And he

couldn't think of a better way to find out than having a reporter dig
around.

Steele met Bailie a few days later at the Country Kitchen Café. She
didn't have any trouble finding the place. The café, the post office,
and a small grocery were all there was to downtown Mesa. When
she arrived, the dirt parking lot was jammed with pickups. Inside,
the men at one table were throwing dice to see who would pay for
the coffee. They wore cowboy hats and boots, and they hollered like
a crowd of conventioneers in Las Vegas. At another table, Tom
Bailie talked about politics and agriculture with another group of
farmers.

The little cafés in Mesa, Basin City, and the other farm towns
served as satellite kitchens and business forums for the farmers.
Anyone who needed a combine or trucks to haul potatoes could
make the circuit of the cafés and hire them from his neighbors.
Problems with crops, the Farmers Home Administration, or with
wives and children were all aired in the cafés. Tom Bailie always felt
comfortable hanging around these places, where he could expect to
meet a cousin, an uncle, or an old classmate from school. And he
didn't mind when the good-natured jokes included cracks about
"the Bailie curse," which, for those who must know, had something
to do with inadequate sexual potency. Being the butt of jokes meant
you belonged in the cafés.

Outsiders did not belong in the cafés. Pale faces and shiny shoes
gave them away as city people. As Karen Dorn Steele came through
the door wearing a conservative dress, every head in the café
turned. Bailie got out of one of the booths and strode over. He wore
faded jeans, boots, and a deep blue cotton work shirt.

"Why, it's Karen Dorn Steele," he said in a big, friendly voice.
"Hey, everyone, this is Karen. She's a reporter from the *Spokesman-Review*," Bailie announced to the men in the café. The men
were suddenly quiet. A few shyly nodded hello. The rest stared into
their coffee cups.

Bailie ushered his guest to a booth. Steele apologized for the long
delay between their talk at Tom Foley's fund-raiser and her trip to
Mesa; it had taken months of research to come up with enough

information to persuade her editors that Bailie might have a story to tell.

After breakfast, Bailie led Steele outside to a beige Ford Bronco, and the two drove west, toward Basin City. Bailie wanted Karen to meet Mr. and Mrs. Nels Allison, whose farm was off Klamath Road, between Mesa and the river. The Allisons had raised sheep in the 1960s. Bailie recalled that over the years, Nels had talked more than anyone else about the deformed sheep. "He was always the maddest about the dead sheep," he told Steele as he drove.

The truck sped down country roads that separated vast, geometrically divided fields of grain like a sharp part in a young boy's bushy hair. A sea of young plants—alfalfa, wheat, corn, and other crops—spread out in every direction. Huge sprinkler systems, five-foot-high metal wheels carrying water pipes and whirling sprinkler heads, crawled across the acres, spraying water that the Columbia Basin Project had diverted from the river.

"Nels was so damn angry," Bailie continued, oblivious to the beauty of the enormous, man-made garden he was passing through. "He would sometimes drink a little bit, over at the café in Basin City, and he'd say, 'Those sons of bitches at Hanford killed my sheep and they almost made me lose my farm.' "

The Allisons' home—a little red farmhouse with white trim—was less than three miles from the river and the boundary of the atomic reservation. Nels was in the kitchen when the visitors came to the door. He was a tall, thin man who wore thick glasses; he had on the same bib overalls that he wore every day for work. At seventy-three, Nels still worked hard, and he had completed a long list of chores before coming in for breakfast. He welcomed Bailie and Steele to the kitchen table. Mrs. Allison poured them coffee and then leaned back against the kitchen counter to listen as her husband began to talk about the deformed sheep.

"We had lots of 'em years ago, right out in that shed out back," Allison began. "They looked like little demons." Most of the deformed lambs had come on a single night. There were lambs without eyes, mouths, or legs. Some had two sets of sex organs, others had none. Some had crooked legs, and some had no legs at all. Others had bones that were fused together, making it impossible for them to be born. Allison said he had to reach into the ewes' wombs and break the fetuses into pieces in order to pull them out. In all, there had been dozens of deformed or dead lambs. Some of the ewes had died as well.

As Allison spoke, Bailie and Steele exchanged shocked glances. This was more gruesome detail than either of them had expected to hear. Spring lambs evoke an image of natural beauty and delight. They are symbols of nature's renewal. But the ghastly creatures Allison described were terrible mutants. When he had finished, Steele sat for a moment in stunned silence. Then her reporter's instincts took over. She asked when the large number of deformities had appeared, and whether there were any records of the event.

Allison thought for long moment. "Jesus, this shit's getting old, sweetie," he said. "I just can't remember."

He paused again, trying to collect his thoughts. As he did so, Mrs. Allison hurried out of the room. In less than a minute she returned, carrying two cardboard boxes. She dropped them on the table. "All you got to do is look it up," she said.

Inside the boxes were ledgers and diaries going back to the 1950s. Many farm wives keep such detailed records; they are invaluable in assessing profit and loss over long periods of time. They also provide a historical account of family life and local agriculture. In this case the deaths of the lambs were recorded in the book for 1962. The record showed thirty-one lost sheep.

Before Bailie and Steele left the little red farmhouse, Steele asked if there were any other farmers who had lost large numbers of lambs in 1962. Nels Allison told her to visit his neighbor Lyle Taylor, who had seen more dead sheep than he had. He told her the Taylors had sent lamb fetuses over to WSU for study. Allison then paused to warn Steele and Bailie that they were touching on a sensitive subject. Many area farmers would rather ignore Hanford than ask hard questions. The Taylors were in this group. "Once I told Lyle they were lettin' some juice out over there. But Lyle didn't want to rock the boat. In them days we just took our lumps."

As the visitors said good-bye and walked out to the truck, Steele bumped her leg. She climbed up into the Bronco, rubbed it, and shivered a little as Bailie started the engine. He asked her if she was cold, and reached over to switch on the heater. It was chilly, for

April. But Steele wasn't cold. She was upset by what she had heard from Nels Allison, and by Bailie's numb response. Years later she would still recall what she then said to Bailie.

"Tom Bailie, do you know anything about radiation and the effects on sheep at all? Do you really know what happened at Utah?" Her tone was impatient, almost exasperated.

Bailie admitted that he knew little about the Utah case, or about radiation in general.

Steele told him that the Allisons' little demons were similar to lambs born to ewes in Utah that had been hit by highly radioactive fallout. "Something terrible has happened here, Tom. Something terrible has happened, I can tell you that."

Bailie didn't know how to react. For years the speculation about deformed sheep and Hanford had been nothing more than idle talk. "The Night of the Little Demons" was a story Nels and others sometimes told, just like the tales people tell about flying saucers or secret societies. They were strange and interesting yarns, but they weren't necessarily true. Besides, Bailie still had some small faith in Hanford and the men who ran it. And he was leery of "antinuclear types" with college educations and cynical attitudes. He tried to argue with Steele, pointing out that deformities and stillbirths are common on farms. As a grain-grower who kept a few cattle, Bailie didn't know a whole lot about sheep. Perhaps it was ignorance, or perhaps it was the traditional prejudice cattlemen bear against sheepherders, but he considered woolly sheep weak and useless.

"You know, a sheep is always the first thing to lie down and die on a farm," he said. "You can hardly keep 'em alive. They aren't like other animals. Hell, with a pig, you can shoot it four times and it still won't go down. But you just look at a sheep the wrong way and it dies."

This attitude made it difficult for him to accept that something extraordinary had happened in 1962. Sheep just aren't very reliable, he thought to himself.

But there was another, more important reason why Bailie wouldn't leap to the conclusion Steele suggested. He was already thinking about the repercussions of Nels Allison's story reaching the food-buying public. Who would buy meat, grain, fruit, or vegetables from radioactive farms? This kind of news could ruin farmers for miles around. Bailie needed more proof before he would accept that his fears about Hanford might be true. So he drove Steele directly to the neighboring farm of Lyle and Melba Taylor.

Melba Taylor, a spry woman in her sixties, had recently been forced to take over the day-to-day operation of the family farm; her husband had been killed when a grain elevator collapsed. Bailie and Steele hopped out of the truck and began talking to Mrs. Taylor in her yard. Bailie introduced Steele and explained that she was working on an article about the problems sheep farmers had experienced back in the 1960s. Mrs. Taylor's memory wasn't clear, but she recalled that there had been a spate of deformed lambs. She also recalled that her husband had sent two spontaneously aborted fetuses to Washington State University, hoping the scientists there could determine what had happened. The lab at WSU never reported any findings, though. She recalled hearing that the carcasses had somehow been lost or misplaced.

Pressing for something that might confirm this story, Steele asked if Mrs. Taylor had any documents relating to the lambs. She said she still had copies of letters her husband had sent to WSU, and minutes from sheep growers' meetings. But as she turned to go into the house to fetch them, she suddenly stopped and turned around. She wanted to know more about Steele and her intentions. Bailie struggled to reassure her, but it was no use. She told him he was digging into things that were better left alone. Nuclear bombs were necessary, she said in an agitated voice, and it would be best just to leave Hanford alone. She told them to leave her property,

No amount of Bailie's backwoods charm would change Mrs. Taylor's mind. Bailie and Steele quickly found themselves back in the Bronco. He suggested they try another of the old-timers, Vernae Hansen. Mrs. Hansen and her husband, Dan, had come to the area with a large contingent of Mormon families who had moved there from Utah after World War II. Dan had worked in a uranium mine near Marysvale, Utah, and had died of lung cancer in the 1970s. (This area may also have received radiation from bomb-test fallout.) It was well known that many uranium miners had been exposed to dangerous levels of radiation. Bailie figured that since Dan had probably been a victim of the nuclear industry, Vernae would be willing to talk openly about Hanford.

When Bailie and Steele arrived, they found Mrs. Hansen was digging in the garden beside her home, a little yellow clapboard house surrounded by carefully clipped shrubs and neat flower beds. A tall, strong woman with curly blond hair that was half gray, Vernae had a prominent nose and piercing blue eyes. She didn't smile when the visitors approached. But she did listen patiently as Tom Bailie once again explained what he was doing. When Karen Dorn Steele said she was trying to determine whether there was a connection between Hanford and problems with sheep in the 1960s, Mrs. Hansen stiffened.

"I think you better ask someone else."

Bailie jumped into the conversation. He didn't want to watch Steele be rejected again. He cajoled Mrs. Hansen, insisting there must be some link between Hanford and problems across the river. "C'mon, Vernae. You know there are problems with radiation, like what happened to Dan. We're just looking at Hanford now, to see if there's something there."

Mrs. Hansen wasn't going to give any ground. She allowed that her husband had probably been killed by the radiation in the mines. But she had declined to join in any of the lawsuits filed by miners and their survivors. She didn't believe in suing the government. The uranium mining, the fallout, Hanford—all of it was necessary, she said, because of the Russians. "It's a necessary thing. If we don't have the bombs we can't deal with the world from a position of strength."

Vernae Hansen was not to be moved. Like many of the area's Mormons, she was proudly patriotic and fiercely private. She was not going to challenge the government, and she resented Bailie's prying into the past. These attitudes were not unusual among the area's old-timers, who, as a rule, tended to be politically conservative and loyal to authority. Bailie and Steele would not get any help from Vernae Hansen, even if she privately believed that something was wrong.

Back in the truck, Bailie suggested coffee at the nearest café in Basin City. As he walked Steele through the door, Bailie recognized many of his neighbors. This time in a more casual way, he tried to get them to talk about Hanford and the sheep. A couple of the older farmers told Bailie that the mystery of the little demons had bothered them for a long time, and they were glad someone was looking into it. But one suggested that he and Steele were missing something more important. He said they should be looking at the farm families, not their animals, and that they should start with Leon and Juanita Andrewjeski's "death map." For several years after her husband was first diagnosed with heart disease, Juanita Andrewjeski had kept track of the illnesses in the area, he said. It was all on a coded map covered with marks indicating cases of cancer and heart ailments.

The Andrewjeskis lived on one of the farms closest to the Hanford reservation, in an area named Ringold. It was a good ten miles from Basin City. On the drive over, Tom Bailie began to reflect on the seriousness of what he seemed to be discovering. As he steered the Bronco down Ringold Road, he began to consider that he was a victim of Hanford. In his mind he could hear the farmer in the café saying, "You need to be looking at the people." Suddenly he let up on the gas. The Bronco gradually slowed from fifty miles an hour to zero. He pulled over to the side of the road and shifted into park.

"Holy shit," he whispered to himself. Then he turned to his passenger. "Karen, I got to tell you something I haven't told you. I told you I was fine back then, but I wasn't. I'm sterile. And that's not all. I was paralyzed when I was a kid. I was in a wheelchair and used crutches for a year. I was born with a hole in my chest, and I had all kinds of respiratory problems. Hell, I was in an iron lung in the hospital. They didn't think I was going to make it. All us kids were always developing sores that wouldn't heal, and little growths on our skin."

As Karen Dorn Steele gently questioned him, Bailie revealed that his father and four uncles had all had intestinal tumors. His grandfather, who had fished almost every day in the Columbia, and eaten what he caught, had died of liver cancer. His grandmother had died of cancer of the colon. His sisters suffered from thyroid problems. His mother and just about every other woman he knew had suffered miscarriages. Some, including a close cousin, had lost as many as six fetuses.

When Bailie was finished, he put the Bronco in gear and drove to their next stop. For most of the way, the only sounds in the Bronco's cabin were the hum of the car's engine and the hollow whine of its oversized tires. Later, Bailie would recall that he felt embarrassed by what he had revealed about his family's medical history. It made him feel as if he came from weak stock, a clan of mutants. He thought that Steele seemed shaken. He would remember that she had said she was sorry about what had happened to them.

They pulled themselves together when they reached the Andrewjeskis' home. Juanita Andrewjeski, a graying woman in her fifties, met Bailie and Steele at the farmhouse door and brought them into the kitchen, where her husband Leon was sitting. On the counter was a small radio receiver of a kind issued by the authorities who ran the WPPSS commercial reactor across the river. Officials had distributed the radios to all the homes within ten miles. They would broadcast a message in case of emergency at the nuclear power plant.

While the others chatted, Juanita spread a map of the Ringold area on the kitchen table. It was marked with crosses that indicated heart attacks and circles that showed cancer cases. She leaned over the table, touched each of the marks, and recalled the farmer who had had a heart attack, or the wife who had developed cancer. In all, there were thirty-five crosses and thirty-two circles.

"You'd expect it among people in their seventies," Juanita said. "But these people are in their fifties." Worse, she added, it seemed that the children of these farmers were also developing health problems. Juanita herself had suffered three miscarriages. Both of her daughters had had hysterectomies while in their thirties. One had a chronic problem with skin sores that wouldn't heal.

The Andrewjeskis had lived directly downwind from Hanford since 1954. They had known the nuclear reservation was across the river when they settled here, but they had understood very little about the work Hanford performed, and had been told nothing of a potential radiation danger. There were no emergency radios back then. No one had mentioned that the milk from their cows could be dangerous to their children, or that there might be radioactive particles in the soil. But over the years, the Andrewjeskis would occasionally see men from Hanford who came to test water or soil, just as Tom Bailie had witnessed as a child. Leon recalled that once, in the early 1960s, he had discovered a long line of government trucks parked on the road beside his fields. Soldiers with Geiger counters had walked up and down the furrows, listening to the raspy clicks of the machines. "You could see them running up and down the fields," he recalled. "I didn't know what the hell they was doing," Leon said. "We still don't know."

Now, years later, Juanita wanted to know if the young lady reporter would be able to answer her questions about Hanford. Steele could say only that she would try. She explained that most of the documents relating to Hanford remained classified, but she promised to chase the story as far as she could.

The Andrewjeskis made it clear they believed that just asking questions about Hanford was a risk. "This is an agricultural community," said Leon. "We sell a lot of grain to Japan. They are very picky. They inspect everything. And they could get very nervous if they think there's something wrong." Nevertheless, the Andrewjeskis were willing to go on record with their concerns.

"We're not interested in this because we want to sue the government or get everyone all upset," Juanita told Steele. "We're more interested in the truth. We'd just like you to help us get the truth."

Bailie and Steele left the Andrewjeski home as the sky was turning dark. He dropped Steele at his mother's house, where she was to spend the night. By the time Bailie got to his own home, Linda had become concerned about her husband's whereabouts. As he came through the door, she asked him where he had been. Bailie thought for a moment, and then decided that he was too confused about what he had heard that day even to begin to explain it. He told her that Steele was writing an article and that he had helped introduce her to some sources. Linda, who was accustomed to her husband dealing with reporters on political matters, accepted the explanation. But she chided her husband for giving so much time to what she thought was an unimportant concern. And she reminded him of his responsibilities. There were bills to pay and children to raise.

The next morning Tom Bailie rose early, as usual, and put on his farmer's uniform—boots, jeans, and a work shirt. He had his breakfast and announced that he was going out to work. He thought there was no sense in upsetting Linda by telling her that Saburo would handle the farm work and that he was going to give another day to the reporter.

Bailie and Steele spent the morning on the back roads of Franklin County, collecting anecdotes about deformed or stillborn livestock. Altogether they found six sheep farmers in the area who said they had lost a total of more than one hundred animals in the spring of 1962. These recollections were more than enough for Steele to be confident in reporting that something had happened, at least to the livestock.

More ambiguous and unsettling were the stories about the health problems of the people who had settled this part of the Columbia Basin. Many of them were "levelers," so named because they had arrived in the 1950s to run the heavy equipment that had flattened much of the land to make it suitable for irrigation. At a café in Homestead Corners, Bailie and Steele ran into an old leveler named Rich Hayes. Bailie recalled that Hayes had a daughter, she would by this time be a teenager, who had been born without an arm. He and Steele began talking with him, to see if he thought the deformity might have something to do with Hanford.

At first, Rich Hayes wanted to reminisce only about the irrigation project. It had been an enormous undertaking. Thousands of acres were reshaped. Entire hillsides were moved so that canals could be built. In the dry, semiarid climate of the Basin, the giant bulldozers, scrapers, and dump trucks had created great clouds of dust that settled on everything and everyone in sight. For years Hayes had worked in the dust storms created by the earth-moving machines. Often the haze was so thick that huge trucks would become invisible to someone standing a hundred yards away. "I leveled farms all over here," said Hayes. "It took me years to cough the dust out of my lungs."

After listening patiently to Hayes's story, Steele tried again to ask him about his daughter, the one with the deformity. Finally he said that yes, he had a daughter who had been born with one arm. However, he insisted that Hanford couldn't be to blame. But as soon as Hayes finished explaining how Hanford couldn't possibly have caused his daughter's deformity, Bailie heard a voice from a booth over by the window. It was Don Worsham, an old farmer who had been Tom Bailie's scoutmaster years ago—Ringold Troop 151.

"You bring her up to my house, Tom," Worsham said, indicating that he was referring to Karen Dorn Steele. He rose to leave the café. "You bring her up right now."

Bailie paid for breakfast, and then quickly drove over to Worsham's farm with Steele. The old farmer was ready with a thick manila folder in his hands. He had long been concerned about the number of cancers in the local community, though local doctors had told him there was nothing to worry about. "You just look at this," he said, "and tell me what *you* think."

He opened a folder filled with yellowed clippings. They were death notices of people from the Ringold area. Worsham said that nearly everyone who had settled in his area in the 1950s had died, except him and his wife, and she had had breast cancer in 1962, when she was just thirty-five years old. He was convinced that all of the farmers in the area knew there was too much illness among both the people and the livestock. But no one talked about it. Like the little demons, the lost babies and the men who had died young were unspoken memories. Everyone seemed to think that if these problems were ignored, they would go away. But Worsham and the Andrewjeskis couldn't maintain the conspiracy of silence. Even if they couldn't explain these losses, they refused to ignore them.

If most of the farmers around Ringold had strange stories to tell, none was stranger than that told by F. R. Chen, one of the farmers Bailie and Steele met in the Basin City café late that day. A stocky, outgoing man of sixty, Chen grew grapes, asparagus, and other crops on a farm that stretched up to the ridge overlooking the Hanford Reservation. He had come to the United States from China just after World War II. With a doctorate in chemistry, he had worked first for an agricultural chemical company in California. In the late 1950s he had come to the Columbia Basin, hoping to buy some land. Each year he had put his name into a lottery the government ran as part of a program to sell off some of the property that had been taken over by the Manhattan Project. Chen would eventually win the lottery and buy 130 acres at sixty dollars apiece. But before he won his land and took up farming, he had worked as a chemist at the Water Authority office in Pasco.

It was at the Water Authority that he learned to fear Hanford. Pasco drew from the Columbia River, downstream from Hanford and the AEC constantly tested the river water and its fish for radioactive contaminants. In 1962, Dr. Chen saw a letter from the commission that warned of the high levels of radiation that had been found in Columbia River fish. The letter did not suggest that the public be alerted, nor did it report that there was excessive radiation in drinking water. (Though the radiation from reactor cooling water would be diluted in the river, it could be concentrated in the flesh of animals.) Chen also recalled overhearing a discussion at the water department in which his supervisors decided that they would follow orders. No public health warning would be issued.

At the time, many of the people who lived along the river, especially local Indians, relied on it as a ready source of food. Like Tom Bailie's grandfather, they fished frequently and ate much of what they caught. Years later, Dr. Chen recalled that he had eaten the fish from the Columbia, too. "But after I read those confidential papers, I said, 'No way am I going to eat that fish anymore.'"

For more than twenty years, Chen drove fifty miles to Walla Walla each week to buy meat, milk, fish, and vegetables. He and his wife boiled their drinking water, and discarded the portion at the bottom of each pot, because that's where he believed the radionuclides would settle. They lived without serious illness, as did their seven children. But all around them, neighbors seemed to suffer from what seemed an excessive number of tumors, respiratory problems, and other illnesses.

As he sat with them in the café, Chen told Bailie and Steele that he felt guilty about not informing the others, but at the time he had been too afraid of the government to speak out. "I had come from China, where government is very repressive, and I had been told that this was secret," Chen would tell Bailie on a subsequent visit. "But what they did was wrong."

Karen Dorn Steele left Mesa and the people she would come to call "the downwinders" with a notebook full of disturbing anecdotes and some compelling questions. In the weeks that followed, she pressed officials at Hanford for information that might confirm or allay the downwinders' fears. Health and environmental specialists at the reservation assured her that Hanford was operating safely, that the farmers had nothing to worry about. The stonewall defense put up by Hanford officials almost killed Steele's investigation. But then she got lucky again. One May morning she came to work and discovered that the day's mail contained a large envelope from the Department of Energy. Inside the envelope were a handful of reports from the 1960s. One of her many FOIA requests had finally been granted.

The documents in the packet hinted at the answers to the questions raised by Bailie and the others. One noted that radiation monitors had been sent to the Mesa area three times in 1962 and 1963. The first time, in April 1962, followed an accident at one of the chemical plants that resulted in the release of 1,200 curies of radioactive gas. Monitors were sent out again after an accident in May 1963. Then, in September 1963, an accident at PUREX resulted in the emission of 60 curies of radioactive iodine 131. Once more, radiation monitoring teams were sent across the river.

The reports acknowledged that something had happened. Radiation, in particular iodine 131, had reached the farm families. One set of documents showed that Hanford officials had paid special attention to milk produced at Ringold following the PUREX release in 1963. Daily sampling of local milk showed that iodine levels had increased more than twelvefold in the six days after the accident. A child in the area who drank milk from local cows was assumed to have absorbed 3,600 picocuries of iodine 131. (The picocurie is a measure of radioactivity. It takes one trillion picocuries to equal a full curie, which is the amount of radioactivity emitted by a gram of radium per second.) Hanford officials chose not to warn residents because this amount was still less than the maximum allowed by federal health guidelines at the time. This occurred at the height of government efforts to downplay the seriousness of radiation from bomb tests, which also affected the milk supply. If the Atomic Energy Commission had warned the Mesa area families about their milk, they would have undermined the larger effort to calm the nation's fear of fallout.

The other documents Steele received showed that since the early 1950s, the Atomic Energy Commission officials and managers of General Electric, which ran Hanford at the time, had been worried about radionuclides in river water. Scientists had obviously been afraid that local residents were being exposed to Hanford's emissions every time they ate fish taken from the river, drank water from local wells, or swam in the Columbia on a hot summer day. River water used to irrigate crops could also have contaminated fruits, grains, and vegetables.

Steele knew enough about radiation to understand the implications of this information. Iodine 131 was one of the most carefully studied radionuclides. There was no question that it could cause thyroid disease—and even thyroid cancer—especially in children and infants. And the September 1963 PUREX accident alone released four or five times more iodine 131 than the Three Mile Island mishap, which had generated international concern. Indeed, these few incidents suggested that the people downwind from Hanford had been subjected to potentially harmful radiation from Hanford.

But to make certain that the information was interpreted properly, Steele contacted an expert at the National Center for Atmospheric Research who was neither a nuclear booster nor a rabid critic. He confirmed, once again, that such radiation is linked to cancer. And he added that there may even be a link between radiation exposure and heart attacks, just as the Worshams and the Andrewjeskis feared.

"Downwinders—Living With Fear" was published in the *Spokesman-Review* on July 28, three months after Steele and Bailie canvassed the farmers of Franklin County. Steele's front-page article raised the level of controversy in the debate over the proposed nuclear waste dump and the very existence of Hanford in Eastern Washington. Again the fears and anxieties expressed by HEAL's Houff and others had been confirmed. Only a tiny fraction of

Hanford's records had been made public, but even these few documents showed that the operation was far from clean. But even more important, on a symbolic and political level, was the fact that Steele's article gave the fear a human face. The face belonged to Tom Bailie, who was pictured above the headline, standing in a field of shoulder-high corn.

The article, and a sidebar titled "The Night the Little Demons Were Born," cataloged the farmers' many experiences with human illness and death as well as their mysteriously deformed and deceased livestock. Juanita Andrewjeski and her "death map" were pictured. Nels Allison's complaints and F. R. Chen's recollections of the water-pollution notice were also included, along with the Bailie family's health history. Tom Bailie had been forthright enough to admit, for the record, that he had been sterile since he was a young man.

The article also included comments from Dr. Bustad, the retired Hanford veterinarian, who had finally agreed to answer a few questions. He said that Hanford could not have emitted the huge amounts of radiation—he said it would require thousands of rems—necessary to cause abnormalities in sheep. But in her article, Steele followed Bustad's comments with a 1977 United Nations report that declared that malformations can be induced by as little as five rems of exposure. Throughout the piece, experts from Hanford were quoted to the effect that the claims of damage to livestock and people couldn't be linked to the reservation. But in nearly every case Steele followed these statements with others, from her substantial list of opposing experts, refuting the Hanford position.

"They were clearly aware of the danger," said Robert Alvarez of the Environmental Policy Institute in Washington, D.C. "There should have been a public warning from the public health department and the federal government not to drink the milk."

Alvarez pointed to the historic betrayal of the downwinders, but it was up to Tom Bailie to frame the current political problem faced by the region's farmers and the nation. "I'm torn," he was quoted as saying. "After farming here for sixteen years, I don't want someone to come in and say, 'Get out, this is a contaminated area.' But I also don't want to be producing contaminated food for the food chain. Maybe they are going to have to choose between Hanford's plutonium and the Columbia Basin Project."

In the weeks and months that followed the first report on the downwinders, Bailie came to understand that few in the farm community and in the Tri-Cities wanted to choose between Hanford and agriculture. For more than forty years the people of the Basin had silently agreed to put aside their worries so that they might have both the benefits of the atom and the bounty of the land. Both were worth hundreds of millions of dollars each year. Both were vital to the region's identity. And they had been able to coexist, as long as no one raised any doubts. Suddenly the issues raised in Steele's article threatened the region's economy and the way residents thought about themselves and their place in the world.

The Department of Energy and local officials did their best to calm the community. Unlike his predecessors, who had kept the press and the public at arm's length, Hanford manager Mike Lawrence recognized the need to defend the department's image and steady the nerves of his neighbors. Lawrence promised to move quickly to provide information about Hanford's past, including responses to HEAL's request for a long list of classified documents. Lawrence was determined to meet the growing public skepticism with a degree of openness never before seen at a nuclear weapons facility. In part this was because he believed that the nuclear community needed the public if it was to survive. But this new openness was also required by the congressionally mandated process for establishing a national nuclear waste repository; Congress had guaranteed that local citizens be given complete information on any potential site's environmental condition before a project could move forward. This meant that before Hanford became the country's atomic dump, its entire history would have to be revealed.

From the start, Hanford's managers were aware that they faced a daunting public-relations challenge. But they also saw an opportunity to interpret the information that would eventually be provided in the most favorable light. Toward that end, the main contractor, Rockwell International, hired additional public-relations people and added $400,000 a year to its PR budget. And

DOE began conducting tours of the Hanford Site, for both the public and the press.

The people of Franklin County received more personal attention. In the fall, Lawrence and several of his key assistants went to the elementary school in Mesa to meet with local people and answer their questions. A few weeks later, Lawrence sent a team of health experts, and a machine called a "whole-body radiation scanner," to provide health screenings for anyone who wanted to be checked. These assurances were only partial, however, because the scanner couldn't measure the amount of short-lived radiation that may have passed through an area resident over the years. Iodine 131 and other such radionuclides do their damage and then decay away without a trace. Nor could the machine detect one of the three basic groups of radioactive substances—alpha emitters, such as plutonium. The scanner could, however, give those who chose to be measured an idea of how much of certain materials—all of them beta and gamma emitters—resided in their bones, muscles, and organs.

On an autumn evening when record cold temperatures sent the thermometer to near zero, the Andrewjeskis and a handful of others went to the Grange hall in Matthews Corner and entered the whole-body scanner. The long, low metal machine looked a little like a miniature submarine. One of the first to go in, Leon Andrewjeski lay on his back and held his body still as he traveled slowly through the machine. Juanita sat close by, listening to the Hanford health worker as he explained that nothing unusual had been found in her body, or her husband's. This was reassuring, but not conclusive. After all, the whole-body scanner could detect only certain radionuclides, and it could not tell them anything about contaminants that had already come and gone from their bodies.

Some vague reassurance was also offered to the downwinders by Dr. Sam Milham, the state epidemiologist whose early findings of excess cancer in Hanford workers had been cited by Karen Dorn Steele. In the weeks following the controversial downwinder articles, Milham conducted a survey of death records in two Franklin County census tracts occupied by about 2,200 people. He reported finding no excess cancers. Of course, Milham was immediately challenged by other experts, who noted that his census tracts did not include Mrs. Andrewjeski's "death mile," and that death records often failed to report cancer if a person died of a more immediate cause such as pneumonia. This point was underscored when Steele wrote a follow-up article on one of the Columbia Basin levelers—the men who shaped the land for the irrigation project—whom she had met on her tour with Bailie. A few months after their meeting, Ed Schutz had died in a Spokane hospital. As Steele reported, his death certificate listed pneumonia as the cause of death, when, in fact, he suffered from colon cancer. Steele used Schutz's death to point out that state regulations did not require physicians to report cancer, and that even the director of a regional tumor registry believed there was no good way to estimate the cancer rate in Franklin County, or any other part of the state.

Steele's report on Ed Schutz, which refuted Sam Milham's death-certificate study, illustrated her tenacity and her growing confidence. Urged on by HEAL and by Robert Alvarez and other nationally known nuclear skeptics, Steele refused to accept the untested claims of the experts, whether they were managers at Hanford or scientists like Sam Milham. In most cases her probing revealed the shades of gray and the contradictions beneath the DOE's arguments. The result was even more uncertainty for the reading public, and frustration for Hanford officials. After the downwinder stories, a Hanford public-relations expert said his department would soon "increase the amount of facts and decrease the amount of fear" in communities surrounding the nuclear reservation. But Steele's aggressive reporting thwarted every attempt that was made to calm the controversy.

Indeed, as the weeks rolled by, Hanford became the subject of even greater public concern. HEAL capitalized on the publicity stirred by the downwinder story and quickly assembled a group of nuclear critics to conduct a symposium called "Human Health at Hanford." More than five hundred people crowded into an auditorium at the Ridpath Hotel in Spokane. They came to hear, among others, Carl Johnson, who had studied Rocky Flats in Colorado, Ernest Sternglass, the University of Pittsburgh radiation health expert, Karl Morgan, a pioneer in radiation health physics, a former DOE waste manager named William Lawless, and German radiologist Bernd Franke. Franke had become well known in nuclear circles for his study of DOE's Savannah River plant in South Carolina, which was similar to Hanford. His study suggested that pollution at Savannah River had caused as many as two thousand excess cancers. He told the Spokane audience that he had recently obtained declassified reports showing that, like Savannah River, Hanford had released significant amounts of radiation. Though the information he had was incomplete. Franke could report that DOE knew that one major release, in 1954, had even reached Spokane.

Franke's revelations about past problems at Hanford and other nuclear weapons facilities were followed by William Lawless's critique of the present operation of the same facilities. A former senior project engineer in charge of waste management at Savannah River, Lawless charged that the federal government had suppressed reports on pollution caused by waste buried at both Savannah River and Hanford. Lawless joined with the others at the symposium in a call for more documents to be declassified, so that the full history of Hanford's releases would be known.

The symposium illustrated the two-pronged attack HEAL would mount against Hanford. First the activists challenged the DOE on scientific grounds, presenting qualified experts who could critique the government's positions. Allen Benson was particularly adept at this, using the Department of Energy's own reports to refute its long-standing claim that Hanford had not sent plutonium pollution off site. But this scientific attack was only part of the HEAL strategy. Just as important was its political argument, which was made on moral rather than partisan grounds. Larry Shook helped lead this effort. At the Ridpath conference he described DOE scientists as devoid of integrity and unworthy of public trust. "I believe that weapons plants like Hanford have become places of great despair," said Shook. "Those who run them hide in fear of humanity's finding out the truth."

The conference ended with a formal call for the Department of Energy to release documents relating to Hanford's off-site emissions since 1943. In a spirit of cooperation and openness, Hanford manager Michael Lawrence said he would try to provide the information.

In Spokane, where Hanford offered no tangible economic benefits, the critics of the nuclear establishment found a warm welcome. HEAL's membership rolls swelled with newcomers who were alarmed by what they heard and suddenly emboldened to ask tough questions of their own government. But people in the farm country around Hanford had a much different reaction to the negative publicity about their nuclear neighbor, as Tom Bailie discovered.

From the day the first downwinder articles were published, certain of his old friends stopped being so friendly. Old men who used to wave and smile from their trucks as they passed suddenly drove by as if they couldn't see Bailie. In the cafés the crowds grew silent when Bailie walked in. No one bothered to tell jokes about "the Bailie curse." The silence was a rebuke. Some made sure Bailie understood how they felt by walking out of the café every time he walked in. When his neighbors did speak about Bailie, many would mock him, calling him "the glow-in-the-dark farmer" or worse. Bailie could handle the sarcasm. But on the occasions when threatening phone calls were made to his home, Bailie was frightened. He was angered when his children were bothered by taunts at school. And there were a few times in the cafes when harsh words almost led to fistfights. After a while, Bailie began keeping a pistol in his car, just in case.

Years later, when they could talk calmly about their reactions, the other farmers told Bailie that they had feared the publicity about Hanford would ruin them. At the height of the downwinder publicity, buyers who had been paying top dollar for buckwheat that would become noodles in Japan flew to the Tri-Cities to investigate. They warned the local farmers that the media reports suggesting the Columbia Valley was polluted by radiation could end their sales to Asia. No contracts were ever canceled, and prices held firm. But nervous inquiries from Tokyo were enough to frighten the farmers.

Other neighbors were annoyed by the media hordes that descended on their community after Karen Dorn Steele's original article. The major television networks all sent reporters and camera crews, and the major news services and magazines sent their people too. Slowly, Bailie became the unelected but oft-quoted spokesman for the community, an ad-libbing emblem of the common man struggling against a huge bureaucracy. After the first few interviews he came to understand that he was serving as a kind of prop—the archetypal American farmer—for journalists who wanted a dramatic angle on the story. He willingly posed in front of tractors and cows and huge piles of potatoes. He would plow a field that didn't need to be plowed, if a photographer asked.

Some interviews were done in cafés, and Bailie's neighbors became scenery. This led to some obvious resentments. In one case, as Bailie sat in a booth in the Basin City café with the network newscaster Connie Chung, he was heckled as he tried to answer her questions for a piece that would be titled "Community Split by the Atom." Every time Chung's crew started to record, someone would shout a protest:

"There's nothing wrong with Hanford."

"It's safe here."

"Let us tell our story, by God. Hanford's safe."

Even when they got the chance to tell their side, those farmers who disagreed with Bailie found it an unpleasant experience. Years later, farmer Roger Danz scornfully recalled the way a reporter had asked leading questions and then edited the film to skew his responses. "The first time, I trusted that they wanted both sides of the story," said Danz, who remained critical of Bailie and always supported Hanford. "After that first time, I never trusted them again."

Others lost their trust in Bailie. An officer of the bank with which he and his family had done business for years advised Bailie to stop granting so many interviews. Bailie asked point-blank if he was being told to shut up. The banker said that was exactly what the bank wanted him to do. "This is your only warning," Bailie recalled the bank officer saying. "Go home and shut up about Hanford." He didn't take this advice and, a few months later, received a notice requesting that all of his loans be paid in full immediately.

Like many other farmers, Bailie was a payment or two behind, but this had never been a problem before. He couldn't help concluding that the bankers had decided to call the notes because they perceived Bailie as a threat to the local economy. He managed to cover the loans and arrange for financing elsewhere, but the anxiety caused by all this was a burden on his family. (Bankers called in loans held by other downwinders who spoke to reporters. Because the farm economy was in a crisis, the farmers couldn't be sure of the connection to the Hanford issue. But the banks offered extensions to their neighbors who were in similar financial trouble.)

Throughout the Hanford controversy, Bailie's family feared reprisals from the community. His wife, Linda, was the most concerned, because she wanted to protect her children from the taunts and stares of neighbors. She also worried at times that her husband was wrong about the danger of Hanford. Her father had worked at Hanford for many years. He had helped build and run the reactors. And when Tom Bailie first went public with his suspicions, his father-in-law told him he was flat-out wrong. The older man said he had been irradiated himself a couple of times, and it hadn't made him sick. Hanford, he insisted, was safe.

Linda Bailie was not as blunt as her father. But she resented the time and attention her husband devoted to Hanford. It often seemed as though every time she came home, she would discover her husband on the phone with a reporter. She came to call the telephone "that growth on Tom's ear." She also worried about the notoriety her husband was generating. Her social life was in the Tri-Cities. She had to deal with the comments from friends in Richland who thought her husband was either misinformed or crazy. She might have to defend him at the dance studio where her daughters took lessons. She was even worried about old friends she had made when she and Tom were adopting their children. These friends were also adoptive parents who had helped the Bailies through the emotional turmoil of adoption. They worked at Hanford and would feel threatened, even betrayed, by Tom's activism. With this in mind, Linda couldn't help asking her husband if he wasn't off track. When she said this, Bailie would often remind her of the number of cats and dogs she had lost to cancer. But while he brushed off her doubts, he couldn't stop worrying that eventually the Hanford controversy might lead to conflict.

It happened on a dark winter morning in January 1986, as Bailie was driving his car along the two-lane highway that runs from the Tri-Cities to Spokane. He had just visited a stockyard where some of his cattle were being fattened. Bailie and his cousin Manton were proud of their growing cattle business. He thrived on the speculative nature of the business. Cattle could make a man rich, if he was smart enough to play the market right.

On the way home that morning, Bailie was passed by a tractor-trailer truck that seemed to slow enough for the driver to check who was behind the wheel of Bailie's car. Moments later a large, old sedan with a driver and one passenger appeared in Bailie's rearview mirror. Bailie slowed to let it pass. The car slowed, and then inched to within a few feet of Bailie's bumper. Perplexed, Bailie pressed on his accelerator to put some distance between himself and the car behind him. But as he sped faster, and faster still, the car behind kept pace. Finally, as the two vehicles careened down a steep hill, the chasing car drew so close that Bailie was convinced it was going to ram him. He swerved to the right, left the roadway, and skidded into a field. The car bounced to a stop. For a moment Bailie sat in a breathless state of shock. Then he noticed that the car that had been chasing him had screeched to a stop on the highway and backed up.

As Bailie sat there, his heart pounding, he saw the sedan stop. As the two men got out, Bailie slid across the front seat of his car, took his pistol out of the glove compartment, and got out on the passenger side. Keeping his car between himself and the two men, Bailie let them see the gun. They turned and left, without saying a word.

In the months that followed, Bailie often reflected on that incident on the highway. He hadn't recognized the men in the car. He couldn't say that they knew him, or that what had happened had anything to do with Hanford. But he couldn't help thinking that he suddenly had more to fear than the slow-working effects of Hanford radiation. For the first time in his life, he was afraid of his own neighbors.

# THE AUDITOR

CASEY RUUD held to a quick pace as he ran along the two-lane road that cut through scrub brush and sand and led to the Plutonium-Uranium Extraction Facility on the eastern edge of the vast Hanford site. He wore just shorts and high-tech running shoes. His plastic Hanford ID badge was clipped to his waistband. As he ran toward the point where train tracks crossed the road, Ruud saw a locomotive pulling one of the lead-shielded freight cars used to carry radioactive materials around the site. He picked up his pace. Beads of sweat trickled from his temples and down his reddened cheeks. He could hear the heavy heartbeat of the engine a few hundred yards away. As he raced to the intersection, he could see the engineer in his cab. He pushed himself to move just a little bit faster, and then faster again. At the same time, the train picked up speed. The runner crossed the tracks in front of the engine, just as the whistle sounded long and loud. As he ran on, he looked over his shoulder to see the engineer waving.

A noon run was part of thirty-year-old Ruud's daily routine at Hanford. Afterwards he would shower and return to his desk. It was no different on this sun-washed day in July 1985. Though Hanford was under attack by the downwinders and the national media, the routine at "the Area," as many workers called it, was unbroken. Practically no one in the Tri-Cities was bothered by the downwinders' claims. Some of the best atomic scientists in the world worked at this facility, and they all said that Hanford was safe. If there were any problems, Ruud thought, they belonged to a distant past.

Casey Ruud had confidence in the scientists, engineers, and production workers who built big, complicated facilities and made

them run. A welder and pipe fitter by training, he had grown up in
the heavy construction trades. His father, John Ruud, had been a
well-known building inspector in Los Angeles. Old man Ruud had
personified the word *stickler*. He was known for holding contractors to the strictest interpretations of building codes. He had also
done some construction on his own—small industrial buildings and
housing. Casey had worked on his father's projects when he was a
teenager. He had concrete in his veins.

When he began working on commercial nuclear power plants,
Casey Ruud (pronounced "rude") was immediately impressed by
the industry's commitment to safety. He had seen it in California,
at the San Onofre nuclear power station. Ruud had worked there
in the late 1970s as a quality-assurance (QA) engineer, inspecting
construction work for the giant Bechtel Corporation. On his first
day at San Onofre he had spotted a serious problem in the sixty-
foot-high stainless-steel lining of a pool that would contain the
cooling water around one of the reactors. To avoid an accident, the
contractor replaced the liner, at a cost of more than $1 million.
Ruud was rewarded with a big raise.

After San Onofre was completed, Ruud joined the community of
"nuclear gypsies" who pulled U-Haul trailers around the country
like caravans, chasing high wages. In the late 1970s and early 1980s,
as the industry contracted, these high-tech itinerants competed for
fewer and fewer jobs. Workers and their families spent months on
the road searching for jobs. Ruud came to the Tri-Cities and
worked briefly on the Washington Public Power Supply System's
Reactor Number Two at Hanford. Then he went back to California
for a short stint at the Diablo Canyon power station. Power-plant
projects were quickly disappearing in the post–Three Mile Island
era. Ruud and his wife, Suzi, dreaded the prospect of moving again
and again in hopes of living off a dying industry. When Diablo
Canyon was done, they returned to the Tri-Cities to open a small
business—a frozen yogurt shop—and at last settle down. Kennewick, with its quiet neighborhoods and good schools, was the
best place they had ever lived. They wanted to stop being nuclear
gypsies and put down roots.

The Ruuds had hoped to escape the boom-bust cycle of nuclear
construction, but the yogurt shop didn't produce enough steady

income. Eventually Casey had to accept an offer to be a QA inspector in the Hanford weapons factories. It wasn't construction, so he didn't have to worry about work running out soon. And the pay was regular. He believed that his father, who had died of cancer a few months earlier, would have told him to take the job. It was the responsible thing to do.

Casey Ruud had been on the job just a few months on that July morning when he raced the yard train, showered, dressed, and reported for work. In a short time he had become relatively well known in the Area. Young-looking even for his age—he had bright blue eyes and a constant smile—Ruud possessed extraordinary energy and an upbeat nature. He tried to make friends with the people he met, even as he inspected their work. Because he could never learn all the details necessary to understand every part of a nuclear facility, Ruud relied on these friends—informants, really—to give him an instant education on whatever part of a plant he was inspecting, and to tip him off when something was amiss. "An insider," he used to say, "is worth his weight in gold."

Like his father, Casey Ruud was a tough inspector, someone who refused to back down until a problem was fixed. On this day his reputation brought Inez Austin to his office, which was actually just a little five-by-five square in a roomful of partitioned desk spaces on the first floor of the drab Rockwell administration building. A roving radiation monitor responsible for checking waste disposal projects, Austin feared that site workers and even managers were dangerously blasé about radiation hazards and less than careful about how and where they disposed of radioactive waste. Though she had discussed the problem with her superiors, no one seemed interested in fixing it. When she heard Ruud was preparing to do an audit of two of her areas—waste-tank farms and burial grounds—she went to see him. Together, she hoped, they might get some attention.

Austin entered the office noiselessly. Ruud looked up from his desk to see a stocky woman with a round, friendly face, short dark hair, and a serious manner. She wore jeans and a work shirt, the standard for those who did the hands-on work out in the Area. Austin, who spoke with a trace of a British accent, told Ruud of a

creeping carelessness that seemed to be affecting the waste-management system at Hanford. Her job included monitoring the disposal
of the liquid wastes, which were stored in 177 steel tanks similar to
oil storage tanks, and the burial of solid radioactive materials,
which included a lot of everyday objects such as gloves, tools, and
other things that had been "crapped up" by radiation. All kinds of
"crapped up" things, from workers' caps to contaminated bulldozers, were buried on the Hanford site. Rumor had it that years ago
they had even laid track into a pit and driven an irradiated locomotive into it. (Government officials have confirmed that railroad cars
have been interred, but are not sure whether a locomotive has been
included.)

Over the years, as members of Congress and others expressed
concern, waste management at Hanford had been subject to
stricter rules. Some of these rules were imposed by Hanford officials; others were the result of state and federal laws such as the
Resource Conservation and Recovery Act (RCRA). Under
RCRA, violations of state and federal rules for handling dangerous wastes could be prosecuted as felonies. Inez Austin wasn't
ready to say that any laws were being broken. But she wasn't
satisfied with the answers her superiors had offered to her questions about certain dump sites.

After a long, vague explanation of what was wrong, Austin suspected she had lost her audience. "Listen, Casey," she finally asked,
"rather than talk about it, why don't I show you?" He thought this
was a good idea. He grabbed a camera from a file drawer and took
Austin outside to a gray government pickup truck. She directed him
to drive a few miles into the desert, to a point where a dirt road
veered off from the paved surface.

As they drove, they crossed a harsh landscape that looked even
more foreboding in the clear, dry, unfiltered Western sunlight.
Before them stretched a vast, semiarid range covered with spiky
sagebrush, low-growing greasewood, and tufts of grass. Tumbleweeds bounced across the road, sometimes catching in the truck
grille. The shells of several retired reactors and their processing
facilities loomed in the distance. Alongside the road were occasional yellow stakes and signs warning of radioactive contamination. In the glare of the desert sun the radiation markers, the empty

concrete carcasses of the reactors, and the crosslike utility poles
that stood along the road made the reservation seem like some kind
of science-fiction graveyard, a high-tech wasteland on some distant,
barren planet.

A few miles from Ruud's office, Austin pointed to a dirt path that
left the main road. They followed it until they came to a stop next
to a Hanford security officer, who was standing beside a parked
patrol car. Behind the officer was a fence, with its gate open, and a
mound of earth about twenty feet high and perhaps fifty yards
across. A dump truck was depositing more dirt as Austin and Ruud
arrived.

As he hopped out of the truck, Ruud tried to disarm the guard
with deference and respect. He and Austin handed over their ID
cards and explained that they were inspectors on a routine assignment. The patrolman peered at the plastic badges and then returned
them. He then told Ruud and Austin to leave. The area was off
limits to everyone, he said, except the truck drivers.

Austin protested. She and Ruud both held special clearances that
allowed them into almost every nook and cranny of the Area; it said
so on the ID cards. She moved closer to the guard and began
arguing with him. Ruud went back to the truck, opened the door,
and took out the camera. He stood on the running board so that
he could get a good view, and took a few pictures of the sand pile.
He then got down, walked toward the big hole, and snapped a
few more.

The guard, whom Austin had occupied with the debate about
clearances, soon noticed Ruud and rushed toward him, shouting.
He told Ruud to get away from the fence. No picture-taking was
allowed.

"Look, I have a pass for this camera. And I'm going to use it,
okay?" Ruud answered.

"No you're not."

Ruud then raised the camera and took a picture of the guard.

"All right, that's it. Give me the goddamn camera and the pictures."

Austin and Ruud started backing up. As he shuffled slowly to the
truck, Ruud kept arguing. When they all reached Ruud's truck, the
officer's attitude softened a bit. Ruud suggested that the officer call

his boss, or the security office to check his pass. The officer agreed to call, as long as Ruud and Austin stayed put.

As the guard turned and walked quickly to the patrol car, Austin and Ruud stood stock-still beside their truck, appearing, at last, obedient. But when the patrolman got into his own car and picked up the radio microphone, Ruud turned to Austin and, in a whisper, told her to get into the truck.

Ruud and Austin quickly sped away, with the patrolman not far behind. Once they reached the paved road, Ruud pushed the accelerator to the floor while Austin looked out the back window for their pursuer. The officer followed them for a short distance, siren blaring and lights flashing, but then gave up the chase and seemed to turn back toward his post.

On the way back to Ruud's office, Austin said she suspected the dump truck had been loaded with sand contaminated some months earlier in a liquid waste spill. The spill had occurred when a corrosive chemical solution mixed with substantial amounts of radionuclides had been misrouted in the complex system of underground pipes that connected PUREX with the tank farms. Thousands of gallons of plutonium-laced waste had leaked into the soil, crapping up a stretch of desert several hundred yards long beside one of the Area's busiest roads. Austin suspected that instead of treating the soil to remove the contamination or placing it in some kind of secure containment, cleanup crews were simply digging it up and dumping it in a pile, where desert winds could carry it in almost any direction.

"Jeez," Ruud said. "There's real plutonium in there." He didn't have to explain the danger of this kind of dumping. There were many ways that plutonium-contaminated soil, improperly dumped, could threaten human life. It could be caught up in a windstorm and blown across the river to Franklin County, or into the city of Richland. Or desert plants could absorb plutonium from the soil. A brush fire could then send the contaminants into the atmosphere. There had even been cases in which animals and birds consumed contaminated plants or water and then spread radioactivity via their droppings. When the contamination involved plutonium—the worst of the radionuclides—the danger was magnified. A human being who came into contact with just one invisible particle of plutonium was, in the view of most experts, certain to get cancer.

Besides posing a public health risk, the dumping discovered by Ruud and Austin could constitute a criminal offense. Under RCRA, those responsible could be prosecuted and jailed. They felt this was probably why no one had responded to Austin's complaints.

Ruud and Austin went straight to Ruud's boss, John Baker. A longtime Rockwellite, Baker had worked in the space program before coming to Hanford. He was a serious man, especially on the job. He was serious about quality assurance, and protective of his people. Both Baker's superiors and his workers considered him competent and conscientious, a solid team player.

Ruud burst into Baker's office, half pretending to be frightened. He told him about the incident with the Hanford patrol, and gave Baker the photos for safekeeping. Baker had been expecting something like this from Ruud. He had hired him with the intention of shaking up the auditing team, which, until Ruud's arrival, had been a rather quiet little backwater. He took the pictures and promised to follow up on the possible violations of company policy.

When they came out of Baker's office, Austin asked Ruud if he had time to see another suspicious dump site. She wasn't sure where this one was, but she had heard enough rumors about it to be confident that it was out there somewhere. The morning's escapade had been more exciting than anything Ruud had yet experienced at Hanford. He eagerly agreed to go back out in search of the second site.

That afternoon, Austin and Ruud took the same government truck out past the gray, hulking Plutonium-Uranium Extraction Facility and into the scrub. Austin directed Ruud first to a small building where some of the waste-disposal managers worked. She had a friend there, and she went inside to get him. After a few minutes Austin brought the man outside to talk to Ruud, who was still sitting in the truck. The man said he had heard there was some "informal" dumping going on a few miles to the northwest, but the road was almost impassable, and he wasn't sure they would find anything even if they went. He pointed them northward, toward the Columbia River, and insisted that if they looked hard enough, they would find a big hole in the desert floor, half-filled with crapped-up stuff. But he refused to go along with them to help them find the dump site. He didn't want to be identified as a troublemaker.

Austin and Ruud then drove around the desert for hours in the gunmetal gray government truck. They followed the main paved roads and then turned off at every dirt path they found. Some of these turnoffs were so rutted they could only drive a few miles per hour. Sliding down into deep gullies and climbing up to the crests of hills, each time they would reach a high point, Ruud and Austin would scan the horizon for some sign of activity.

There was plenty of time for talking, as they looked out over the vacant landscape. Austin told Ruud that she was the daughter of an air force officer who had been stationed in England when she was very young. She had admired the by-the-book style of military people, and she tried to approach her work in the same way. But, she said, it was hard to buck the prevailing attitude at Hanford, which held that only the timid obeyed the rules when it came to radiation exposure.

Years later, Austin recalled what she had felt then about the Hanford mentality. "They were just plain macho when it came to radiation. Take the tank farms. They expected you to just hold your breath and run past areas where there was radiation. They said it saved the time you would use up putting on the protective suits. It just seemed careless to me, but I didn't push it. You know, you don't want them to think you're holier-than-thou. God help you if they think you're not on the team."

On that summer afternoon in 1985, Austin and Ruud spent three hours looking for the second dump and becoming hot, tired, dirty, and frustrated. Ruud suggested they go back to the waste-management office and ask for more information. When they arrived at the small building, Austin again went inside. But this time it was a young woman who came over to the truck to talk with Ruud. Ruud was purposefully vague as he described what he was trying to find, but the woman knew exactly what he meant, and seemed more than willing to help. "I'd follow the railroad tracks behind T Plant," she said. "That's where I'd go if I was trying to hide something. Nobody ever goes out there." As Ruud started the truck and backed it up to leave, the young woman called after him, "Remember, think railroad tracks!"

Ruud and Austin drove out to T Plant, which had been one of the first chemical processing facilities built at Hanford. It had been converted to a decontamination facility. Much of the area around it was marked with yellow radiation warning signs. The two inspectors found the railroad tracks behind the building, but no sign of a disposal area.

Near T Plant, Austin pointed to a rutted trail that veered away from the railway. Ruud suggested she get behind the wheel and drive along the path while he stood in the back of the pickup to get a better view. He climbed into the bed of the truck, stood on the sidewall, and braced himself against the roof of the cab. A bang on the roof of the truck signaled Austin to proceed.

Austin drove the truck at about five miles per hour, rolling through the sagebrush and tumbleweeds as Ruud bounced up and down in the back. She was careful to stay on the path, avoiding the worst of the holes and bumps so that Ruud wouldn't fall out of the truck. Suddenly she heard a pounding on the roof. Ruud leaned over the open window and said he had seen something, a mound, about a mile ahead.

When they reached the spot they discovered that a huge pile of earth had been removed to create a pit about thirty feet deep and fifty yards across. Small yellow warning signs with the familiar radioactivity symbol—a circle surrounded by three triangles—were posted on stakes around the edges of the hole. Austin rolled the truck to a stop and sat for a moment, just looking at the pit. Ruud climbed down from the pickup bed.

Austin grabbed the camera off the seat beside her and got out of the truck. The two walked up to the pit and stared down. Inside they saw pieces of steel, concrete blocks, discarded work gloves, and other miscellaneous bits of trash, alongside scores of rusting fifty-five-gallon drums labeled RADIOACTIVE WASTE. It looked as if truckloads of crapped-up stuff had simply been poured down the side of the pit and left in a jumbled pile.

Ruud took the camera from Austin and walked around the hole, photographing it from every angle, but making sure they didn't get too close. "What do you think it is?" he asked as he walked around. Austin could only guess. She thought that some of the materials might have come from PUREX or PFP. Or, she said, the dump could contain items that had been buried at other locations and then removed during an environmental cleanup project.

When they had finished, Ruud and Austin again took the pictures to Baker. This time he told them to give the photos of both sites to an environmental specialist in the auditing department. The specialist, and Austin, would press the case further.

That night, Ruud went home to the split-level cedar house that he and his wife, Suzi, had bought in a new subdivision in Kennewick. They had chosen the neighborhood because it was full of young families and close to the elementary school their children had attended during their first stay in the Tri-Cities. Jason, their older son, was a nine-year-old immersed in Little League, soccer, basketball, and the tame adventures available in the neighborhood. Six-year-old Kelly was about to start first grade, and their second son, Blaze, was just two.

On most nights Casey Ruud would greet his pretty, dark-haired wife with a kiss and answer her first question with a half-mumbled "Fine, everything was fine today." Like most Hanford workers, he was prohibited from discussing the substance of what he did in any detail. He could talk about his daily run, or whom he had seen at lunch. But he couldn't offer a detailed description of the equipment he may have inspected that day, nor could he discuss the audits he was scheduled to perform. In the tradition of Hanford, Casey Ruud had become a husband who rarely talked about his work.

On this night, however, after his long journey in the desert with Inez Austin, Ruud arrived home to tell his wife that he had had one of his rare good days at work, and that he felt he was at last being put to constructive use. "We found something pretty big, Suzi," he told her. "I'm just waiting to see if they're going to do something to fix it."

A few days later, Ruud and John Baker received a positive response to the complaints they had filed with their superiors. Several high-level managers in the waste-disposal operation had been transferred or had resigned because of the discoveries Ruud and Austin had made. The remaining managers promised to follow the rules for proper decontamination and disposal of solid and liquid wastes. Ruud considered it a mild response, since in all likelihood both the disposal crews and their bosses had violated RCRA and placed Rockwell in legal peril. But at least something had been done about the problem. Ruud was encouraged because it appeared to him that Rockwell was trying to play by the rules.

In the months that followed his adventures in the desert, Casey Ruud and John Baker developed a plan for a series of audits that would cover most of the important facilities at Hanford, including PUREX, PFP, and the tank farms where millions of gallons of dangerous liquid wastes were stored. Most of the previous audits had involved reviews of reports and forms, and rather literal on-site investigations. Under Baker's direction, Ruud would spend most of his time in the field, talking to designers, production workers, and engineers. For the first time, Baker would have someone with construction experience and years spent in the commercial nuclear business eyeballing the work done in the Area.

This aggressive approach suited Baker. A former navy man, he believed that risky operations such as plutonium manufacturing should always be done by the book. Auditors existed to make sure the rules were followed. This view had been hardened by the pivotal event in his navy career, an accident that occurred aboard the aircraft carrier *Boxer* in 1952. Baker and several other sailors had been trapped inside a belowdecks compartment by a raging fire that was the direct result of a fellow crewman's error. The crewman had failed to make sure that an airplane's guns were unarmed, and had accidentally set off a single round. The resulting fire killed two of Baker's friends. He escaped only by dashing through the flames moments before the others were engulfed. More than thirty years later, Baker still mourned the loss of his friends and lamented that the safety systems in place on the ship had somehow broken down.

After his navy days, Baker spent the rest of his working life in the quasi-military world of government contractors. His little office at Hanford was decorated with pictures of the aircraft he had

helped build for the army, the air force, and the navy. He also
displayed mementos from NASA, where he had worked on several high-profile projects. Rockwell's space operation had been his
last home before Hanford. It was also the site of his second dramatic brush with disaster. Baker had worked on the tragic 1967
Apollo mission that ended when a fire inside the capsule killed all
three astronauts. He recalled how engineers had recommended
ways to reduce the danger of fire and improve escape routes.
(With nothing but pure oxygen in the capsule, and a hatch that
could only be opened from the outside, the astronauts didn't have
a chance once the fire was sparked.) The safety experts who had
foreseen these dangers and suggested different designs had been
overruled by higher-ups.

Despite the tragedy, and the sense of guilt he shared with thousands who had worked on Apollo, Baker still considered those
NASA years the high point in his career. He loved to tell stories
about the space program. And Ruud was always willing to listen
when Baker recalled how astronaut Gus Grissom used to drive his
sports car right onto the sidewalk in his neighborhood, or how
Eugene Sirnan would dive into the details of engineering problems
to solve even the least technical concern.

"The astronauts were gods," he would say, a faraway look in his
eye. "Anything they wanted, they got, and I mean anything. But,
hell, they were the ones taking the biggest personal risks. There's
nobody like them today. They were bigger than life."

At NASA, and at Hanford, Baker fit comfortably with the many
ex-military men who held key management jobs. This flow of per-
sonnel from the military to major contractors explained in part the
culture of Hanford, a culture that valued the chain of command
and loyalty above almost everything else. Baker subscribed to these
values. He was loyal to those under his command and to the authority of his superiors. In particular, Baker believed in Rockwell's
commitment to safety. Paul Lorenzini, Rockwell's manager at Hanford, spoke often about the need for both safe operations and
quality control. Baker believed that Lorenzini had given him a
mandate to pursue these goals. And in the back of his mind was the
knowledge that one safety violation—on the *Boxer* or at Hanford—could cost lives.

Nowhere was safety more important than in a process called "design control." The design-control system was supposed to guarantee that work done at any Hanford facility complied with certain standards. Welds had to be done in such a way that they could withstand stress. Pipes had to stand up to the pressure of the corrosive liquids they would carry. Vessels had to be designed to prevent a criticality—the spontaneous, deadly flash of high-energy radiation that can occur when too much plutonium is collected in one spot. Baker had heard rumors suggesting that design-control standards were routinely ignored. He had heard that many engineers in the Area were "Hanfordized," which meant that they had a casual, seat-of-the-pants attitude and ignored design guidelines. Hanfordization was the dark side of the can-do spirit that had made Hanford work during World War II. At that time, engineers and mechanics were creating one-of-a-kind machines, and they often made up the rules as they went along. But over the course of forty years, standards had been set by the nuclear industry. Hanfordized workers would tend to ignore these standards in favor of their own judgment. To see if Hanfordization was a real problem, Baker asked Ruud to determine whether workers complied with a special nuclear engineering code called NQA-1—for Nuclear Quality Assurance Standard Number One. If his auditor discovered that NQA-1 was being followed to the letter, then Baker could be confident in the basic design of plant equipment and major repairs. If NQA-1 was being widely ignored, then Hanfordization was real.

The NQA-1 engineering review—also called the "design-control audit"—was just one in a series of audits Baker and Ruud would pursue in the coming year. Ruud was also scheduled to look into a rather technical area called nuclear materials control, or NMC for short. NMC was a system of accounting procedures designed to prevent both criticalities and the loss or theft of plutonium. It was one of the most security-sensitive programs at Hanford.

As they prepared their schedule of audits, Ruud and Baker discovered they were a good match. Baker had wanted to conduct more assertive inspections, but had never had an auditor with the right background. Ruud had the necessary experience and temperament for the job. He was a good listener, and he always seemed to make friends with workers on the site who could teach him the workings of a complex plant or production process.

Design control and nuclear materials control were to be the focus of Ruud's work in the coming year. But first Baker gave him a smaller assignment, a kind of warm-up exercise, that would fore-shadow the kinds of discoveries he would encounter in the larger audits. This small review involved checking the criticality alarm systems at PUREX and PFP, where the plutonium that was born in the inferno of N Reactor was refined and finally fashioned into solid "buttons" of weapons-grade atomic explosive. PFP was per-haps the most sensitive and radiologically hazardous work environ-ment at Hanford. Because workers dealt with so much plutonium, criticality was a special concern. The plant was equipped with radi-ation detectors and special alarms that would sound a loud "ah-oo-gah" warning if a blue-flash criticality event was about to occur. If an alarm sounded, workers had just seconds to evacuate before receiving a lethal dose of radiation.

The detectors, the special containers, and the precise work rules that prevented criticalities were monitored by a group of safety experts who worked in a small building near the plant. Ruud went there looking for someone who might guide him through the audit. He found Paul Ritman, Ph.D., a scientist who specialized in com-plicated analyses of design and production problems. Ritman agreed to walk Ruud through both plants and explain how the alarms worked and how criticality risk was assessed. On their tours, Ritman and Ruud would ask technicians to hold radioactive testing devices near the alarms, and watch as the horns began to blare and the workers cleared out. Ruud discovered that the alarm system was basically sound, and the technicians charged with preventing criticalities knew what they were doing. In theory, these safety specialists had taken into account all of the possible problems that would lead to a critical mass and imposed the proper safeguards. Of course, Ritman had told him, there was one factor that no one had taken into account.

"What's that?" Ruud asked.

"Earthquakes," Ritman replied.

Ritman went on to explain that some of the buildings were not seismically safe. One substantial earthquake, similar in magnitude to others that had occurred in Eastern Washington in the past, could cause many of the Hanford buildings to collapse. Ritman said he couldn't be sure what would happen in an earthquake. It could be that nothing beyond structural damage would occur. But a building collapse could also dump large amounts of the plutonium together, creating a criticality big enough to kill hundreds of people.

The NQA-1 standard required that nuclear facilities be designed to withstand "seismic events" or earthquakes greater than the most violent quake locally recorded. Ritman couldn't be certain, but he said he had heard that neither PUREX nor PFP, the large plutonium-handling canyon buildings, met such a standard.

When Ruud reported back to John Baker, he told him that the criticality alarm system was sound. He also told him about Ritman's offhand remarks about earthquakes. Baker was interested, but not enough to push for more. Ruud's original audit plan called for a review of the alarm system. He had completed the task, and there were other audits to be done.

Though Ruud wanted to try to confirm Ritman's earthquake story, he had to agree with Baker. There were too many other important audits to be done. In particular, he wanted to review the design-control system on site. It would be impossible for him to look at large numbers of designs for repairs or new equipment and then locate each one in a facility to make sure the work was done correctly. So he decided to visit key facilities, select three engineering projects at random, and follow them. If the random check turned up NQA-1 violations, he thought, it would be reasonable to assume that Hanfordization was indeed a problem.

Ruud began in an office at the tank farms. The secretary pointed him toward a grizzled old engineer who sat at a government-issue metal desk that was flanked by file cabinets. The auditor explained that he wanted to look at three "design packages," envelopes that contained the documentation and calculations done for every engineering change or improvement. With those in hand, he could then go into the field and make sure the work had been done according to the plans.

The engineer reached into a drawer and handed Ruud three envelopes. The first one was for the design of a high-pressure steam pipe. Ruud identified it as a "Safety Impact 1" job, the kind of repair that could kill nearby workers if it failed. Ruud was familiar with these kinds of steam lines; he had worked on them himself in commercial plants. He also knew that the design package should include calculations to prove that the right materials were being used. Any good engineer should know which kinds of pipes and other materials would work, but the calculations were required. When Ruud asked for them, he was told they weren't necessary. "I didn't have time for calculations," the engineer told him. "I just did it with best engineering judgment."

Ruud protested, and the engineer's back stiffened. In a terse confrontation that Ruud would recall years later, word for word, the engineer informed him that simple projects that were needed to keep production going were done on an ad-hoc basis. There was no time for calculations, or for peer review by other engineers. And as far as the old veteran was concerned, this system of relying on the judgment of experienced Hanford hands worked. "We don't have time for that shit," Ruud would recall him saying. "This is how we do business."

After visiting the tank farms, Ruud went to PUREX and picked out three more engineering packages. One was for a mixing device used to keep radioactive liquids from settling and going critical. Again he discovered that key calculations were not recorded and included in the engineering package. He also found that after it was built, the device had to be modified because it didn't work.

The last phase of the design-control audit was done at the Plutonium Finishing Plant. There a young new engineering supervisor handed Ruud three design packages. As Ruud flipped through them he asked about the engineers who had done the work. This was another conversation he would remember, word for word.

"Where's the engineer for this one?"

"He quit."

"How about this one?"

"He quit."

"And this one?"

"He quit too. He couldn't handle this place, so he left."

The implication was that the engineers had been frustrated by Hanfordization.

The final design package Ruud had asked about was for a small change in the ventilating system inside PFP. It involved ductwork at a work station called Hood 9B. The duct drew air away from the hood, where plant operators used remote-control devices to handle plutonium. Ruud wanted to see the finished product. The engineer took Ruud to the production line and Hood 9B. What he saw was an exhaust system designed to cool an area where temperatures would otherwise exceed 150 degrees. Special "high-energy particulate air filters" inside the hood caught airborne radionuclides before they could leave the work station and be circulated outside. The workers near the hood explained that when the filters got clogged with plutonium, they were changed. They would push a new filter into a slot in the hood, dislodging an old one, which would then fall out and be disposed.

The engineering packet Ruud had selected covered a remodeling of the filter "change-out" system. But something about it didn't look right to Ruud. He knew that the hot air would cause the metal duct to expand, and that the whole mechanism might jam. The system could have been designed with special supports to offset the problem of heat. But there were no supports, and Ruud wanted to know why. "Where are the calculations?" he asked. Once again, there were no calculations.

Not only were there no calculations for the changes on Hood 9B, but Ruud discovered that the overall plans for the production lines—the schematic drawings that showed where all the equipment was located and where the various pipes, wires, and ventilation system led—were substantially out of date. (These drawings are often referred to as "as-built" drawings.) Numerous repairs, additions, and rerouting of equipment hadn't been recorded in the as-built plans. Based on the drawings, engineers couldn't be certain of the exact locations of much of the plant's mechanical equipment.

The Hood 9B problem and the out-of-date general diagrams violated Ruud's idea of good engineering practices, at least as they were defined by NQA-1 and his experience in the nuclear power industry. But everyone he talked to suggested that this was simply the way things had always been at Hanford, and that he was making too much of it. Then, after spending days with engineers and their staff, Ruud was pulled aside by a high-level engineer—someone he occasionally hung out with—who insisted that their discussion be confidential.

This informant—Ruud jokingly called him "Deep Throat," after the shadowy Watergate figure—said that a "quick-fix" approach to maintenance and improvements in the plant was required by upper managers. He said that engineers followed a "top-ten hit list" sent down from on high. The hit list focused the staff on jobs that maintained production, to meet the government's demand for plutonium. Safety was a secondary consideration.

The engineer went on to tell Ruud that many of Hanford's engineers had tried to slow down the design process so that they could satisfy NQA-1 requirements for calculations, documentation, and peer review. But the heavy workload and deadlines set by production managers made it impossible for them to follow proper procedures. They were continually forced to fall back on their "best engineering judgment," a euphemism for bypassing standards. Rockwell received bonuses—in addition to the normal fee the Department of Energy paid the company for running Hanford—whenever production goals were met or exceeded. In the drive to meet the goals and win the extra money, the engineer said, safety might be compromised.

"It's all screwed up, Case," said Deep Throat. "It's the whole system."

When the design-control audit was over, Ruud reviewed his findings. Random checks at all three facilities—tank farms, PUREX, and PFP—had revealed that engineers routinely violated the most basic requirements for safe design. In each case they added new equipment or made repairs without calculations or review by other, qualified engineers. At PFP the as-built sketches were so out of date that they were practically useless. And at all three facilities, engineers and operators didn't seem to care that their work was substandard. All this was taking place in a defense facility where mechanical breakdowns could lead to spills and contaminations that could cost millions to repair, or contaminate the environment, or even kill every human being in sight.

Ruud was certain that any one of these discoveries, if made at a civilian nuclear power plant, would have led to an immediate shutdown. The Nuclear Regulatory Commission, which oversees civilian atomic plants, would have required the operator to fix the problem, and prove it was fixed, before restarting. But Hanford was not a commercial facility, and Ruud couldn't be sure that Rockwell's managers would respond to his findings the way the San Onofre managers had responded when he found the flaws in the steel lining of the reactor containment pool. Ruud considered management's response to the discovery of the two illegal waste dumps to be halfhearted. Then there was Dr. Paul Ritman's story about seismic safety. If Hanford managers were willing to ignore the possibility that many of their critical facilities could not withstand an earthquake, what else might they ignore? Technically, his audit findings seemed to require an immediate shutdown. But he had worked on site long enough to know that Hanfordization was real. If he called this one by the book, he would face an immediate challenge from the managers at all three facilities. Ruud wasn't even sure that Baker would support him.

All of this weighed heavily on Ruud as he wrote his final reports. During this time he was even quieter than usual at home. Suzi would ask about work, and Casey would say he was dealing with some big problems, but wouldn't go into any detail.

As fall turned to winter, Ruud finished interviewing operators, managers, and engineers. He drafted a report that declared that the design-control system on site was essentially "out of control." Such a declaration would present the top Rockwell executives with the option of an immediate shutdown or a crash program to bring the engineering processes up to standards.

Ruud was still undecided about whether to submit this draft report to Baker when, on a day in early January, he was invited to one of the conference rooms in the Rockwell administration building. The space shuttle *Challenger* was about to be launched. Rockwell was a major contractor for the space shuttle program, and many of the company's top people at Hanford had some connection to the aerospace division. Some had even worked on the shuttle, before transferring to Hanford. They were proud of their work, and they reveled in the power and beauty of the sleek spacecraft and its giant booster rocket.

Several dozen people crowded into the conference room, where a television had been set up so they could watch the *Challenger* launch as it was broadcast live. Much of the country would be tuned in because this time the rocket would send aloft a civilian schoolteacher, Christa McAuliffe, along with the regular astronauts. The *Challenger* mission marked an especially confident moment in the American space program. With the addition of a civilian crew member, NASA had symbolically declared that space travel was becoming safe, dependable, routine. This feeling—that flying into space was becoming a normal event—was reinforced by the fact that the shuttle itself looked and operated much like an airplane. It rode into space straddling a rocket, but, unlike the early space capsules, which fell like rocks into the sea, the shuttle could fly back to earth on its own wings, land at an airstrip, and then be sent back into space.

As the countdown neared completion, Ruud squeezed into the conference room, where a large TV showed a broadcast from the launch site. All around him, veterans of Rockwell's space projects talked, drank coffee, and nibbled on the pastry that had been laid out on a table. When the mission-control announcer on TV began the final countdown, they grew quiet. They heard the voice run through the numbers "ten, nine, eight . . ." They saw the smoke and flame of the rocket igniting and heard the roar of the engines. They watched intently as the rocket punched through some clouds and then followed a gentle arc into the sky. But then, just seconds into the mission, came an unexpected billowing of smoke and confusion in mission control. As the television announcers struggled to find out what happened, there were some in the Hanford conference room who felt the truth in their stomachs. The *Challenger* had exploded.

In the months that followed, investigators would trace the worst space disaster in history to faulty seals on rocket boosters and to officials who had approved the launch over the objections of technical experts. Rockwell would not be implicated directly in the loss of the *Challenger*. But on that January morning, as he sat with the

Rockwell veterans, Casey Ruud experienced an epiphany. He thought about the dangers inherent in great technical challenges, and the reasons why engineering codes must be enforced. He reflected on the problem of Hanfordization and his fear that Rockwell managers were putting production before safety. He began to think of himself as someone separate from the Rockwell team.

# NOTHING TO HIDE

ON A CLEAR, cold morning in February 1986, while the nation was still in shock from the *Challenger* disaster, Hanford manager Michael Lawrence appeared in a small conference room in the Richland federal building, and calmly began to dismantle the wall of secrecy that had shielded America's plutonium complex for more than forty years. As a surprised group of reporters and activists looked on, workers wheeled out box after box of documents. Lawrence took just one complete set, comprising nineteen thousand pages, and put it on a table. It was five and a half feet tall. Here was the Department of Energy's response to the concerns of the downwinders and others, he announced. Here was Hanford's secret history.

At the time, Lawrence couldn't know all that the papers contained. Archivists, national security experts, and scientists had actually reviewed the papers and recommended those that could be released without compromising national security. But even though he hadn't read all the documents, Lawrence was confident in his agency, confident that there were no serious problems in the reports, no "smoking gun" pointing to serious problems. And he was amused to think that his critics—Karen Dorn Steele and the people from the Hanford Education Action League—might be overwhelmed by the white paper mountain before them. There was so much material in each set that people had to help each other carry them out.

As he watched Steele and the others grappling with the stacks of paper, Lawrence felt victorious. In the months since his appearance at the Unitarian church in Spokane, he had become even more convinced that it was time for Hanford to emerge from the shadow of secrecy. Lawrence had promised a new openness—he often referred to it as a "change in the culture" of Hanford—and he had made good on that promise. This gesture won him instant praise, even from his harshest critic, HEAL, whose spokesman declared that the federal government was "increasing their credibility with the people of the Northwest."

The release of the nineteen thousand pages marked a turning point in long-standing Department of Energy policy. Lawrence had broken with the tradition of strong nuclear managers who in the past were regarded as warlords ruling carefully protected domains. Whether at Hanford, Savannah River, Rocky Flats, or Oak Ridge, these managers had operated in almost total secrecy. Lawrence believed that eventually all of the department's operations would have to come out of the darkness. He was happy to be the first. In the glow of the TV lights, he became the white knight of Hanford, a telegenic hero bureaucrat who seemed to be creating a new relationship between the public and the federal nuclear weapons establishment, one marked by cooperation and trust.

The early news reports on Lawrence's sweeping release of Hanford's historical records relied on summaries provided by the Department of Energy. These summaries noted that in the preceding twenty-seven years the public had received no significant dose of radiation from Hanford. Indeed, "the impact of Hanford isn't zero, but it's minimal," noted a Department of Energy official who was quoted by Karen Dorn Steele. Michael Lawrence went even further, insisting that even though radiation had occasionally leaked past the borders of the site, the papers showed that Hanford hadn't harmed anyone. Hanford, he said, had "nothing to hide."

This didn't mean that the plutonium factory's record of operation was spotless. On the contrary, the summary confessed that until the last old reactor closed in 1971, their "single loop" cooling systems had routinely deposited radioactivity in the Columbia River. The Hanford papers also detailed a number of incidents in which radiation had been released into the air. But while these occurrences were noted, there was little in the summaries to indicate that any lasting harm had been done. The summaries left the impression that releases into both water and air were diluted to the point of near harmlessness. (Dilution was the solution, the nuclear establishment always said.)

Given the volume and technical quality of the declassified reports, and the magnitude of the story, Steele and other local journalists had no option but to report, more or less unchallenged, the government's interpretations. The simple fact that the Department of Energy had unloaded so many previously secret reports was news in itself. The newspapers couldn't wait while outside experts or even their own reporters waded through the materials themselves. They had to go with the story.

But on that first day in the new era of openness, Steele noticed something strange in the official summary—the reference to negligible pollution over "the past twenty-seven years." What about the period before that, the years from 1943 to 1957? Steele already suspected that this early period of plutonium production had been the dirtiest. After all, the technology was still new then, and the pressure of the Manhattan Project and the Cold War had been most intense. But there was no mention of this time in the summaries. Steele made sure to mention this gap in the second paragraph of an otherwise positive story about the department's openness. This caveat put the government on notice; Steele was not satisfied with their version of the truth.

The activists at the Hanford Education Action League were not satisfied either. In the days following the release of the nineteen thousand pages, they divided up the documents and pored over them, trying to piece together a more complete understanding of Hanford's past. Steele also worked around the clock, wading through the raw data in search of important information omitted by the official summary. She was motivated by two concerns. First, she suspected that the Department of Energy was trying to soft-pedal what had happened at Hanford in the early years of operation, before that twenty-seven-year period mentioned in the summary. Second, she lived in journalistic terror of being scooped by rival reporters. Hanford had become an important topic for the Seattle and Portland papers, and Steele wanted to maintain her lead in the friendly battle to be first with the biggest stories.

As she worked day and night, Steele once again became a distant, puffy-eyed figure whom her daughters Blythe and Trilby regarded with both concern and pride. Once again they would find her asleep on the sofa in the morning, surrounded by Hanford. But this time they were not worried about her safety, and they understood the importance of the work. They were proud, even if their mother seemed distracted, consumed once more by the chase.

Steele was assisted by Timothy Connor, a free-lance reporter hired by HEAL to do research. Connor had much in common with Steele. As a child, he too had lived abroad, in the Panama Canal Zone. As a third-generation "Zonian," Connor had been raised to regard the little colony as a bit of America. But like Steele, he had learned early on that what was real and true was open to interpretation. In Connor's case, it had come with the discovery that many Panamanians resented the American community that bisected their country. This experience had filled Connor with a mistrust of government. His appetite for journalism was probably inherited. His grandmother had edited a small paper in Idaho, and according to family lore, a distant relative had worked with the legendary editor Horace Greeley. Connor had left Panama to attend Washington State University, where he gained some notoriety for uncovering a secret slush fund in the athletic department. He first became interested in Hanford in 1983, while working as a local newspaper reporter in the small town of Ellensburg, about forty miles north of the atomic reservation. Frustrated by his editors' lack of interest, he quit his job and, even though no magazine or paper would back him, began investigating the history of the secret facilities. By 1985 he was living in the basement of his parents' house, selling tickets at a Spokane theater to finance his obsession. Late in the year, HEAL started paying him to do research. When the documents were released, he and Steele agreed to work together to speed up the review process.

In their first few days with the documents, the two worked like miners sifting through tons of earth to find raw gems. They would scan the sheaves of documents and call each other when they made discoveries, so that they could compare the weight and clarity of what they had found. They made their most spectacular find in the first week.

Connor came upon it first, in a 1950 report titled, dryly, "Radioactive Contamination in the Environs of the Hanford Works for the Period October, November, December 1949." His attention was drawn initially by a map that appeared to show radiation measurements taken in a wide area around Hanford. A note accompanying the map referred casually, in lowercase letters, to something called the "green run." The investigators would attach sufficient importance to it to capitalize it.

"A significant increase in the I-131 activity on vegetation occurred immediately after the dissolving of the green run on Dec. 3," the document stated. "Table 2 summarizes the results of the vegetation sample program for the period previous to and the period immediately after the green run." Table 2 showed that radiation levels higher than the government-established limits had been measured as far north as Spokane and as far south as the California-Oregon border. The contamination was worst closest to Hanford. In an area that included hundreds of square miles of farmland bordering the site, the samples had shown radiation at ten to twenty times the safe level.

As Connor read on, he found other pieces of the Green Run puzzle. On page twelve: "5,247.5 curies released in December from 200 west area." (Connor knew this was the area where the T Plant was located.) "These figures include the radioactive gases formed during the experimental dissolution of one ton of irradiated uranium cooled only 16 days," the report continued. "This experimental green run was performed on Dec. 2, 1949. A detailed discussion of the complete data of this experiment is included in a report issued under separate cover."

On page 28: "One ton of green uranium was dissolved on Dec. 3, when an estimated 5,050 curies of iodine 131 and 4,750 curies of xenon 133 were formed in the dissolver at this time. Estimations of the amount of this activity actually liberated to the atmosphere and a more detailed appraisal of its deposition pattern and concentration may be referred to in a special report on this operation." (The figures for xenon were officially classified secret in 1986, and were mistakenly included in the released documents.)

There was little more valuable detail. But Connor knew enough about radiation and weapons production to understand that the Green Run had been extraordinary. In normal production, "green" uranium rested for ninety days to allow certain elements, such as iodine 131, to decay and become less harmful. Processing green uranium, in an era before sophisticated filters had been developed, guaranteed that a substantial amount of iodine 131 and other radionuclides would go up the smokestacks of T Plant and into the air. From there, as the shaded map indicated, it apparently spread in every direction, falling on plants, animals, houses, and people.

There could be no doubt that the radiation had spread far and wide. In one Hanford document it was noted that a weather balloon loaded with Geiger counters had broken free of its tether and floated off in the very middle of the Green Run. It was eventually found in the town of Pleasant View, Washington, fifty-five miles to the east. There was also ample evidence that dairy cows were grazing the downwind area during the experiment, and as Hanford documents suggested, the cows and every other living thing in the region received a radiation dose eighty times official limits.

If it wasn't a smoking gun, at the very least the Green Run was evidence that in one instance in 1949, Hanford had irradiated the environment outside the fence. The amount suggested by the report—5,050 curies—was hundreds of times the amount of radiation released by the Three Mile Island accident. This made the Green Run one of the biggest radiation releases ever to occur at an atomic facility. But worse, thought Connor, was the fact that this release was not an accident. It was a deliberate and—given the extensive sampling of radiation levels on vegetation all over the region— carefully considered experiment.

As the reporter and the researcher slowly came to understand the technical details of what they were reading, they also began to consider the moral and political implications of this information. In 1986 the United States was still locked in the Cold War arms race. But they felt sure that few citizens, save perhaps a handful of extreme hawks, would accept their government endangering thousands of civilians for the sake of the weapons program. News of the Green Run would inevitably raise more questions about the conduct of the arms race. It would also provide ammunition for the Reagan administration's political opponents, who constantly questioned the arms buildup.

But most disturbing was the realization that specific individuals had chosen to proceed with the Green Run. Connor and Steele both concluded that Hanford's operators understood the risk they were taking with public health. Among the documents in the nineteen thousand pages were several referring to the radiation threat posed by operations like the Green Run. Another HEAL researcher, Jim Thomas, found a memo warning of the dangers, written by Hanford health scientist Herbert Parker and distributed just months after the Green Run. In his memo, Parker urged caution on those who would increase uranium production by reducing cooling time. If the Atomic Energy Commission were to repeat the Green Run, Parker wrote, the government might have to pay compensation "for possible injury to animals over a wide area." (This memo would be of special interest to Tom Bailie and the farmers downwind. It also caught the attention of the Utah sheepherders, who had been told by the old Atomic Energy Commission that their animals couldn't have been harmed by similar bomb-test radiation.)

The Parker memos troubled Thomas, who soon assumed from Connor the chore of reviewing the documents for HEAL. He worked alone, in the Spokane Public Library, which had received a full set of the papers released by Mike Lawrence. Thomas's cheeks would flush with anger when he was confronted with a situation he considered unjust. Thomas, who had once studied for the priesthood, was serious-minded and devoutly moral. He lived by his conscience. In the early 1980s he was so deeply involved in the Catholic peace movement that he joined a twenty-month "peace pilgrimage," walking from Seattle to Bethlehem. One of his fellow marchers was Father George Zabelka, a onetime military chaplain who had been spiritual shepherd to some of the men who dropped the first atom bombs. In the 1940s the priest had told the fliers to act without guilt, for they were engaged in a just war. But by the time Thomas met him, Zabelka had experienced a profound change of heart. He had come to regard atomic weapons as inherently evil, and Thomas would recall that on the peace walk Zabelka spoke remorsefully of the way he had justified the bombings.

Jim Thomas had been profoundly affected by George Zabelka, his own fear of the Reagan buildup, and the antinuclear stands taken by America's Catholic bishops. He had returned to Spokane in the early 1980s to find that the international controversy over nuclear technology was being played out in his hometown. He soon became a very active member of the Hanford Education Action League. Eventually he would become HEAL's chief researcher. No one outside the federal bureaucracy knew more about Hanford. But even as he gained expertise in technical matters, Thomas never lost his moral perspective. It was, in the end, political morality—not scientific or economic concerns—that drove his obsession with Hanford and the larger nuclear arms issues.

After reading the Green Run document, it seemed obvious to Thomas, Connor, and Steele that the experiment had created substantial pollution, that Hanford's operators knew the public could be affected, and that a deliberate decision had been made to keep the danger secret. They were stunned by the idea that anyone would experimentally release so much radiation so close to farm families, cities, and towns. They couldn't understand why it had been done. The answer to this question probably lay in the separate reports referred to in the documents. But this report was not among the nineteen thousand pages. It was still classified.

As she worked on an article about the Green Run, Steele learned that the new openness announced by Mike Lawrence had its limits. Keith Price, the Battelle scientist who headed the group that had released the nineteen thousand pages, refused to discuss the Green Run in any detail. He wouldn't say who had ordered the experiment, or how it was decided that no warning would be issued. All he told Steele was that it had been done to test certain instruments, and that it was still a sensitive subject.

It was left to outsiders to put the Green Run in context. State officials said they were never told about the experiment, and that such releases would not be allowed today because the iodine release would likely exceed radiation exposure regulations. Sam Milham, the epidemiologist, called the experiment "stupid." And like everyone else Steele interviewed, Milham wanted to know why it had been conducted.

In the absence of any explanation from the Department of Energy, speculation was rampant. The most provocative notion was advanced by Bob Alvarez and other antinuclear activists, who guessed that the Green Run had something to do with a secret radiation weapons program that had been directed by former air force general Curtis LeMay. A tough, cigar-smoking fighter pilot, LeMay was a driven man who had overseen the bombing of Japan—including the atom-bomb drops—during World War II. The hawkish LeMay would go on to become presidential candidate George Wallace's running mate in 1968. But in the late 1940s and early 1950s he was head of the Strategic Air Command, the air force's nuclear arm. In this capacity, LeMay had explored the idea of using highly radioactive by-products from Hanford's reactors as weapons. The radiation would be delivered in special bombs. Once on the ground, it would contaminate enemies and their environment. The Green Run, Alvarez guessed, had been related to this weapon research.

While Alvarez and others tried to imagine the reason for the Green Run, the downwinders worried about its effects. Laura Lee Bailie, Tom Bailie's mother, told Karen Steele that she was most concerned that the food in the region had been contaminated. She wondered aloud about the connection between the Green Run and her son's childhood illnesses. Chastened by his neighbors' reaction to his earlier interviews, Bailie tried to stay out of the media limelight. But other downwinders spoke of their fury and outrage. The anger extended even to members of Congress from Oregon and Washington State, who promised an investigation of the Green Run incident and the more than thirty years of official silence that followed.

As the Department of Energy continued to refuse to provide more information, it appeared that members of Congress were the only ones who could hope to get the full story. Mike Lawrence promised to give them a secret briefing on the experiment, but he warned that much of the information remained classified (for national security reasons) and could only be known by those who, like some members of Congress, held high-level security clearances.

The justification for the Green Run could have remained a mystery to the general public were it not for Carl Gamertsfelder, a seventy-four-year-old retired Hanford radiation-control manager whose name appeared in small print on one page of the Green Run documents. This time, Steele was beaten on the story. Reporters for the Portland *Oregonian* tracked Gamertsfelder to his retirement home in Knoxville, Tennessee, where he told them that the experiment had had nothing to do with LeMay's exotic radiation weapons. But it had related to the intrigue and espionage of the Cold War. The United States had been trying to spy on Soviet weapons factories from the stratospheric perspective of exotic surveillance aircraft. The aircraft, and monitoring stations at sites bordering the Soviet Union, could be equipped with devices that would measure the pollution coming out of Russian plutonium plants. But in order to know how the emissions related to the volume of uranium being processed, the Americans needed to simulate Soviet manufacturing methods. To do this, they ran the T Plant Soviet-style, shortening the cooling period and allowing higher levels of pollution. They then measured off-site radiation and worked out a formula that would turn readings from monitoring devices into estimates of the enemy's bomb-production rate. Since the Soviets processed green uranium, in order to stay competitive in the arms race, Hanford had to conduct a Green Run too. (Of course, without documentation, no one could be sure that this explanation was accurate. Years later, HEAL would continue to suggest that there was more to the story. Jim Thomas theorized that the U.S. scientists had to perform the Green Run in the way they did because their instruments were not sensitive enough to detect small emissions.)

The Gamertsfelder story—displayed prominently in the Portland paper—was one of the few Steele failed to get first. Chastened by the setback, she called Gamertsfelder to see if she could get something more out of him. The old Hanfordite seemed delighted by all the attention he was suddenly getting. "Gosh, it's sure taken a lot of years for this to become declassified, hasn't it?" Steele later recalled him saying. Gamertsfelder told her the Green Run experiment was originally designed to disperse radiation over a wide area, perhaps as far as Minneapolis and beyond. But bad weather conditions, including unexpected rain, had contained the radiation. "It didn't go far," Gamertsfelder said. "We really plastered the lower Columbia Valley."

If the Green Run had been the only major incident at Hanford, it still would have been a shocking revelation. But as winter turned to spring, Jim Thomas and Karen Dorn Steele kept combing through the nineteen thousand pages and continuing to make startling discoveries. They turned up evidence of many other releases, some of which were much larger than the Green Run. In all, they estimated, more than one million curies of radioactivity—the largest accumulation of atomic industrial pollution then on record—had been deposited in the air, water, and soil. Hanford, it turned out, had plastered the Columbia Valley over and over again:

- In the 1940s, hundreds of thousands of curies of iodine 131 were released into the air from ongoing operations as Hanford rushed to build the bomb.

- From 1952 to 1954, a Hanford processing plant called Redox repeatedly showered Richland, Mesa, and much of Eastern Washington with ruthenium particles, which are highly carcinogenic. The radioactive contamination was so heavy that access to part of the Hanford site was restricted to protect the workers.

- In 1956, two separate incidents led to radioactive iodine emissions that were detected as far away as Spokane.

- During a three-month period in 1957, an average of 34,000 curies of radiation per day were flushed into the Columbia River along with the reactor cooling water. Even after operating improvements were made, 18,000 curies per day entered the river during one stretch of time the following autumn.

Hanford's environmental performance improved in the 1960s, but mishaps were still quite common. An entire pound of uranium was sent into the river in 1963 during high-power operations, which engineers knew would rupture some fuel slugs. This release raised the radioactivity level by 150 percent as far as ten miles downstream. In the 1960s the river was contaminated by the fission products of 1,300 different ruptured reactor fuel slugs. (These incidents may explain the discovery of a fifty-five-foot radioactive fin whale that died off the Oregon coast in 1964. At the time the British journal *Nature* reported the find, but not the source of the contami-

nation.) Various other fires, ruptures, and accidents sent hot particles into the air and the water, threatening workers, wildlife, and
neighboring citizens.

Although officials had often considered warning the public, each
time they chose instead to be silent. Indeed, Hanford officials and
the national nuclear establishment repeatedly denied that any nuclear facility posed a threat. One widely distributed Atomic Energy
Commission film from the 1950s explained that the government
was on top of environmental issues. "One of the foremost considerations of the AEC is the safety of these people who work and live
in cities near atomic plants," the narrator of the film says as pictures
of the Tri-Cities flash on the screen. "Waste material which might
be potentially dangerous must be removed and stored safely. This
is vitally important." Of course, at the time the AEC was already
exempted from all national, state, and local environmental standards by the 1952 Atomic Energy Act. And safe storage amounted
to nothing more than steel tanks, which were susceptible to leaks,
and drainage ditches.

For nearly forty years the public had generally accepted the
assurances from the government and the nuclear experts. In the
meantime the government remained silent, acknowledging none of
the serious radiation problems at the nation's seventeen atomic
weapons facilities. Even when they knew that radiation was falling
on the local population, officials at Hanford consistently decided
against advising the public.

Working alone in the Spokane public library, Jim Thomas became increasingly indignant as he read the documents describing
these decisions. He was particularly disturbed by a 1957 memo
innocuously titled "Aspects For River Navigation Through Hanford." Riverboats carried grain, produce, and other materials along
the Columbia. The report warned that crews routinely drank water
from the channel, water that might be contaminated. While they
considered warning the boat operators, Hanford officials eventually
decided to keep mum, because "public relations might suffer."

More than thirty years later, as the revelations of incidents,
accidents, and experiments continued, public relations remained
the major concern for the people who ran Hanford. When the
Green Run scandal hit the press, Keith Price and Joseph Soldat,

one of the few scientists who had been around for the experiment, urged people to remember that the experiment had taken place at the height of the Cold War. Those who could recall that time understood the sense of urgency, even fear, that surrounded the weapons race. At the monthly meeting of the Richland chapter of the national Health Physics Society, scientists from Battelle and the Department of Energy complained that they had been inundated with calls from anxious citizens. Department of Energy physicist Erik Erichson told the health physicists that he had reviewed the documents and he was certain "there was no attempt by anybody to hide anything."

Many of those who defended Hanford tried to weather the controversy by relegating the dangers to a distant past. Others, like Mike Lawrence, argued that the problems of the past, the Green Run in particular, were not so serious, even when they violated radiation limits of the time. After all, the releases that had taken place during the war years—1944 to 1945—had been even more substantial. Indeed, the level of radiation emitted by the Green Run could have been considered acceptable just a few years earlier, as Hanford raced to end the war.

Time and again, Lawrence tried to get people to understand rather than condemn the old AEC for decisions that must have seemed reasonable at the time. During the Manhattan Project, those in charge certainly believed that some risk was necessary if America was to acquire atomic weapons before the Germans and the Japanese. Years later it became clear that neither enemy was close to producing the super weapon. But at the time, the Americans believed that the Germans in particular were on the brink of making a bomb. After all, the German effort was led by some of the world's greatest physicists, including Otto Hahn, who had been the first to recognize that atoms could be split—fissioned—with astounding results. And though the Japanese lagged in science, their suicidal defense of the islands on the approach to Japan made it clear to many American strategists that finishing the war without the bomb would create a sea of blood. Given these facts, Lawrence refused to condemn those who led the Manhattan Project and allowed some radiation pollution. Lawrence also refused to view those who approved the postwar Green Run as irresponsible or evil. The way he saw it, his peacetime predecessors had considered the effects on downwinders, limited the amount of radiation that was released, and planned releases for times when winds would dilute the emissions. During the Green Run, a sudden change in the weather had meant that some unexpectedly high concentrations of radiation fell on populated areas. But Lawrence saw no malicious intent on the part of the government, and he was certain that given the tenor of the times—with the Russians appearing ever more bellicose and threatening—the Green Run had been necessary. In one TV interview, Lawrence suggested that even with the problems of the 1940s and 1950s, there was little to worry about. "Nothing is without risk," he said, "and the risks in the early days were certainly greater than they are now. But basically there is still, I think, evidence of safe operations during that entire period of time."

In the downwind community, many were prepared to accept Lawrence's analysis, especially if it meant they could protect the value of their lands and crops. Tom Bailie's neighbor and friend Steve Halvorson appeared on one TV newscast, standing in a field of cauliflower. He said he had lost twenty thousand dollars in sales because consumers had been frightened by the Hanford publicity. He blamed antinuclear activists and a few hysterical fellow farmers. "They have no idea of what they're talking about, and it's costing people money," Halvorson complained. "The downwinders here that are so worried about it are still eating the food that's grown here."

Ultimately, neither those who believed they were harmed by Hanford nor those who thought the downwinders' fears were nonsense could be sure they were correct. No one had ever conducted a comprehensive health study of the population near any weapons facility, let alone a specific survey of the Tri-Cities region. But soon after the documents were released, the federal Centers for Disease Control announced that it would study the effects of Hanford's emissions. This study would take many years, but it promised to provide some answers for the downwinders, and it could possibly settle long-standing scientific and political disputes over radiation and health. The CDC's action and the arguments made by Mike Lawrence might have calmed the public if it weren't for a historic event that took place half a world away. On April 25, as Rockwell executives returned from lunch in downtown Richland and thousands of Hanford workers tended to their daily duties, their counterparts in a Ukrainian atomic settlement called Chernobyl were in a panicky struggle with an out-of-control reactor. It was already the early morning of April 26 in the Soviet Union. Plant operators had deactivated certain safety equipment—including an emergency cooling system—to run an experiment. Officials wanted to test the ability of the power plant to make enough electricity, using the inertia of spinning turbines, to respond to a catastrophic loss of power. Poor operator training and a fatally flawed protocol for the experiment led to the reactor's overheating to the point of disaster.

The definitive book on what happened at Chernobyl was written by Grigori Medvedev, a Soviet nuclear expert. His second-by-second account, titled *The Truth About Chernobyl,* shows how poorly trained workers followed ill-conceived orders to an inevitable outcome. According to Medvedev, the crucial moment arrived at 1:23 A.M., when a control-room operator named Akimov pushed the red button that was supposed to activate machinery that would reduce the reactor's power. Instead, Reactor Number 4 experienced a sudden energy surge. Radioactive gases and superheated steam reached astounding levels of pressure. At 1:24 A.M., the world's first nuclear power plant explosion blasted Number 4 apart and sent much of the disintegrated core—an estimated fifty tons of highly radioactive materials—into the night sky. This was more than ten times the mass of radioactive elements in the Hiroshima bomb. Indeed, the emissions were so substantial that a week after the explosion, Soviet airline workers still discovered contamination on high-flying jets that passed over the Ukraine. (Akimov himself actually survived the blast, but died of radiation poisoning two weeks later.)

Soviet officials immediately understood the ramifications, both domestic and international, of what had happened. The plant itself continued to burn, sending more toxins into the atmosphere. Nearby communities were being rendered uninhabitable. Putting out the fires at the plant and moving thousands of people would take an enormous effort. Outside the Soviet Union, the Chernobyl explosion deposited radiation on people, property, livestock, and produce throughout much of Europe. It also cast a pall over the worldwide nuclear establishment. Officials in every country with atomic power had said that such an explosion was almost impossible. But the impossible had happened, and the result was death and destruction.

In the United States, the nuclear industry rushed to calm the public. American reactors were nothing like those in the Soviet Union, they noted. Chernobyl Number 4 had been an old-fashioned graphite reactor with no containment building. The designers of America's commercial nuclear power facilities had long ago abandoned graphite because it could ignite at high temperatures. They also housed their atomic cores in special earthquake-proof domes to contain radiation and protect the public in the event of an accident. These and other differences suggested that the West was far ahead of the Soviets when it came to nuclear safety, and that American power plants were so different from Chernobyl Number 4 that comparing them would be like comparing an adding machine to a computer.

Almost everyone in the atomic establishment made this argument, except for a Hanford-based engineer, Ersel Evans, who told the *Tri-City Herald* that the Soviet reactors were really not so bad. The lack of containment "doesn't mean they are inherently less safe," said Evans. And, he added, the people running the Soviet plants "are as brilliant as ours."

These statements would have baffled many outside the Hanford community. After all, the best way to protect the image of the American nuclear community would be to separate it from the Soviets. But inside the Tri-Cities, it would be obvious to everyone that Evans had to defend the Russian technology. Because, although most of the country didn't yet know it, Hanford's own N Reactor was similar in design to the one that had exploded in the Soviet Union. Like Chernobyl Number 4, N Reactor had been built out of graphite blocks. It was also the only American reactor that, like Chernobyl Number 4, produced both electric power and plutonium. Commissioned in 1963, N was also one of only five large American reactors that lacked containment domes. The other four were at the Department of Energy's Savannah River atomic weapons complex in South Carolina.

In the days that followed the Chernobyl explosion, a HEAL

researcher, who remembered reading an article about Chernobyl's design in the magazine *Soviet Life,* alerted reporters to the similarities to N Reactor. The Department of Energy office in Richland and Hanford's contractors were subsequently besieged by reporters who wanted to know if a Chernobyl-type disaster could happen at Hanford. Of course the Hanford experts insisted the answer was no. They pointed to the redundant safety system built into N Reactor, the superior training of its workers, and its long history of safe operation. Mike Lawrence described N Reactor as so superior to the Chernobyl machine that it was practically "meltdown-proof."

These reassurances were not enough to calm public concern. In comments to the press that were widely reported, Timothy Connor of HEAL challenged much of what the Hanford experts said. Connor argued that in some ways the Chernobyl unit was safer. Reactor Number 4 was much newer than N Reactor, for example, and some of its emergency protection devices were superior. And, it would later be revealed that the Hanford unit, designed to last about twenty years, had reached the end of its useful life. As the controversy seemed to spin out of Mike Lawrence's control, Secretary of Energy John Herrington stepped in. A lawyer-politician who was highly conscious of the department's image problems, Herrington did what many politicians do in response to a crisis—he appointed a commission. The panel, headed by John Roddis, former president of New York City's Consolidated Edison utility, would review N Reactor's condition and suggest what might be done with the Hanford reactor. Until the review was completed, N Reactor continued to operate.

The government's response to Chernobyl was calculated to calm the public. But even when journalists presented the reassurances of the American officials, it was almost always in the context of a report that emphasized how similar N Reactor was to the Soviet reactor. This was a natural angle for the media to pursue in the wake of the Chernobyl catastrophe, a fact that throughout 1986 frustrated public-relations officers at Hanford.

"Everyone always took the obvious story, which led with pictures of the Atomic Lanes bowling alley and concluded that the Tri-Cities was some strange, blindly pro-nuclear place," Jerry Gilliland would recall years later. As the unflappable public relations director for Rockwell, Gilliland, forty-two years old at the time, had to cope with a controversy that never seemed to abate. Whether it was the downwinders, the document release, or Chernobyl, it seemed as if every time the fire died down, more fuel was added. "It was a feeding frenzy," he said of the media interest.

It was at about this time that Gilliland began to think that the very future of Hanford as an operating nuclear center was in doubt. For months he had felt ambivalent about his own work and the overall integrity of Hanford. A former newspaper reporter with a serious cast of mind, he had been recruited to Hanford the year before by the head of Rockwell Hanford, Paul Lorenzini. Gilliland brought with him a reputation as a scrupulously honest if somewhat stodgy journalist, a Clark Kent who never turned into Superman. He had also made it a condition of his employment that he be given immediate access to factual information whenever a problem arose. Gilliland was preoccupied with doing the right thing. As a reporter he had avoided sensationalistic stories, preferring long, explanatory pieces to front-page scandals. As a public-relations man he was determined always to tell the truth. This sensibility was honed in the Mormon Church, in which he was raised, and he kept it sharpened with almost constant reflection on the morality of his work.

"I had been personally appalled by the revelations about the Green Run," he remembered. "That was a terrible thing they did. The people could have protected themselves, but nothing was said." Gilliland's disillusionment grew when key people at Hanford failed to tell him everything he needed to know about N Reactor's similarities to Chernobyl Number 4. Indeed, in the first days after the explosion in the Ukraine, Gilliland unintentionally misled reporters, telling them that N Reactor had an effective containment building. He was forced to apologize to them when he found out that N Reactor had no containment building to protect area residents.

Having been misled by his own colleagues Gilliland began to believe that the people of Hanford were incapable of dealing openly with a public that was growing ever more frightened of atomic pollution. The gap between what the public found acceptable and the attitude within Hanford was growing wider and wider. At the height of the Chernobyl story, Gilliland admitted his worries to his wife, Leslie. One evening they discussed it after driving past the New England–style saltbox home they were building in one of Richland's best neighborhoods. It was to be identical to a home they had left behind in Olympia when Gilliland had been hired by Rockwell. He told her that the problems at Hanford were bigger than he had expected, and that the workers and managers didn't seem ready to adapt to new standards of openness. He said he might resign to avoid ever having to lie again to the press. Though they made no decision that night, Gilliland discovered that to his wife, the house and the big Rockwell salary were not the most important things. "Do what you have to do," Leslie said. "You don't have to have this job."

The revelations about Hanford's past and Chernobyl had a direct effect on the Gillilands and thousands of other Tri-Cities families whose lives were bound up in the atomic facilities. Some worried about the future of their jobs. Others began to reflect on their roles in what Hanford had done. The Hanford crisis also rippled across the country; while watching the network news and reading their hometown papers, thousands of people who once worked at Hanford, or lived nearby, had to wonder if they had been unknowingly affected by the radioactive releases.

June Stark Casey was one of the many who, in the spring of 1986, were jarred by the revelations. Thirty-six years before, when she was a college student in Walla Walla, Casey had gone home to The Dalles, Oregon, for Christmas, feeling more tired than she had ever felt in her life. She slept day and night, and always felt cold. Her family doctor in the Columbia River town diagnosed her exhaustion and chills as hypothyroidism and promptly put her on medication. While her general condition improved, she soon noticed another symptom that was even more disturbing: hair loss. Great clumps of her thick, curly brown hair started appearing on Casey's brushes a few months after Christmas 1949. Horrified, she tried every kind of treatment that doctors could imagine including hormone injections. Nothing worked. Her hair continued to fall out until she was bald. The baldness, and her continued bouts with exhaustion, remained a mystery as she finished college, found work as a teacher in Oakland, California, married a school counselor named Desmond Casey, and settled into a comfortable middle-class life in a house overlooking San Francisco Bay. Even as her life took on all the trappings of normalcy, she remained troubled by illness. She suffered a miscarriage in 1970 and a stillbirth in 1972. Skin cancer and a degenerative spine disorder came later.

After decades of sickness, Casey believed her mystery was solved on a warm Sunday afternoon—it was Mother's Day, 1986—as she sat on the sofa in her living room, reading the paper. An article on the Green Run brought Casey back to 1949 and her college days in Walla Walla. Suddenly she had a plausible explanation for what had happened to her. According to the article, the Green Run documents showed that Walla Walla had been blanketed with radiation from Hanford. Casey knew enough about radiation to surmise that the iodine and other radionuclides that fell on The Dalles had probably caused her illnesses.

As she sat on the sofa, the newspaper in her hand, June Stark Casey began to cry. She was flooded by many emotions. One was relief. She had always wondered if her symptoms were psychological, somehow resulting from a flaw in her character. Now she knew otherwise, and could let go of the self-doubt. But Casey also felt profoundly betrayed. All her life she had been a loyal, patriotic citizen. She had been raised in the Catholic church, and remained devout. When she retired from teaching, she had thrown herself into charity work, raising money for everything from cancer research to historic preservation projects. She believed in the goodness of others and the basic integrity of the bedrock institutions such as the church and the government. When she found out about the Green Run, this changed.

In the ensuing weeks, June Casey poured herself into the task of learning everything she could about Hanford. She contacted the editors of the local paper, who put her in touch with the Washington-based author of that first article. From there she found her way to Karen Dorn Steele, HEAL, and an organization called the National Association of Radiation Survivors. She read books such as *Killing Our Own,* written in part by Robert Alvarez, and she began

asking questions of her friends and family. She remembered a so-
rority sister who gave birth to a deformed baby in 1951, and a
neighbor whose child developed cancer in 1945. At about the same
time, her brother had developed a seizure disorder. None of what
Casey learned, or remembered, proved that Hanford had injured
her or anyone else. But her crash course in atomic history changed
the way she thought about herself and her country. Her priorities
changed. She couldn't bear the small talk at cocktail parties or
the frivolity of charity banquets. She ended her charity work and
devoted herself to groups working for peace and nuclear disarmament.

Though June Casey's experience was extreme, it was not unique.
Across the country, people who had once lived near Hanford read
of the experimental and accidental radiation releases and were forever changed. Whether they were affected physically or psychologi-
cally, they were nevertheless victims of the atomic age who shared
a common sense of anger and disillusionment. Others experienced
a similarly painful awakening in October 1986, when a congressional committee revealed that the government had conducted many
secret radiation experiments on human beings in locations spread
nationwide. Over the years, hundreds of people had been fed radioactive substances or exposed to airborne contamination. Some subjects drank radioactive milk. While most of these events occurred
in the 1940s and 1950s, one human experiment was conducted as
late as 1967, at Hanford. In that case, fourteen people were either
fed or injected with promethium.

Hundreds of those who were directly affected by Hanford joined
Heal, so they could learn as much about Hanford as they could,
while being sustained by the support of a group dedicated to their
concerns. Although education remained the group's main activity,
Heal also provided a meeting place for those who felt the need to
grieve their physical losses and their loss of innocence. "I felt such
grief and sorrow," Casey would recall years later. "It wasn't so
much anger as it was deep, deep disillusionment. But I did feel
anger every time I heard someone talk about what had happened
as if it was a mistake or an accident. It wasn't. It was an atrocity,
and it was deliberate, and that was the hardest part to understand."

As scattered former residents of the downwind area such as June Casey came to realize what might have happened to them, the people of Franklin County had to consider what Hanford might have done to their entire community. Farmers and townspeople were suddenly aware that Tom Bailie was more than a headline-grabbing politician. The documents released by Mike Lawrence proved to them that Bailie had been right about Hanford's past. The Chernobyl tragedy made them worry about its future.

The analyses offered by various experts further alarmed the residents of the farm belt around the nuclear reservation. Some of the most disturbing news came from a sociologist at Boise State University who announced that thyroid and breast cancer levels in three downwind counties had been unusually high in the 1950s and 1960s. Professor Michael Blain found the cancer statistics in a federal publication called the *Atlas of Cancer Mortality for U.S. Counties.* In the atlas, seven counties downwind from Hanford were highlighted in bright colors, indicating high levels of thyroid and breast tumors.

Blain contacted the media and presented his discovery apparently as a disinterested academic. In fact he was a longtime opponent of nuclear weapons and well schooled in the use of science in political debate. An avid reader of Bertrand Russell, Blain had joined the philosopher's Ban-the-Bomb movement as a college student in the early 1960s; he had gone on to collaborate with Dr. Carl Johnson on a study of the health effects of atomic facilities in Idaho. Even though Blain believed that Johnson's studies often inflated the incidence of cancer near nuclear facilities, he thought that this thumb-on-the-scale method was justified.

"To the public, this might be a scandal," he would explain later. "But the nuclear industry was doing the same thing. And in scientific debates, they can always try to prove you wrong. But that doesn't mean you have to tell them how to do it." In the case of Hanford and cancer, Blain went to the press with his statistics in order to put political pressure on the government officials who could fund in-depth studies of the health of the downwinders. In 1991 he would publish an academic paper titled *Rhetorical Practice in an Anti–Nuclear Weapons Campaign,* which described the movement as a "victimage ritual." As with all rituals, symbols were more important than facts, and the antinuclear forces used "melo-dramatic rhetoric"—words such as "contamination," "cancer," "pollution," and "secrecy"—to portray themselves as innocents fighting against an evil force. Blain described how the activists, modeling themselves after Gandhi and Martin Luther King, would try to turn federal officials into demons and make the nuclear fight a matter of morality, not science.

In the wake of Chernobyl and the Hanford revelations, experts and activists followed Blain's theoretical model, creating what amounted to a tidal wave of frightening speculation. In some cases, this happened inadvertently. When the Richland chapter of the American Nuclear Society held a symposium intended to calm public concern, Hanford officials were confronted by farmers and members of HEAL. The questioners practically forced the pro-nuclear scientists to acknowledge that any radioactive release—no matter how small—could increase the risk of cancer in local com-munities. At the same meeting, the Hanford scientists confirmed that workers at the site suffered higher-than-expected rates of cer-tain cancers. Both of these statements contradicted long-standing government statements about the absolute safety of the atomic operation.

While the experts from Hanford reluctantly confirmed the health risks posed by the radiation releases, a host of outside authorities were brought to Spokane in May of 1986 by a local lawyers' group that put on a public symposium called "Hanford: The Public and the Law." Many of the experts pounded the government with criti-cism and alarmed the public. The German researcher Bernd Franke declared that Hanford had definitely caused hundreds of thyroid cancers and precancerous tumors. Larry Shook, one of HEAL's early activists, compared the Department of Energy with sinister Soviet bureaucracies. Robert Alvarez, who was spending a lot of his time in Eastern Washington, demanded that N Reactor be shut down because, without a containment dome, it failed to meet gov-ernment safety standards set for commercial reactors.

These critics were opposed by Department of Energy officials and other pro-nuclear spokesmen, who had been invited in the spirit of fairness. The pro-nuclear speakers reminded the more than one hundred people in the auditorium that there was no certain proof that Hanford had hurt a single downwinder. Such cause-and-effect was almost impossible to prove, so Hanford's supporters could always fall back on the claim that after more than forty years of operation, not one area resident's death could be traced directly to the atomic reservation.

At the meeting, Donald Jose, a lawyer who had successfully defended the government against lawsuits brought in other radiation cases, led the defense of the atomic industry. Jose argued that the more than one million curies of radiation released by Hanford had probably not caused any excess cancers. He warned the audience to resist jumping to conclusions about what had happened in the past and who was to blame.

As he sat in the audience and listened to this argument, Tom Bailie grew angrier and angrier. Although he had served as a living symbol of the Hanford controversy for nearly a year, it was the first time Bailie had actually attended an event with so many antinuclear activists. Like most of the farm people he knew, he was uncomfortable with the "peacenik" aura that surrounded HEAL, and he had avoided an alliance with the Spokane group until this moment. Bailie still considered himself a loyal, patriotic American who viewed nuclear weapons as a necessary if unpleasant fact of life. But in the pursuit of the truth about Hanford, he had increasingly found himself allied with the antinuclear community. And as he heard the defenses offered by Hanford's supporters, Bailie experienced a change of heart. For the first time he came to view the nuclear establishment as potentially evil, and he accepted his alliance with the 1960s-style activists of the antinuclear side.

When Jose finished speaking, Bailie, his face flushed with fury, raised his hand. "I'd like to say something, and I'd like to say it now," he said loudly from his chair in the audience. Robert Alvarez, who was on the stage, offered him a microphone. Bailie jumped onto the stage and turned to face the auditorium.

"I got to say, I'm mad," Bailie began. "You people are animals. You've gone beyond the line of morality. Nothing they have done before or since can redeem the Hanford scientific community for

what has been done to the downwinders of Eastern Washington."
After forty years of silence and deception, Bailie concluded, "We
need the truth."

Bailie's red-faced anger was shared throughout Franklin County
as every morning's newspaper seemed to bring more revelations of
secret pollution. Even some of the farmers who had originally
shunned Bailie in the cafés had begun to wonder about the health
of their families and the condition of their lands. In interviews with
reporters, farmer Allan McAffee said that the government was
literally killing people who lived downwind. McAffee took a photographer from the Seattle *Post-Intelligencer* into a pasture where
a dead cow lay belly-up, its legs splayed and its head extended.
Although the cow could have died of a number of causes, McAffee
said he wanted the carcass tested for radiation poisoning. His suggestion—that perhaps Hanford killed the cow—was as dramatic as
the photo the paper published of the farmer next to the fallen
animal. But the cow's death was never conclusively connected to
radiation.

As the press again swooped down on Mesa and the surrounding
area, others who once shunned Tom Bailie were now ready to
recount for reporters their stories of miscarriages, stillbirths, and
illnesses, which they now blamed on Hanford. A local druggist
noted that the demand for thyroid medication was so great that it
was one of the few pharmaceuticals he ordered in bulk. Other
residents spoke of a cancer epidemic. In one typical TV broadcast,
Bailie stood in a wheatfield with Connie Chung, who was now
becoming a familiar face around Mesa. In the program, Chung
related the history of secret radiation releases, and she compared Hanford's N Reactor with Chernobyl. Then she invited Bailie to speak.

"All my father's brothers have had cancer," he said. "My father
has had cancer. My mother has had some cancer. My two sisters
have had cancer surgery, and it seems like I spent most of my
growing-up years in the hospital." The implication was clear, if
unstated: Hanford caused cancer.

Because Washington State did not require doctors to register
cancer cases, there were no solid facts to prove or disprove the
conclusions of frightened downwinders. But it didn't matter that

the facts were insufficient proof for their claims. In 1986 and 1987, with the help of the media, the Hanford story fast became a powerful modern myth, a narrative that contained so many convincing elements that the facts were secondary. First there were the farm families. Seemingly simple, trusting, loyal Americans, they represented the traditional small-town ideals of honesty, hard work, and independence. The second important element of the Hanford myth was the secret atomic technology operating at the site. Like Pandora's box, nuclear knowledge promised the riches of the universe but held, as well, the potential ruin of the innocent. Finally the myth contained enemies, the intellectually superior but tragically overreaching technocrats, who also fit an American archetype. The scientists and bureaucrats who ran the plutonium complex could be seen as brilliant fools whose hubris had created a disaster for the common people.

Ironically, the human face that came to represent to many the dark side of the Hanford myth belonged to Michael Lawrence, the former white knight among nuclear managers. Despite his brave efforts to part the veil of secrecy, in the eyes of Hanford's critics and many everyday citizens, Lawrence became Hanford's evils made flesh. It fell to Lawrence to explain that there were similarities between N Reactor and Chernobyl's Number 4, but that the Hanford reactor had extra safety devices. It was also Lawrence's duty to try to explain the dark secrets of Hanford's past. As he struggled to do this, he came to be associated with the institution's transgressions.

In the Department of Energy's executive offices, high in the Richland federal building, Lawrence's closest aides resented the negative publicity and bristled at the downwinders' attacks. Many had been skeptical about Lawrence's decision to release the documents in the first place. This kind of openness ran counter to Hanford's culture of secrecy, and it had been widely assumed inside the department that the site's history would be misinterpreted. During the turmoil that followed, Lawrence's assistant, Edward Goldberg, complained privately to him that today's managers were being blamed unfairly for the wrongdoing of the past. But Lawrence insisted that Hanford and the entire Department of Energy would have no future if it couldn't come to terms with its past. "We are paying the price now," he said. "But it's the right thing, and we'll be beyond this when all the other Department of Energy sites are still trying to figure out how to do the same thing."

Lawrence kept himself calm with his convictions and with his long-distance running, which served as an antidote to stress. And more than once he amused himself when he noticed how much recent events reminded him of his favorite movie, *The Wizard of Oz*. A great sparkling city of the future, Oz was the domain of a humanly flawed wizard whose magic depended on the faith of his subjects. Sometimes the Tri-Cities could seem like just such a fantastic place of the imagination. Anyone else comparing Hanford with Oz would assume that Mike Lawrence was the Wizard. He sat atop the Hanford techno-bureaucracy, and he was supposed to be in charge. But as events began to run out of control, Lawrence actually felt more like Dorothy. "And I sometimes wished," he confessed later, "that I was back in Kansas."

While it may have felt like a fantasy, the problems Hanford's manager faced were real. He had to be concerned about protecting the energy department's image and his own reputation. He tried to do this by arguing three points at once. The first was that nothing seriously dangerous had taken place. The second was that, given the context of the times, the government could justify its actions. Finally he would point out that the problems all lay in the past, that the department now followed ever more stringent safety and environmental rules.

Of course, these arguments were all self-serving and open to criticism. Despite what Lawrence might say, there was no doubt among health physicists that the radiation that drifted across the Hanford fenceline could, and probably did, cause cancer or birth defects in animals and human beings. There was also growing public skepticism about the urgency of the Cold War buildup. Not everyone believed that the arms race of the 1940s and 1950s justified the kinds of risks that had been taken at Hanford. Finally, as Casey Ruud's audits showed, Hanford could not claim entirely clean and safe operations even in 1986. In fact, Hanford continued to pollute the soil and groundwater, more than 150 temporary waste-storage tanks continued to pose a threat, and precious little contamination had been cleaned up.

Nevertheless, in interviews and public appearances, Lawrence repeatedly defended Hanford. He argued that in the 1950s, America had been threatened by the Soviet Union, and had rightly sought more and bigger weapons. The men and women of the Atomic Energy Commission, and later the Department of Energy, had performed an essential duty as best they could. Lawrence would not condemn his predecessors. Likewise, he refused to agree that Hanford had injured its neighbors.

Lawrence's loyalty to the atomic pioneers of the past, and his firm position on the health effects of the radiation releases, reflected the consensus of opinion in the nuclear cities. As a career Department of Energy manager Lawrence may have had no other option. Perhaps he could not even imagine doing things differently. Any Hanford insider who criticized the actions of his predecessor would be viewed as an ungrateful child unworthy of his inheritance, or as a weakling who let human emotion override his intellect. For the sake of his professional future and his position in the Tri-Cities nuclear culture, Lawrence had to preach the company line.

But though the hard-line approach played well in the Tri-Cities, it seemed cold and uncaring when juxtaposed on national TV with testimony from Tom Bailie and other downwinders. To make matters worse, while the downwinders were pictured on TV standing in fields of golden wheat, Lawrence was usually interviewed in his austere government office, sitting behind a bare oak desk. In a gray suit, white shirt, and tie, he looked like everyone's idea of a bureaucrat, especially when compared with the farmers in their flannel shirts and fertilizer company caps. And while the TV reporters gave downwinders and others wide latitude to tell their stories, they subjected Lawrence to the kind of aggressive questioning that can make almost anyone seem like the accused.

On one CBS news program, "West 57th Street," Lawrence sat stiffly in his suit while the reporter bore down like a prosecuting attorney. Lawrence used his standard argument about the risks inherent in any large-scale project and the absence of any proof that people had been harmed. The workers, he noted, were healthy. The reporter responded with a withering description of how Hanford had threatened innocent civilians. The more than one million curies of radiation released by Hanford couldn't be considered a small risk, he pointed out. And no one had studied the health of the downwinders, especially children and pregnant women, who were most susceptible to radiation.

"In fact," the reporter continued, "Hanford's neighbors could have received much higher radiation doses than the workers. Because radioactive releases came from towering smokestacks, they were blown away from the plant, downwind and toward an unprotected population that included infants and small children, who are ten to one hundred times more vulnerable to radiation than adults."

None of Lawrence's explanations could overcome the stories of the downwinders, the photographs of ominous-looking uranium facilities, and the suspicious tone of the reporter. In this and many other forums, Lawrence was forced to answer powerful imagery with a kind of technocrat-ese. It was an utter mismatch. He failed to defend Hanford's past, and he failed to protect its future as a plutonium producer or a waste repository.

Lawrence and his allies must have felt strangely naked to the criticisms of outsiders. Indeed, for the first time in history, much of the power to determine Hanford's image, and ultimately its future, lay in the hands of outsiders. The CDC would investigate Hanford's effects on human health. The so-called Roddis Commission, appointed by the Secretary of Energy, was looking at the future of N Reactor. Finally, a citizens' committee named by the Department of Energy and the governors of Washington and Oregon would oversee a review of the nineteen thousand pages of documents and try to assess the atomic reservation's effect on the environment. These studies would take a great deal of time, but the simple fact that they were being planned meant that Hanford's shield of secrecy was cracked and that its very survival was in doubt.

Of course, for those who had campaigned to get the truth about Hanford, the revelations about the Green Run and other incidents caused mixed emotions. Karen Dorn Steele's instincts about Hanford had been proved right. But she still had an enormous undertaking before her. Only a fraction of Hanford's past had been revealed in the documents. Given the serious problems revealed so far, Steele had to wonder if those reports that remained hidden behind the door of national security were even worse.

But though Steele's professional passions were stirred by the truths leaking out of Hanford, Tom Bailie and the other downwinders were affected more personally by the revelations. Bailie felt vindicated. He knew, at last, that his suspicions had been justified. And many of his friends and family asked him if he could now let go of his crusade. At first he thought he could. After all, he had won.

But gradually he found that his obsession with Hanford was burning stronger than ever. Despite the objections of his wife and children, Bailie seemed compelled to talk about little else. Years later he would admit that he had continued his crusade as a kind of emotional therapy, a way to soothe his anger at the federal government and his feelings of helplessness. He felt helpless to change what had happened in the past and helpless to protect himself, his family, and the community from whatever lay in the future. Always his mind was filled with questions: How many babies had been lost to miscarriages caused by Hanford? How many cancers lurked in the bodies of the thousands of downwinders? How could they know if Hanford's current operations were safe?

Bailie wasn't the only one who couldn't seem to get over Hanford. Down in Oakland, June Stark Casey obsessively continued to gather books, articles, and even documentary films on nuclear technology. And even some of Bailie's neighbors, the ones who had shunned him in the past, began to form a chorus of complaint that could be enlisted any time a reporter or TV camera crew came to town. They didn't trust Mike Lawrence and they didn't trust Hanford. And they didn't believe they knew all of the truth about what had been done to them.

# MAD AS HELL

IN THE vacuum-quiet wilderness of the Hanford site, the emotional power of the revelations about the facility's past and even the shock of Chernobyl seemed to disappear. No one felt personally responsible for the ecological sins of the fathers that had been revealed by reporter Karen Dorn Steele, or for the losses suffered by downwinders such as Tom Bailie. And no one could have suspected that Hanford would soon be embroiled in an enormous public controversy relating to its current operations. In the momentary calm, the men and women who worked in the Area held to their daily routines and to their faith in America's superior technology.

It was mostly boring work; that was the remarkable thing about Hanford's top-secret mission. Making plutonium was a relatively simple process. Almost anyone with a high-school diploma could be trained to work at Hanford. It was like being in the army; as long as you followed proper procedures, the job got done through the combined efforts of thousands. Day in and day out, Hanford workers followed procedures. Even when something unexpected happened, there were procedures and routines that governed how they would respond.

In April 1986, at about the time when the world was obsessed with Chernobyl and graphite reactors, one of these unexpected events—an Unusual Occurrence, or "UO" in the official language of Hanford—occurred at the Plutonium Finishing Plant. At about ten-thirty on the night of April 15, a second-shift worker was assigned to change an air filter in Glove Box 9B (also called Hood 9B.). Glove boxes were workstations where technicians placed their hands in long rubber gloves attached to openings in a protective wall. As they peered through thick windows, they worked with the

146

weapons-grade plutonium, remaining safe from contamination. Box 9B was like a glass greenhouse, about five feet wide, fifteen feet long, and seven feet high, placed in the middle of a large white room. Greenish plutonium nitrate solution entered the greenhouse through pipes. Workers wearing white jumpsuits with gloves and booties used the remote-controlled tools to begin converting the solution to the grayish powder that would eventually be formed into metallic plutonium "buttons" the size of hockey pucks. The cylindrical air filter that the worker was supposed to change kept radioactive particles from entering the system of air ducts and fans that cooled the workstation. A constant flow of air was necessary because besides being intensely radioactive, the plutonium solution was literally hot. Without ventilation, temperatures inside the hood would exceed two hundred degrees.

Filter changes were routine. A fresh filter in a stainless-steel housing would be pushed through an opening in the duct. As the new one was inserted, the old one would be dislodged. A worker could reach a gloved hand into the duct, remove the old filter, and dispose of it as radioactive waste. But on this night, when a technician in a standard white jumpsuit pushed the new filter in, the old one didn't fall out.

This had happened before, so when a few more pushes failed to dislodge it, the worker used a tried-and-true method to fix the problem. He grabbed a pair of pliers and, working through the rubber gloves, yanked on the old filter. It broke. Part of it came out, but the technician was left with the tedious task of pulling out the remaining shreds of metal one by one. This chore was made more difficult by the fact that he couldn't actually see what he was doing. He could only reach into the duct and feel his way around. The work was slow. He had to reach up into the filter while wearing the bulky rubber gloves. And he had to be especially careful. The filter was completely crapped up. Any direct contact with the pieces would mean immediate contamination.

With midnight approaching and his shift nearly over, the first technician put down the pliers inside the hood and prepared to hand the job off to the next crew. But as he withdrew his hands from the gloves, he discovered a small puncture wound on his left palm. Somehow he had brushed up against one of the sharp pieces of the old filter. It had pierced his glove and his skin. Given the high concentration of radioactive particles on the old filter, he knew the wound had to be contaminated, and so did his supervisor. The man was rushed to a Hanford clinic, where doctors cut away a small area of flesh near the wound, taking with it microscopic amounts of plutonium. Although the treatment was apparently a success, the worker could never be certain that a particle had not entered his bloodstream, where it could, many years later, cause cancer.

While the first worker was in the clinic, a second cautiously struggled to finish the job. His supervisor recommended using a Vise-Grip rather than ordinary pliers. This second technician was able to grab the remaining part of the filter setup and rock it loose. But when he removed it from the duct, he too was wounded when a shard of metal cut through his rubber glove and sliced the little finger of his left hand. Again a man was raced to the clinic. Again doctors had to remove a small portion of flesh so they could get all of the atomic poison.

All of this was documented in detail in a formal document called a UO Report, as were the recommendations for preventing future injuries. The problem with the filter was blamed on poor design and improper procedures. Under "lessons learned," the UO Report noted that workers could use better "hand protection" (heavy leather gloves), and that the duct system should be redesigned and rebuilt to "allow easier removal of the filters."

Serious plutonium contamination was rare enough that when Rockwell's executives heard about the incident, they decided to use it as an object lesson. They prepared a video lecture on the incidents at Glove Box 9B, which became required viewing for every employee. Though the managers were concerned about the well-being of their workers, the video also served to focus attention on the workers rather than on the design of the filter system. In the video, Rockwell chief Paul Lorenzini explained that the workers had been injured because of sloppy procedures. They hadn't worn the thick leather gloves that were available. The message was obvious: The workers were to blame. They had been less than serious about safety and had paid a price.

When the incident at Glove Box 9B occurred, Cascy Ruud happened to be in the middle of yet another audit. He was checking on one of the most sensitive jobs on site: nuclear materials control, or NMC. The nuclear materials control system was supposed to guarantee that plant operators knew where every bit of plutonium was located at all times. If one of the buttons of weapons-grade material was shifted from one room to another, NMC auditors had to monitor the move and record it. A missing button could mean that a terrorist had stolen material to make a bomb or to poison a big-city water system. The NMC system was also responsible for preventing inadvertent criticalities. This could happen at a workstation, in one of the vaults where finished buttons were stored, or in the hallways at PFP, where canisters holding buttons were placed on little red wagons and pulled from room to room.

For weeks Ruud had wandered around various facilities, keeping track of the people who were supposed to keep track of the hot stuff, from the liquid plutonium solution down to the finished buttons. In the first days of the audit, Ruud felt confused. He found so many problems that he was certain he had misunderstood something basic about the NMC process. But as he continued, he realized that the system for tracking and securing the plutonium was coming apart at the seams.

One day he arrived at PUREX—the Plutonium-Uranium Extraction Facility—to find fifty-five-gallon drums containing plutonium nitrate solution scattered in the hallways. No one seemed to know where the barrels had come from, or where they were going. And the records that were supposed to be with every shipment of plutonium were missing. Ruud traced the barrels to security officers who admitted that they had lost track of the drums, but were certain they would turn up eventually.

The misplaced drums were not the only problem. Ruud next discovered that the special copper seals that were soldered onto the closed drums, like wax seals on a letter, were being used by unauthorized workers. These seals, which prevented tampering with the plutonium, were crucial to the security process and should have been locked away. Instead they were in an open drawer, where anyone could pick out a new seal to replace one that had been broken.

Ruud found the same kinds of security problems when he followed the plutonium trail to PFP. They resulted in part from the fact that the plants were running full bore. Indeed, so much plutonium was being produced that workers were running out of places to put the stuff. Ruud walked into PFP to find drums of solution stored in hallways where scores of people passed by on their daily routines. These were the same hallways traversed by the little red wagons that carried the finished buttons from room to room. One afternoon, while Ruud was watching, a technician pulling a wagon parked it in a hallway full of fifty-five-gallon drums. Normally he would have left the wagon in a space marked on the floor, which would have kept it away from other radioactive materials. But with all the improperly stored drums, there was no place where it could be parked away from all the drums. The frustrated worker left the wagon in the middle of the hall, an obvious violation of the procedures established to prevent criticalities.

As he investigated these problems, Ruud discovered that the overseers for the plutonium—called principal custodians—were chronically swamped by the volume of materials being produced. They couldn't keep track of it all. This was made clear during a visit to the vault where the plutonium buttons were stored.

After passing through various security checkpoints, gates, and huge locked doors, Ruud came to the area where the buttons awaited shipment to other weapons manufacturing facilities. He asked for the paperwork on a number of shipments. Then he asked how auditors could be certain that the proper custodians were signing the materials in and out. The officer on duty directed Ruud to a file of signature cards, like the ones banks sometimes use to verify the signatures on depositors' checks. Ruud compared the names signed on security documents with the cards until, like a surprised teller, he found a mismatch, then another, and another. The papers showed that during one five-day period the signature on a batch of shipping forms was different from that on the signature card for the woman who was supposed to be the custodian on duty. It was also during this period that some of the largest shipments in the history of Hanford had taken place. Ruud guessed that the custodians had been so overworked that someone had bent the rules.

The signatures were clearly different. On the card, and on other documents, all the letters were slanted in one direction. On many of the forms for the five-day period, the letters were tilted the opposite way. But when Ruud found the woman behind the name, she denied that her signature had been forged. She said she had been very busy dealing with the large numbers of shipments, and so her signature had become messy. But though she insisted her forms were correct, she offered another important concern. If the signatures didn't look right, she asked, why hadn't someone else caught it?

The auditor brought all this back to his boss, John Baker. Both men knew that these discoveries would put Ruud once again on a collision course with management. But they felt they had no choice. Ruud and Baker felt like doctors who had been asked to perform an annual physical exam and had discovered the patient had cancer. They were obligated to act. Ruud sat down to write an audit report that would blame production pressure for a breakdown in safety and security. He planned to demand that managers certify that the problems he discovered were corrected or cease operations. Although he expected a fight, he still nursed faint hopes that what Baker and others had told him about Rockwell's desire to improve the attitudes of Hanford old-timers was true. If this was so, he thought, they might heed his warnings.

In the middle of writing his NMC audit, Ruud was called to a conference room to watch the safety videotape prompted by the problems at Glove Box 9B. As he watched, Ruud realized this was *his* Glove Box 9B, the very same workstation and the very same cooling system that, months earlier, he had cited as an example of shoddy design. Watching Paul Lorenzini blame the workers for their injuries and then lecture them on following proper procedure, Ruud grew angry and impatient. This was a coverup, he thought. The primary cause of the injuries was bad design. And he had warned management of the problem before the workers were injured. When the tape was finished, Ruud raced over to the Plutonium Finishing Plant to have another look at Glove Box 9B.

At the workstation, the people on the day shift told Ruud that they didn't believe their co-workers were responsible for the injuries. Every time a filter had to be changed, they explained, they encountered the same problems. To make matters worse, when a filter got stuck, the design made it very difficult to reach the broken pieces and pull them out. The two injured workers had tried to use the leather gloves, but the bulk of the gloves made the work impossible.

"We tried to tell them when they built the damn thing to take their time and build in a support for it," Ruud would later recall one of the workers saying. "But they said, 'Fuck it. Just put it in. Make it go. We don't have time for that shit.' "

Ruud was already compiling a case against Hanford. With the problem of Glove Box 9B, his fading faith in Rockwell's intention to reform the old hands disappeared. He was no longer concerned about keeping the peace and being a team player. He believed that after forty years of operations, Hanford had declined to a point where accidents could happen at any moment. But it wasn't just a matter of the physical plant being old. In their isolation from the rest of the nuclear industry, many of Hanford's workers had become desensitized to the dangers of their work. And the Lorenzini video, in which workers were blamed for something Ruud believed was management's fault, was the last straw. It seemed as though no one was willing to fix what was really wrong. Back at his office, Ruud vented his anger at John Baker.

Baker couldn't explain away the problem, nor did he want to. He was as concerned about safety as anyone else. The fatal fire on the USS *Boxer* was never far from his mind. He had hired Ruud to raise a little hell, and he was going to let him do it.

"Casey," Baker asked, "have you ever heard of this thing called 'management by walking around'?" Baker went on to explain that Rockwell had instituted a program for speeding the review of important issues. Anyone at the site could investigate a problem and write a personal appraisal that would go directly to upper management. They called this "management by walking around," a term borrowed from a popular book on business management. On May 8, Ruud sent the following memo to his superiors.

SUBJECT: MANAGEMENT BY WALKING AROUND

The puncture wounds of serious nature (as indicated by Paul Lorenzini in the safety film) occurred at PFP during the change out of filters in the exhaust system for RMC line Hood 9B due to the inadequate design of the filter housing units. The housing units were not supported, causing a sagging effect resulting in binding of the filters during change out.

This same exhaust system was cited during a recent Design Control Audit as being deficient because calculations/analysis and independent design verification to assure adequacy of design [were] not performed. The seriousness of the potential impact of inadequate designs was explicitly pointed out to upper management.

To date, the PFP Unit Plant Engineering Manager has received no input concerning the results of the noted Design Control Audit, nor has the filter housing unit been redesigned and supported to preclude any further susceptibility to puncture wounds.

Although the above are specific cases, the audit determined that the same problems exist generically for all Rockwell Hanford Operation Facilities.

*C. O. Ruud, Lead Auditor*
*Safety and Quality Assurance Audits*

In the dry language of Hanford, the four paragraphs in Ruud's memo were as much an attack on Rockwell's managers as Martin Luther's ninety-five theses were an attack on Rome. Ruud was demanding that the residents of Mahogany Row—as the Rockwell executive suite was called—acknowledge that serious injuries had occurred because they had ignored his warnings. Worse, the same problems that had caused the injuries at Glove Box 9B existed all over the site.

The managers who received Ruud's memo should not have been surprised. Earlier, while the world outside had been dealing with the revelations of Hanford's past and Chernobyl, Ruud had wrestled with his superiors over the findings in his design-control audit. Ruud had described the design program as "significantly out of control" and had called for immediate corrective action. Corrective action would mean a halt to all design and installation of new equipment as well as major repairs, while a new system for reviewing designs was put in place.

The design issue mattered to Ruud because he believed that it was vital to safe operations. It was at the point of design that replacement parts and new devices could be made safe or dangerous. The case of Glove Box 9B proved what could happen with shoddy design. At its worst, bad design could lead to criticalities, large-scale contaminations, serious injuries, and even deaths. In one case Ruud had stumbled upon, the poor design of a vessel that held plutonium solution had allowed it to overflow and flood an entire workroom with radioactive liquid. In another case, a drain had been designed in a way that radioactive waste was routed directly into the earth below the Plutonium Finishing Plant.

At the end of his original design-control audit memo, Ruud had concluded that the problems were caused by, among other things, the pressure to meet production deadlines and the fact that too many engineers "are Hanfordized and cut corners. . . ." He offered two ways to resolve the audit satisfactorily: stop work, or notify the Department of Energy of the problem and begin a program to bring the design program into compliance with nuclear industry standards. Neither of these options was attractive to the managers who received Ruud's report. The first would ruin Rockwell's effort to reach production goals. The second would commit the company to a very costly and time-consuming effort to bring the facilities up to NQA-1 standards. Rockwell officials said that they had already notified DOE of this problem and had begun working on a plan to resolve it. Still, some insiders thought the plants were so old and so neglected that there would never be enough time or money to bring them up to snuff. Indeed, past efforts to get the energy department to spend money upgrading plants like PUREX and the Plutonium Finishing Plant had been killed by the agency's budget-makers.

The engineers, managers, and department directors who received Ruud's design-control audit understood how difficult it would be to comply with its terms. But in the Rockwell hierarchy, safety auditors held a peculiar power. An auditor had the authority to order

the immediate shutdown of any facility. Plant managers were required to respond to the findings in audit reports in a timely fash-
ion. And no audit could be closed—indicating a resolution of the
problems found—without the individual auditor's consent.

But if Ruud had his superiors over a barrel, he had also placed
himself in jeopardy. Some of the people he was pushing were likely
to push back. He could find himself reassigned or, worse, they could
arrange to have him fired for some trumped-up reason. It was this
unstated danger, well understood by all Hanford workers, including the auditors, that helped keep them in line—which is why
Ruud's aggressive approach shocked some of his superiors. Even if
everyone knew about the troubles covered in the audits, document-
ing them on paper and forcing management to deal with them could
be career suicide.

Ruud understood this danger, and so did his wife, Suzi. Sometimes when she heard him talk about his confrontations with the
people who were supposed to be his superiors, Suzi would become
both frightened and angry. She feared that Casey would be fired at
any moment. Visions of losing her home and security often moved
her to tears. In these moments, which usually arrived late at night
as they lay in bed, Casey would try to comfort her. But his promises
were based on nothing more than faith. He assumed that John
Baker would try to protect him, but he knew that Baker's power
was limited. Baker could not guarantee Ruud's career, and ultimately Suzi would have to live with her fears. So, too, would Casey
have to live with his own doubts. Even as he tried to convince his
wife that everything would be all right, he secretly doubted his own
words. But he was not willing to confess that he, too, was deeply
worried, that Suzi wasn't alone in her fear.

On the outside, the Ruuds tried to hide the stress from their
children and neighbors. When they went to their favorite restaurant, the Hanford House in Richland, they smiled and spoke cheer-
fully to the friends they met. Casey continued coaching his son's
soccer and basketball teams. And he ran every day. The running,
sometimes fifteen miles or more, was a meditative practice. Sometimes as he ran, he would imagine talking to his father about his
problems. And if he tried hard enough, he could still hear the old

man telling him always to do the right thing. Without these runs, and the reflections on his father's honesty, Ruud used to think, the stress of his job would have driven him crazy.

The stress was most intense during the meetings held to review his audits. These were a kind of target practice for the managers, who did their best to pick Ruud's work apart and delay responding. But Ruud would not be deterred. In one particular session on the design-control audit, held in the main conference room at the Rockwell administration building, he kept insisting on a response— either a plant shutdown or major changes in procedures—until one of the engineers exploded.

"You know and I know that we are not in compliance," he said, slamming down his clipboard. "We are not going to be in compliance, and DOE doesn't have the guts to tell us we're not in compliance. So fuck it," he said, throwing Ruud's report on the conference table. "I'm not responding to this."

In the eyes of this engineer, and many others, the federal government had asked Rockwell to make plutonium without the funding necessary to meet every safety and environmental concern. Although it was official policy that Hanford comply with NQA-1, the government didn't press the issue because compliance was practically impossible. And although an order invoking NQA-1 would shut down Hanford, this wasn't just a matter for local concern. Ruud was messing with the geopolitics of the Reagan administration, which was using its nuclear buildup to pressure the Soviet Union into concessions at strategic arms reduction talks. If the production lines at Hanford stopped, the entire nuclear arms complex would be affected.

These points were reinforced in private meetings Ruud had with high-level managers who made it clear that the government depended on outside contractors like Rockwell to do the things public officials could not. Some jobs were so important, and so sensitive, that a certain amount of secrecy and risk-taking was acceptable. Behind closed doors on Mahogany Row, one tough-talking executive explained that Ruud could not expect that going past Rockwell, to the Department of Energy, would get results. Not only was the government uninterested in funding the proper upgrades, he was told, but the government expected Rockwell to do what it took to keep the production lines going. This meant that public officials had "deniability." They could blame the civilian contractors if anything disastrous occurred. "Our job," Ruud was told, "is to make these decisions for them."

Ruud nevertheless refused to close out the audit. But he did agree to a compromise. The plants could keep operating, and DOE would be kept in the dark, until September. In the ensuing months, Rockwell would put together a plan to answer Ruud's concerns. The executives said it was their best offer. Ruud accepted it. And with his acceptance of this compromise, it must have seemed to his bosses that Casey Ruud had gone away, at least for a few months. But the management-by-walking-around "memo" signaled a resumption of hostilities. It was immediately followed by a second salvo, the nuclear materials control audit report:

"There's a serious problem with the degree to which nuclear materials custodians either understand their duties and responsibilities or choose to comply with them," wrote Ruud. The problem again was pressure to produce, he concluded. "The overall program is assessed as less than adequate in assuring control of nuclear materials as described by DOE and Rockwell . . . immediate management attention is necessary to achieve an adequate level of compliance." Ruud demanded that managers shut down operations at the Plutonium Finishing Plant if they could not be sure the plutonium was being safeguarded.

By labeling this last item a "priority finding," Ruud made sure that this audit would reach the high-rent district of Mahogany Row. On May 30 it landed on the desk of Assistant General Manager A. Clegg Crawford, a gruff, imposing, fifty-three-year-old engineer who had risen in the Rockwell ranks to become the number-two man at Hanford. At six feet two, and 225 pounds, Crawford had a deep baritone voice that he used to great effect when demanding performance from others. Crawford was nothing but tough. He had been raised on the legend of his father, who was orphaned at age eight and had survived alone for several months in a shed. His son had served as a submariner in Admiral Hyman Rickover's nuclear navy and then followed a well-worn path into atomic industry. One of the high points of Crawford's career had been when he worked as one of the leaders of the team that responded to the emergency at the Three Mile Island nuclear plant and limited the damage. Crawford's team had figured out how to release safely the hydrogen gas pressure building up inside the plant and thereby prevent the kind of explosion that would happen later at Chernobyl.

When he came to Hanford in 1981 to help restart the old plutonium production facilities, Crawford believed that nuclear weapons were "one of the great things that had happened in the history of the world." He was certain that the A-bombs dropped by President Truman had saved millions of lives in World War II, and he believed that America's growing strategic weapons arsenal made the prospect of another world war so terrible that it blunted Soviet aggression. He considered restarting the Plutonium-Uranium Extraction Facility a patriotic duty, and he plunged into the task.

Crawford was met by a work force he considered sullen and uncooperative. With more than a dozen different union bargaining groups and frequent changes in contractors, Hanford was beset by labor problems. Crawford loved to tell the story of a crew assigned to pump atomic waste from one tank to another. Work rules required that the four men wait for hours for an electrician to come and plug in a pump motor. When the electrician finally appeared, he did one minute's worth of work—the only work he did that day. By then it was time for the crew's lunch break. In five years at Hanford, Crawford had struggled to rebuild worker pride and improve productivity by opening communication between bosses and workers and emphasizing quality work. He believed he was succeeding, and the record-setting pace of plutonium production told him he was right.

On the afternoon when Casey Ruud's NMC audit arrived, Crawford was sitting at the oversized desk that dominated his carpeted office. On the wall behind him was a framed collection of the business cards of some of the men Crawford admired—John D. Rockefeller, Henry Ford, Howard Hughes, Thomas Edison, and others. The wall also held a mockup display of different atomic fuel elements. On a bookshelf stood a gumball machine. The most important object in the office was the large blackboard Crawford used to keep track of projects and work out difficult problems.

There was nothing on Crawford's blackboard about Ruud's audits. Indeed, he had never heard of Casey Ruud. But when the audit report arrived, Crawford began reading and chewing his fingernails. By the time he had finished reading, he was enraged. He quickly wrote a memo of his own, addressed to Ruud's superiors. It was typed not on Rockwell stationery but on notepaper with a heading that read, "From the Desk of A. Clegg Crawford."

GENTLEMEN: I have just had the dubious honor of reading Audit J-86-04 relative to nuclear materials management and it frankly makes me mad as hell. When you consider the efforts we have put forth to upgrade our nuclear materials management processes and you consider that this audit points out we are not following our own procedures I become more than angry, I get furious.

Crawford demanded that the problems raised in the audit be resolved in ten days, and he noted that those responsible would suffer the consequences in upcoming reviews of their job performance.

Copies of Crawford's "mad as hell" note circulated widely. John Baker saw it, and so did Casey Ruud. Both men were encouraged by its tone. At least on paper, Crawford seemed to be tough enough to do what was necessary to clean up Hanford. And in the weeks that followed, the official responses to the NMC audit indicated that the problems were being fixed. Clegg Crawford seemed to be the leader that Baker and Ruud had been hoping to find.

But soon Ruud's sources inside PFP reported something different. Many of these sources were Ruud's running partners. A group of more than a dozen men—draftsmen, engineers, technicians— had mapped out a three-and-a-half-mile loop around the huge Plutonium Finishing Plant. At lunchtime they would take several laps together. Often, between heaving breaths, one of his fellow runners would tell Ruud about problems inside the facility. "If they're telling you it's all fixed, that's a bunch of bullshit," Ruud would recall one of them saying. "Half the time they still don't know where all the plutonium is."

In July, as the ninety-day deadline that was set by the auditing rules arrived, Ruud went to Baker and asked if he could return to PFP and check on the response to his findings.

"Go get 'em," Baker replied.

Ruud drove across the area in hundred-degree heat. He passed through the security checkpoint at the door of PFP, donned a white jumpsuit, and began his inspection. The first person he met was a principal custodian who recalled him from the spring audit tour.

"What the hell are you doing here?" the man said. He seemed frantic, even bewildered. "I can't talk to you. I can't believe you're standing here right now. I've lost two drums and I don't know where they're at. People have been in my vaults. They're open. They're taking stuff out and I don't know where it's at."

Ruud followed the custodian to the guard post by the vault, passed through another checkpoint, and saw that the heavily gated storage room was wide open. Drums were backed up in the hallways, half of them belonging to this custodian, half to another. Many of the seals on the drums were broken. Others had no seals at all.

This time Ruud didn't even bother to go back to his office to report what he had found. He called Baker from the phone at the guard desk. "It's all gone bad, John," he said. "We've got to meet with the plant manager. You've got to come over here and see this right now. Immediately. Not in an hour. Now."

Ruud knew that the plant manager had been committed to fixing the problems in the original audit. He had told him all along that he was working on solutions. Obviously ninety days had not been time enough. When Baker arrived, the two men went into the manager's office and issued an ultimatum.

"You've got no option but to shut down, I'm telling you that right now," Ruud began. Baker backed him up.

"Casey, answer me one question," the manager responded. "Why is it that you're picking on PFP?"

"It's because I come over here to go running with my buddies," Ruud answered, with a chuckle.

After much negotiation, the men agreed to wait one day, to give the plant staff a chance to set things right. When Ruud and Baker came back the next day, nothing had changed. The plant manager said he couldn't order that the production line be closed. "It's above me," he said. "It's more than I can do."

There would have to be more meetings before any serious action could be taken, but Ruud pressed the case. In the following days he and Baker negotiated with the next level of Rockwell managers. Again the managers were reluctant to shut down the facility. Again they played for time. A full three months after the audit and Clegg Crawford's "mad as hell" letter, the Mahogany Row managers suggested that a review team be formed to examine the problems. There was nothing in the standard audit procedure calling for such a review. Ruud had a right to insist on a shutdown. But he didn't. In part because Baker asked him to, and in part because he wanted to be fair, Ruud agreed to join a committee that would double-check his work.

The committee found the same problems and more. In one case they discovered that audits of the plutonium inventory had come up short. Something was missing. Normally the operators would have been required to call security officials and lock up the plant, keeping everyone on the premises until the books were balanced. But it was a Friday afternoon, and a lockup might have stretched through the weekend. Managers decided to let people go home, and the pluto-nium was later found. Nevertheless, a breach of procedures had occurred.

While the committee probed this issue and others, Ruud used his time to develop yet another serious criticism of PFP security. Months before, he had shared a ride to work with a woman who was a technician on the Remote Mechanical line. A casual conver-sation turned serious when she told Ruud that she thought it was possible to spirit plutonium out of the plant. She said the weak link in the security chain was at a laboratory where finished buttons that were discovered to have imperfections were cleaned.

Ruud had chosen not to follow this lead earlier, because he didn't want to seem overly aggressive. But with his own sense of frustra-tion building, he decided to follow up the tip. He traced the ship-ment of a single plutonium button from the production area to the lab, which was outside what was called the security "envelope." Inside the envelope, the plutonium was subjected to constant surveillance. But once it was transferred to the lab, security loosened; no one would try to account for it until it was again returned to the envelope. Because lab workers routinely brought samples of radioactive materials into and out of their work area, security officers were often required to turn off their radiation detection devices when these employees passed through checkpoints. During one of these moments, a button could leave the lab along with a sample. It might be days before anyone realized it was missing.

Such casual handling of plutonium would not be as hazardous as it might seem. Though technically lethal, the buttons were alpha-emitters; their radiation would penetrate only a few layers of skin. That was why the cans on the little red wagons were adequate containers. Unless a person inhaled or otherwise ingested a particle, handling the finished product was relatively safe. And the buttons that came out of the lab were so well cleaned that the likelihood of ingesting a particle was small. But their comparatively safe condition made them easier pickings for terrorist thieves inspired by a revolutionary cause or a million-dollar ransom.

Another auditor suggested to Ruud a second way for someone to get a button out of PFP. The custodians responsible for nuclear materials also supervised the packaging and disposal of waste such as crapped-up gloves and tools. A button might be placed in a waste barrel, sealed, and trucked out. It could be retrieved somewhere in the desert between the plant and a burial site. This scenario would require that several workers collude, but as Ruud said in presenting this idea to his superiors, it's not unusual for terrorists to collude.

More than a week passed as Ruud looked into these security gaps. In that time, management had still not responded fully to his audit. In fact, with the evidence of security lapses, Ruud had even more reason to insist that production stop until the problems were fixed. On August 18, with Baker's support, Ruud decided to exercise his power. He wrote a "Stop Work Action Letter," a formal document that would require PFP and PUREX to shut down. Baker called his boss, Jim Albaugh, who told him to bring the letter up to Mahogany Row. Albaugh would have to sign the letter, and he indicated that he would. At last, Ruud thought, the tussle over his audit would end.

Later, Ruud couldn't remember whether Albaugh actually had

his pen in hand when Clegg Crawford walked into the room. He may have simply announced that he was going to sign. Either way, it was a remarkable coincidence. At this key moment, Crawford appeared and Albaugh's hand was stilled.

"So, what are you gentlemen up to?" Crawford asked.

As Albaugh explained, Crawford took the letter off the desk and began reading. "Casey and John," he said, "let's go in my office and talk."

Letter in hand, Crawford walked them to his office suite. Once they arrived, he said he was going to take charge of the problems at PFP. He grabbed the phone and told his secretary to arrange for the PFP managers to be in his office the next morning. In the middle of this call, he held one hand against the mouthpiece and said to Ruud and Baker, "I'm going to kick some ass about this."

Baker and Ruud were impressed. This was obviously a man of action. Seeing his opening, Baker asked Crawford if he also knew about the design-control audit, which was still unresolved. Crawford agreed to get involved in the design program's problems as well, and he invited Ruud and Baker to a management meeting the next morning, where, he promised, they would see how fast a big organization could move when it was kicked by a tough boss.

The big meeting was held around a conference table on Mahogany Row. The assembly included the people in charge of security, audits, nuclear materials, and engineering, and the plant managers for both PFP and PUREX. They were all men, and they all arrived wearing the drab suits of the Rockwell executive corps. Ruud, who had worn his usual sport shirt and cotton pants, began with a presentation of the audit findings, which had been confirmed by the follow-up team. The principal custodians were still overwhelmed. The seals for plutonium barrels were not properly controlled. Accounting of materials was sloppy. And now, it seemed, there were gaps in security.

When Ruud finished, Crawford held up the Stop Work letter and said, "Folks, we've got to do something to solve this." A plant shutdown would probably be reported by the media. Crawford was worried about negative publicity because Rockwell was in the middle of a fierce competition for the contract to operate Hanford's facilities. Under orders from Washington, Mike Lawrence had rearranged the way things were organized at Hanford, cutting the number of major contracts from seven to three. If Rockwell won the new contract, it would add several additional facilities, including N Reactor, to its responsibilities. This bigger contract was worth $800 million. With this in mind, Crawford was loath to let Ruud's audits cause an unnecessary shutdown or bad publicity.

Around the table, various men volunteered to take care of the problems raised by auditor Ruud. The PFP manager insisted his people could resolve the audit findings. Others confessed that Ruud had raised important issues, but they believed a complete shutdown was unnecessary. Coincidentally, work at the Remote Mechanical line inside the plant was already stopped so that plutonium-handling problems could be fixed. The fact that this line, the heart of the operation, was already closed no doubt led many at the meeting to conclude that a full stop-work order was unnecessary.

Slowly the group reached a consensus. There would be no shutdown. Crawford assigned tasks to the men around the table. Each was asked to bring his department in line. And he asked Robert Heineman, the director of safeguards and security, to supervise the entire process, making weekly checks to determine whether progress was being made. Finally he directed one of the men at the meeting to write a report on the meeting, which would be signed by all the participants. The report would state that everyone in the meeting agreed that some problems remained, that they were being addressed, and that it was not necessary to stop work.

"Is that okay with everyone?" Crawford asked.

Around the table, heads nodded in agreement, including John Baker's. But Crawford wanted to make sure this problem would go away. So he asked Ruud, in particular, if he agreed. Years later, Crawford and the other executives in the room would insist that Ruud had quietly nodded his head in assent. John Baker would say he couldn't remember the details of what happened. Ruud would swear that he made it very clear he vehemently disagreed.

"All I could think was, 'My career is over,'" Ruud would recall. "Then I said, 'Gentlemen, I believe you live in an ivory tower. Unless somebody's either killed or somebody puts a plutonium button on your desk, you won't be able to see the problems. And you are the cause of the problems.' " In Ruud's version of events, it was clear that he would not sign off on the meeting's minutes.

If it wasn't clear that day, it soon would be. Following Crawford's directions, a two-paragraph note was circulated to all those who had gathered in the conference room. It said, "A proposed draft of a Stop Work Action Letter was discussed and all present agreed that such a letter was not warranted. No audit finding revealed a serious compromise to the safeguard of special nuclear material." This document bounced from one office to another, gathering initials of agreement, until it reached Casey Ruud. On August 26, 1986, Ruud responded with a memo of his own. In less than sixty words he refused to initial the report and protested its conclusions about the Stop Work Action Letter and the audit findings. Again, Ruud was refusing to go away.

In the midst of this battle, one angry executive asked Ruud if he had written an anonymous letter describing problems at Hanford that had gone to Rockwell's top Hanford boss, Paul Lorenzini, and to the governor of the state of Washington and a *Seattle Times* newspaper reporter named Eric Nalder, among others. Ruud said he had had nothing to do with the letter. But in the midst of a situation in which he felt powerless, the letter suggested a way out.

That night, Ruud and Suzi went shopping. A new school year was beginning and the children all needed clothes. When they got to the department store, the kids all went in different directions, leaving their parents to wander the aisles. Suzi hadn't seen much of her husband in the previous weeks. Without spilling too much detail, he had told her of the battle over his audits. She knew he was discouraged, even bitter, about what was happening. And she was worried. Every day it seemed he came home to report another argument with his bosses. She feared that one day he would push too hard and they would simply fire him.

"I don't think I can win this fight alone," he told her after she prodded him.

"Well, you've got John Baker, and you've got me," she replied.

That wasn't enough. Suzi Ruud's husband was convinced that

nothing would change at Hanford unless people outside heard about the problems. He was sure it was his last chance to do something before a catastrophic accident occurred.

What the managers at Rockwell didn't understand was that Casey Ruud would never give up. He couldn't. Giving up would be a repudiation of his own father, the Los Angeles building inspector who couldn't be bought by crooked contractors or intimidated by company goons. In Ruud's mind, the executives at Rockwell were nothing compared with the dangers his father had stared down. And the stakes in this confrontation, which included the lives of workers and the Hanford environment, were too high for Ruud to ignore. Like Crawford, he was mad as hell. So there, in the Fred Meyer store, Ruud decided he would call the *Seattle Times* reporter.

That evening, Ruud dialed the phone and was surprised when the person who answered said that Eric Nalder was in, working late. He trembled a bit as the call was connected.

"Eric, my name is Casey Ruud," he began.

"Wow!" came the response from the other end of the phone. "I've been meaning to call you. I've heard about you and I've been trying to get to the bottom of the story, but they won't let me have the records."

"I think I can help," Ruud said.

In the next few weeks, Ruud quietly made copies of his audits, carefully replaced the originals in his office files, and brought the duplicates home in his briefcase. He then sent the copies to Nalder one at a time. In Seattle, Nalder could tell with just a cursory reading that he was looking at some very controversial documents. But the engineering terms and bureaucratic tone made him feel as if he were reading a foreign language after just a few lessons. Nalder enlisted help from an engineering professor at a local college, who offered some translation. But he relied on Ruud to walk him through the documents during long, late-night telephone conversations.

These conversations also gave Nalder a chance to build a relationship with Ruud, who was still nervous about dealing with the press. By secretly talking to a reporter, Ruud was violating Rock-

well rules. The company expected employees to report any over-
tures from the press. And although no one had ever said that a
worker was barred from giving interviews, they didn't have to say
it. Everyone knew that the press was the enemy and contact was
forbidden. As he dealt with Eric Nalder, Casey Ruud felt afraid.

He kept insisting that Nalder use the documents, but keep him
out of the story. If Ruud was going to leave his job, he wanted it
to be his decision. He had his family to consider. "You can't tell
anyone where you got this stuff, and everything I tell you is off the
record," he repeated. "You can't quote me."

On the other end of the phone, Nalder promised Ruud everything. He pledged to keep his sources confidential, and he promised
to protect Ruud in any way he could. Nalder would do this by
making a flurry of requests for documents. He would pester Rockwell's public relations office and place direct calls to other people
involved in the audit disputes. All this would be a diversion, activity
intended to suggest that he was still trying to get the information
Ruud had already given him. In the event that Nalder was able to
go public with what he had, Rockwell's managers could not be sure
just who had given him the goods. "We can create a smokescreen,"
Nalder said. "I think it will protect you."

# CASEY AT THE BAT

By THE END of September 1986, Casey Ruud felt as though the world had been lifted from his shoulders. Convinced that Rockwell would not be moved from within, he had stopped trying. He had stopped pressing upper management for responses to his audits. He had stopped keeping track of the deadlines for their compliance with his audits. Now it was all in Eric Nalder's hands, and for the first time in a year, Ruud felt relaxed.

On an early-autumn evening, Ruud left his house after dinner and drove to downtown Richland to play tennis with one of his running buddies from Hanford. They didn't talk about work; they just bashed the ball back and forth until the setting sun turned the sky rosy red and the dry desert air blew cool. On a night like this, Ruud could remember why he had settled in the Tri-Cities. In this modern, virtually crime-free community, it was easy to find the good life. From the tennis court Ruud could see the tall, blocky Richland Federal Building, where the Department of Energy kept its offices. When the match was over he noticed that the lights were still burning in one of the upper floors.

It was after eight o'clock when Ruud walked in the front door of his home. Just as his kids rushed to greet him, the phone began to ring. Suzi called from the kitchen. It was John Baker. When Ruud took the phone, Baker told him he wanted him to come to the Federal Building for an emergency meeting. He couldn't say what it was all about. "But I'm not asking you to come," he added, "I'm telling you." Ruud changed into a fresh sport shirt and jeans. While his children complained and his wife wished him well, he quickly left for the Federal Building.

Ruud's footsteps echoed off the walls of the vacant lobby of the darkened Federal Building. After checking his badge, the guard waved him through the metal detector and toward the elevators. He was expected. Waiting upstairs were about fifteen Rockwell managers, most still in business suits. When he walked into the paneled meeting room, Ruud felt like a fourth-grader who had been called to the principal's office. Here were all the people he had peppered with audits, memos, and complaints. The usually protective John Baker glanced at Ruud from the opposite side of the room. Baker feared what could happen when a worker compelled by his conscience was ignored. In the aftermath of the Apollo fire, a whistle-blower had come forward to complain about parts that had been installed in the spacecraft without proper clearances. The press found the man and he became an instant national figure. But after his moment of celebrity, the whistle-blower died in a mysterious car wreck. Baker had always wondered if the pressure, or something more sinister, had gotten to the man. Here, once again, Baker could see a strong-minded young man battling an enormous institution. He was certain Rockwell would survive, but he wasn't so sure about Ruud.

At the start of the meeting, one of the executives explained that a reporter had been asking a lot of questions, questions he could have asked only if he had obtained copies of the audits and the Unusual Occurrence reports from the incident at Glove Box 9B. Jerry Gilliland, the public-relations chief, said Eric Nalder of the *Seattle Times* had ambushed Paul Lorenzini over the telephone with a barrage of questions based on the audits. Gilliland also believed that Nalder had copies of the Stop Work Action Letter and the management-by-walking-around memo. Ruud and the others had been brought in that night to listen to a tape recording of the reporter's questions and develop answers they would give Nalder when he arrived in the Tri-Cities the next day.

As he sat down in one of the high-backed swivel chairs that ringed the conference room, Casey Ruud's heart began to pound. He didn't know what he would say if he was asked, point-blank, if he was Nalder's source. But as the meeting wore on, it became clear that no one was going to ask. Ruud breathed a quiet sigh and relaxed a little.

When the tape player was switched on, Ruud could hear the familiar voice of Eric Nalder going through the issues he had discussed with him during long telephone conversations in the previous weeks. At almost every turn in the interview, Lorenzini told Nalder he didn't know enough of the details to answer a specific question, and promised that his staff would have it for him the next day. The men in the conference room played the recording question by question, stopping after each one to ask Ruud his impressions. They also wanted Ruud to concur with the answers they were constructing for Lorezini to give Nalder the next day. This was a tedious task because Ruud still refused to agree that the audit findings were resolved.

For example, in the case of the plutonium contamination at Glove Box 9B, one engineer asked Ruud if his concerns couldn't be softened, since there was some doubt about the cause of the plutonium puncture wounds. "Your audit did not define that specific element of that hood thing anyway," he said, "and that problem occurred because they didn't use the gloves."

Ruud couldn't agree. He argued that the original design was the problem, and that it still had not been fixed. Across the table, several of the managers said they couldn't believe that such a small repair had yet to be made. It had been seven months and two injured men since Ruud's original warning. More than one of the managers in the room had promised to fix it. When they asked for a status report from the engineer who had been put in charge of the job, he blanched. Ruud was correct. Nothing had been done.

"Of course it hasn't," Ruud interjected mischievously. "It's not on the top-ten hit list."

During a break in the meeting, Ruud got up to get a drink of water at a fountain in the hallway. One of the executives followed him. In the privacy of the corridor, as Ruud bent over the stream of water, he couldn't help asking the question that was on everyone's mind. He wanted to know who had sent the documents to Eric Nalder.

"It could be a lot of people," Ruud answered. "All I can tell you is you've got a lot of people in the organization who are very dissatisfied with how these problems are dealt with. It could be anyone." It wasn't exactly the truth, but Ruud felt he hadn't lied, either. Like the managers who were responsible for addressing his audits, he had just offered a creative response.

Back in the conference room, the group returned to the task of reviewing the tape and suggesting answers. If they were to head off a negative story, they needed to convince Nalder that the audits were being dealt with, even if they hadn't been resolved. When they reached the design-control audit, the men around the table agreed that they could tell the reporter that substantial progress had been made toward establishing stiffer design standards and procedures. They asked for Ruud's blessing. Again he refused.

The frustration was obvious in the faces of the other men. As Ruud issued one objection after another, one older engineer seated in a chair pressed up against the wall could no longer contain his anger. For forty years the great machine that was Hanford had been run by its corps of engineers. They were the people who made things work for a nation full of citizens and politicians who didn't understand the first thing about physics, chemistry, or mechanical engineering. Now they were being pushed around by some upstart underling. "This kid is not even a draftsman," he fumed. "Why are we even talking to this guy! He's not in the know. He's the problem!"

No one answered. They didn't have to respond because everyone understood that Ruud was essential to the Rockwell public-relations strategy. They needed to be able to tell the press that the auditor in question was satisfied. With Ruud on their side, they could extinguish the controversy Nalder sought to inflame. And even if Ruud didn't agree with all the answers devised at the late-night meeting, the men in the room wanted to make him feel part of the Rockwell family. If he hadn't already talked to Nalder and they could make him feel even the slightest loyalty, they might prevent him from going public with his complaints.

The meeting ground on for hours. Styrofoam coffee cups littered the conference room table. Experts from various departments came and went as the group moved from one issue to the next. Outside, the traffic on the streets of Richland grew lighter. The lights went out at the Wendy's restaurant across the street.

High inside the Federal Building, Casey Ruud was growing tired and bored as the tape recording was slowly played. He suspected the others felt the same. Then something happened to pique their interest. Out of the tape recorder they began to hear a pinging sound along with the voices. It was a high-pitched, hollow tone, like the sound of sonar in an old war movie. It came in a steady rhythm—ping, ping, ping—under the conversation on the tape. Soon they heard Nalder ask about the noise.

"That's just a submarine," laughed one of the voices on the tape. It wasn't Lorenzini, but someone else who shared a speakerphone hookup with Nalder.

"Well, you know that in the state of Washington it is a felony to tape-record a conversation without the knowledge or consent of the other party?" Nalder said. "Are you aware of that?"

After a long pause, there came an answer. "Eric, we'd like to inform you that we are recording this conversation." Nalder feigned outrage, then agreed to permit the recording in exchange for a copy of the tapes.

In the conference room, Ruud couldn't suppress a smile. Neither could many of the others. In fact, for a brief moment everyone took a bit of delight in the sound of the reporter pushing the big bosses around, and they played this part of the tape over a few times. Someone said that Nalder sounded like a tough guy. Someone else noted that the ping-ping of the recording device really did sound like the sonar on a submarine.

It was well after midnight when the punch-drunk group got to the end of the tape. It was clear that very few of Ruud's complaints could be described as resolved. Nevertheless, one of the executives telephoned Paul Lorenzini to report that their work with Ruud was done. They all waited there as their boss drove over from his home, which was nestled beside a fairway at the posh Meadow Spring Country Club. Lorenzini, tall, with silver hair and a perfect smile, arrived dressed in an oversized sweater and blue jeans. Ruud, who viewed the executive suite as a foreign land, couldn't help thinking that Lorenzini was the picture of success and self-assurance. For a moment Ruud imagined Lorenzini had spent the night sitting in the family library reading and smoking a pipe. Perhaps there had even been a dog at his feet.

These fantasies vanished from Ruud's mind as Lorenzini began to speak. He called the young auditor "a member of the team" and said he respected the work he had done. Ruud was impressed. Lorenzini was a well-spoken man who understood the technical issues at hand. For a moment Ruud felt as if he did want to be part of this man's team.

As Lorenzini did everything he could to help Casey Ruud relax, the others in the room seemed to grow even more anxious. When the boss asked them what progress had been made, he was greeted with silence. Lorenzini posed the question again, asking whether the group was stalemated on any of the issues. Again there was silence, until Ruud spoke up. For the next fifteen minutes he told Lorenzini that the problems in design and nuclear materials control were still festering. He told him about Dr. Paul Ritman and his views on seismically unsafe buildings. He even told him about the barrels of plutonium backing up in the hallways of one of the plants.

After listening to Ruud and the others, Lorenzini said there would be more work done that night, but Ruud was free to go. As the young auditor left, Lorenzini made a point of standing up and shaking his hand.

The next morning Eric Nalder couldn't help feeling a little paranoid. This feeling came over him whenever he flew over the Cascades in the little two-prop commuter planes that connected Seattle and the top-secret nuclear fortress of the Tri-Cities. He felt it too when he rented a car and wheeled out onto the highway that led to Richland. As he drove, he kept glancing in the rearview mirror to see if he was being followed. He was sure the fear was appropriate. He had made the mistake of tipping his hand to Rockwell too early in the game. They might have called Hanford security, and who knew what kind of wiretaps and surveillance they could muster? Nalder had to assume that he was being watched and that he was never more than one move ahead on the game board.

Investigations were a kind of game for Nalder, as they are for most good reporters, which is something their prey never seem to understand. For the predator, it's nothing personal. Nalder didn't care if his opponent was a politician on the take or a government contractor he suspected of dangerous operations. All he wanted was to get enough on-the-record testimony and enough documenta-

tion to publish a story that would withstand a lawsuit. In this case
he had made the mistake of beginning his work by going directly to
Rockwell public-relations people and asking for Ruud's audits. As
a corporation, Rockwell didn't have to give him anything. It was
the government—the Department of Energy in this case—that was
required by law to make documents available. Nalder's slipup had
almost guaranteed that Rockwell would keep the audits secret indefinitely. And it had informed the powers that be at Hanford that
he was on the hunt.

Big organizations, big machines, and big projects like Hanford
had fascinated Nalder since he was a boy. Now forty-one years old,
he had been raised in an age of scientific wonders, a time when
young boys came to admire the beauty of high technology and the
masculine genius of the scientists and engineers. Nalder's abiding
interest in great human endeavors had much to do with the Grand
Coulee Dam. Born in 1945, he was the son of the fourth man hired
for the dam project. His memories from early childhood included
countless visits to the dam with his father, who eventually rose to
be manager. The Grand Coulee Dam blocked the Columbia River
and turned one of its ravines into a reservoir 150 miles long. The
largest dam project in the United States, the Grand Coulee had
generated much of the electric power used by Hanford in the war
years. Besides visiting the dam, little Eric Nalder had accompanied
his father on visits to the Hanford site, about seventy-five miles to
the south. The curly-haired boy would stand by quietly as his father
talked to Atomic Energy Commission officials about their electric
power needs.

When Nalder was a teenager, the Bureau of Reclamation loaned
his father to a foreign service project in Afghanistan. He helped the
Afghanis build an irrigation system. His wife, son, and two daughters came along. In Afghanistan, young Nalder was confronted
with the good and bad effects of American attitudes and policies
abroad. Like the others, he learned to question authority and look
behind patriotic rhetoric. Afghanistan also bred in Nalder a sense
of adventure. Some of his most vivid memories were of exploring
the countryside with his father and the local men. On one hunting
expedition he had shot a wild boar in a sort of rite of passage. That
night he had slept in the wilderness, sheltered by the body of his kill.

These worldly experiences were never far from his mind, and they gave Nalder the kind of self-assurance that some critics would call egotism.

Nalder had come back to the Northwest to study for his degree at the University of Washington in Seattle. He was drawn by the excitement and power of journalism. Later, working at Seattle newspapers, he built a national reputation as an investigative reporter. A self-confident man with curly reddish brown hair, brown eyes, and a strong, square jaw, he was not easily intimidated. Unlike Karen Dorn Steele, who was fascinated by history and the struggles of everyday people like farmer Tom Bailie, Eric Nalder was motivated mainly by the thrill of the journalistic hunt. He relished the role of exposing government wrongdoing. He knew that soon the public would learn that Hanford's troubles were not all in the past. The Green Run scandal had been perpetrated in another time, by men long gone from power. But, as Nalder knew, the controversy over Casey Ruud's audits would have a more profound effect on Hanford and the Tri-Cities. Indeed, for a while he may have been the only one who could even speculate that the very future of the Hanford complex would soon be in doubt.

On the day when he flew into the Tri-Cities, Nalder arrived at Rockwell's headquarters building with a box full of documents under his arm. He was met by a group of men who were weary from the long night of preparation at the Federal Building. John Baker was there, along with audit department head Jim Albaugh, PR man Jerry Gilliland, and Bob Heineman, who was in charge of nuclear materials security. They were joined by Ron Gerton, a Department of Energy overseer. None of them could have been prepared for the theatrics to come.

Eric Nalder may have been a kind and loving father, a good husband and friend. But in his professional life he was not what one would call a nice man. He came on like a prosecutor in a high-profile murder trial, part bully, part confidant, part high-minded preacher. Nalder thought of interviews in terms of power. He always started gently, but planned to turn stern. His role model was the FBI man played by Charles Durning in the film *Dog Day Afternoon*. "It's all wild and funny until this FBI agent comes in and takes control," he later said, describing the movie. "All of a sudden he's telling these kidnappers how they should behave. It works. It works when I do it, too. It's like I say, 'I'm the boss here, and you guys are working for me now, and I expect you to perform.' Sometimes you do it so well you've even got the secretaries in someone's office working for you. I love it."

This was the pattern Nalder followed, as the tape recording he made of this meeting with the Rockwell managers reveals. Consider an exchange over the simple matter of defining the audit process, which can be heard in the first minutes of Nalder's interview. The object of this inquisition was Jim Albaugh, who spoke in a soft, patient monotone, responding to a seemingly innocuous question.

"Several years ago DOE and Rockwell made the decision that audits would no longer be formally transmitted to DOE," Albaugh volunteered. "This was to assure autonomy of our audit process and that we would not be writing our audits for DOE, we would not be in any way changing words, not being frank, not being open, not being totally candid with the people we were writing the audit against."

"What are you worried about with DOE?" Nalder asked, suddenly turning icy. "Why wouldn't you be candid with DOE if you work for them?"

"We are candid with DOE."

"You just said you would lose some of the candor."

"There is a concern there would be some pressure not to put the frankness in that we might want."

"Don't you think you ought to be frank with the U.S. government?"

At this point Gerton, the Department of Energy's overseer, rushed to rescue Albaugh, explaining that the audit process was part of Rockwell's internal practice, not a government requirement. All this took a good ten minutes, and it didn't move the interview along in any substantive way. But it put Nalder's prey on notice; this was to be an adversarial exchange, and he would accept nothing at face value. Even Gerton found himself entrapped by Nalder's carefully orchestrated disagreeableness. When he finished explaining that DOE wasn't interested in hovering over Rockwell's shoulder, Nalder used this to suggest the government was lax.

Maynard and Laura Lee Bailie sit with their infant son, Tom, on the steps of their farmhouse, 1947. Although they didn't know it, the Bailies were already becoming some of the most irradiated civilians in U.S. history.

Tom Bailie, age eighteen months, in front of a wheat field on the family farm. Hanford technicians frequently inspected fields like this one and discovered radioactive hot spots. Their findings were kept secret.

Maynard Bailie's farm, 1949, the year of the top-secret Green Run. Just a few miles from the Hanford site, the Bailie property lay directly in the path of the Green Run emissions.

Tommy Bailie, age three, with a playmate. The unexplained bone deformity in his chest, apparent at birth, had become more pronounced.

Fish and game, which Hanford scientists knew to be contaminated, were a regular part of many downwinders' diets. Here Maynard and Tom Bailie, age four, hold a rabbit shot for food. Behind them is a family cow grazing on irradiated grasses that would no doubt produce contaminated milk.

At right is Tommy Bailie, age four, during the early stages of his mysterious paralysis. Eventually he would be confined to an iron lung and recover only after months of bed rest.

Pollution problems and a history of secret radiation releases have been discovered at many DOE facilities. The dirtiest of these include Hanford (shown as Richland), Savannah River, Rocky Flats, and Fernald.

The N Reactor site, the most modern plutonium-production reactor at Hanford, is also the facility most like the Chernobyl Unit that exploded in the former Soviet Union in 1986.

Karen Dorn Steele, reporter for the *Spokane Spokesman-Review,* in the paper's newsroom. Beginning with rumors about dead livestock, her articles on Hanford and the downwinders helped break down Hanford's wall of secrecy.

*Chris Anderson*

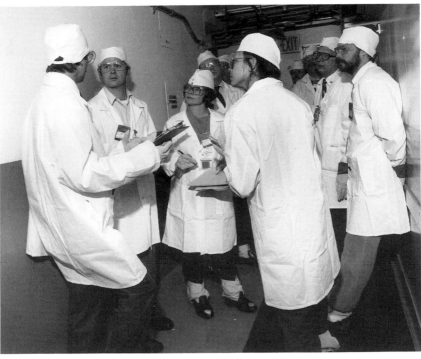

*DOE photo*

Pictured in the center of the group, Karen Dorn Steele participates in one of the first public tours of the PUREX facility at Hanford. The tours were part of the government's public-relations effort in response to Steele's articles.

In 1992 a billboard at the main entrance suggests Hanford's commitment to the environment. At the time, Hanford was widely considered to be the most polluted place in America.

Still radioactive in 1993, Hanford's B Reactor, the world's first large-scale nuclear reactor, was guarded by a high fence and signs warning of radiation.

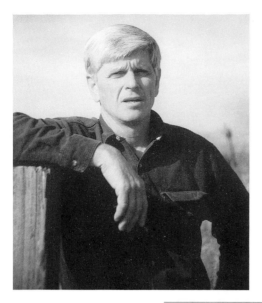

Tom Bailie, in 1992, in the overgrown yard of the farm where he was raised and where, as a boy, he was heavily irradiated.

Juanita Andrewjeski stands in the rural cemetery where her husband, Leon, was buried in 1992. She blames his death, in part, on Hanford.

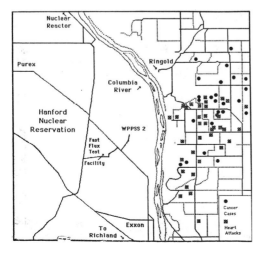

The "death map" kept by Juanita and Leon Andrewjeski in the 1980s. Each mark shows a death due to cancer or heart disease.

Reporter Eric Nalder, *top,* and Hanford safety auditor Casey Ruud in 1992. Nalder's reporting on Ruud's discoveries of mismanagement and safety problems led to the shutdown of Hanford's plutonium production facilities.

DOE photo

John Herrington, secretary of energy from 1984 to 1988, foresaw the fall of the nuclear weapons complex. He warned officials of the Bush administration that cleaning up the lethal wastes of the weapons industry would cost "everything you've got."

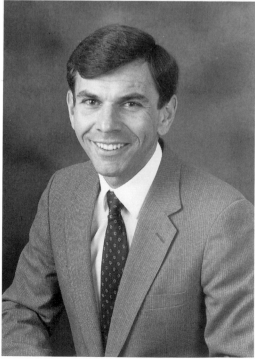

DOE photo

Michael Lawrence, manager of Hanford, from 1984 to 1990, struggled to respond to the revelations of Hanford's long history of pollution and official cover-up. Once the "war lord" in charge of one of the nation's most important defense facilities, he ultimately oversaw its demise.

"Isn't the security of nuclear materials important?" he asked briskly.

"Everything out there is very important," Gerton replied.

"I'm asking this because DOE has been accused in some quarters, and I have no proof of this, of being a see-no-evil, hear-no-evil outfit," Nalder continued. "What I hear consistently from safety people is DOE stays at headquarters and doesn't do a very good job of coming out to see what Rockwell is doing." Nalder was essentially right. Under President Reagan, the number of DOE inspectors had been reduced to save money. Those who remained spent most of their time checking paperwork, not touring the Area.

"Let me ask you," Nalder added, "do you think you could stand up to a congressional investigation on this?"

"That's nothing new for us," answered Gerton. "We were back talking to Dingell's committee just a few days ago. We welcome the opportunity to talk about what we think is a good system." Congressman John Dingell of Michigan was chairman of the House Committee on Energy and Commerce, which oversaw the Department of Energy. By mentioning Congress, Nalder had reminded everyone in the room that Democratic lawmakers were always willing to air the Republican-run DOE's problems in the glare of a committee hearing. This could adversely affect the company's bid for a new contract. Though he didn't mention it, Nalder had already been in touch with aides to Congressman Dingell, and he believed that a series of negative stories based on Ruud's audits might lead to hearings on the problems at Hanford. Many in the company, including John Baker and Paul Lorenzini, understood this possibility too.

The Rockwell team patiently endured three hours of questioning. They persevered because they believed they were right when they said the plants were operating safely. And they did have plausible arguments to counter Casey Ruud's complaints. In the area of nuclear materials control, for example, all of Ruud's criticisms had to do with accounting and surveillance practices. He had never documented the actual loss of plutonium or a near criticality. This point was made by nuclear materials security expert Robert Heineman, who said that Ruud's audit findings were not serious enough to stop work at any of the plants.

The same was true, they said, when it came to the problem at Glove Box 9B. The Hanford men insisted that the most important cause of the accident was the workers' failure to follow procedure. Although they admitted that the vent system had not yet been rebuilt, they claimed other steps had been taken to protect workers. Here Nalder asked whether Casey Ruud had agreed that the problem had been resolved satisfactorily. He also used the opportunity to pretend that he didn't know Ruud.

"Has this Casey Ruud fellow been told all this?" asked Nalder. "Does he now agree that his memo was wrong?" (At this and other moments in the interview, he pretended that he didn't know how to pronounce Ruud's name. He referred to "this Ruud character" and repeatedly mentioned that he would like to meet him.)

John Baker admitted that Ruud was not in agreement. "No, I believe in his mind he would still consider it a design problem," said Baker. Nalder would later say that the others hadn't seemed to understand the underlying meaning of what Baker said. They seemed to believe that the matter was closed and that Ruud's opinion was no longer so important.

As they struggled to persuade Nalder, the Rockwell men drew elaborate diagrams of equipment and pulled out reams of documents to make their case. According to company reports, Hanford had never run better in terms of worker safety and emissions. At the same time, plant output had exceeded expectations. Rockwell had surpassed milestones set by previous operators and regularly earned glowing appraisals and large bonuses from the government.

As the end of the interview approached, Eric Nalder softened a bit. He jokingly asked if he could be put on the regular mailing list for all audits. He also asked once more if Casey Ruud was satisfied with the responses to his audits. Again John Baker said that Ruud had concurred with many of the responses to his complaints, but he added that some of the audits remained open.

Nalder was convinced that after many months, the design and safety problem Ruud had discovered had not been fixed. Ruud had identified serious lapses in Rockwell's management and potentially disastrous problems in plant design and operations. These remained open issues long after they should have been resolved. Finally, Nalder was distressed by the way the DOE man had risen to Rockwell's defense. As a reporter, he was suspicious of anything that seemed so cozy and complicit. He expected the government to hold its contractors to strict standards, to stand as a taskmaster, not an ally.

Before he left the meeting, Nalder chose to distract his opposition the way a squid distracts its foe with a jet of blinding ink. Still seated at the conference table, he scratched out a note on a napkin. It read, "Mr. Ruud, Please call me at the *Seattle Times* collect to at least talk without quote, so I can better understand the audit process." As he departed, Nalder gave the napkin to Jerry Gilliland, and asked him to pass it along to the shy auditor. Gilliland agreed, and he did arrange for Ruud to get the note.

It was late on a Friday afternoon when Eric Nalder got back to Seattle. He would work into the night to write the first audit story for Saturday's paper. That piece, which was finished by 9:00 P.M., was printed with a headline reading, AUDITS SAY HANFORD PLANTS UNSAFE. It began with a paragraph explaining that intense production pressure had jeopardized the safe operation of Hanford facilities, but work went on despite an auditor's warnings. Paul Lorenzini was quoted as saying there was no cause for alarm, but his reassurances seemed pale compared with the drama of the rest of the article.

Nalder and his editor, Tom Brown understood this was an incendiary story. With the Chernobyl disaster barely four months old, any suggestion of problems at Hanford would create a public uproar. But even as they were finishing work on this first article, they turned their attention to the second act. Every good newsperson knows that a good story must be followed the next day by an article on further developments. Besides, the Sunday *Times* was a statewide paper with a circulation of half a million, nearly double Saturday's readership. But Nalder needed a peg, some bit of additional news on which he could base a Sunday story.

As midnight approached, Nalder and Brown racked their minds for some new angle that would justify a second piece. Frustrated, Nalder took a walk outside the newspaper building, which is in an ivy-covered, factorylike brick box in downtown Seattle. Nalder walked past idling newspaper trucks, waiting to take out the Saturday edition, and then back inside. Before returning to talk with Brown, he stopped at his desk and shuffled through a mound of papers. There, in an overnight-delivery envelope marked with Casey Ruud's return address, he discovered his peg. It was an audit Ruud had conducted the previous year on welding and fabrication practices. Though not as dramatic as the others, it concluded that undersized welds were a serious problem at Hanford, and that the inspection of welds was slipshod.

Calling them at home, even after midnight, Nalder was able to get Rockwell public-relations officers to offer boilerplate rebuttals to the weld-audit issues. (One of them would later complain to Nalder that he had disturbed him and his wife at a rather intimate moment.) As he wrote the Sunday story he began with the new element, the welding audit, but then repeated everything in his original article in a way that made it seem even more dramatic. Finishing work the next evening, Nalder stayed at the office long enough to go down into the bowels of the building and grab one of the first copies as it rolled off the thundering presses. He went home exhausted, after thirty-six hours of work.

In the Tri-Cities, the blows struck by Eric Nalder were met with stiff resistance. Rockwell gathered local reporters together for a press conference at which Lorenzini attacked the *Seattle Times*. Not only was the paper wrong about the seriousness of the audit findings, he said, but they were wrong about the opinions held by the auditor in question. Casey Ruud, Lorenzini insisted, was satisfied with the company's work on his audit findings and would not support the allegations in the *Times*.

Lorenzini's appearance was a profound statement to the Tri-Cities community. As the leader of Hanford's main contractor, he was behaving like a general who has gone to the front to direct his troops. His presence at a press conference indicated that the threat to Hanford was so serious that the defense could not be left in the hands of junior officers. This level of status and esteem was something Lorenzini had aspired to since he was a boy working in his father's fast-food restaurant, called Whizburger, in Portland. He recalled well the pain in his father's voice when he had described the hardships he had faced as an immigrant. The son became determined to hold a respected position in life. Lorenzini had been the first person to earn a doctorate in nuclear engineering from Oregon State University. He also held a law degree.

Lorenzini had worked for Rockwell for much of his adult life. Joining the firm in 1969, he had been immediately assigned to study nuclear reactor safety. In those early years at Rockwell he had become certain that it was possible to make atomic power plants so safe that accidents were almost impossible. After several promotions, Lorenzini got to put his convictions to work as a spokesman for nuclear power in California and head of the speakers' bureau for the American Nuclear Society. In this first brush with the politics of the atom, he fought against a well-organized campaign to ban nuclear power by referendum vote. The antinuclear drive was led by a group of sixties-style activists, some of whom were inspired by Eastern spirituality. With Lorenzini out front, a coalition of utilities and construction companies answered with a sophisticated advertising campaign and beat the initiative by a wide margin.

Perhaps more than almost anyone else at Hanford, Lorenzini had reflected on the larger philosophical issues affecting the atomic community. In his view, the civil rights movement, Watergate, and the Vietnam War had eroded the basic values held by the nation. Many Americans had turned to nontraditional religions and philosophies and away from old-fashioned Christian ideals. These wanderers had also attached themselves to environmental causes that ran counter to Lorenzini's conservative Christian notion of man's dominion over nature.

"They believe that nature is the essence of God," he once explained. "Therefore they believe that when we invade the natural realm, we enter something that has a spiritual dimension to it and therefore we should minimize the amount of what we do, even if it means we compromise quality of life and ourselves. The effect is to devalue human life."

As a proponent of a nuclear technology, Lorenzini considered himself a defender of American strength and human progress. "If you see the world as a world in which man was created by a personal God and all these resources are here for his use, you see technology as acceptable," he would tell his friends in those days. "If your worldview is that God and nature are the same, you will reject technology." This analysis of his opponents served Lorenzini well.

In the battle over Casey Ruud's audits, Lorenzini believed that the facts didn't matter as much as public relations. He had to calm public fears that were exaggerated by visions of Chernobyl and Three Mile Island. At the same time he had to make sure that Hanford didn't become a public-relations nightmare for Rockwell International. As operator of the Department of Energy's Rocky Flats weapons plant, Rockwell was already taking a beating in the press for reports of illegal dumping and worker harassment. A spate of bad stories about Hanford would further dirty the company's image and threaten its position in the competition for the $800-million ($4 billion over five years) consolidated contract. Mike Lawrence had already contacted Rockwell seeking copies of Ruud's original audits, and at least two Northwest congressmen were suggesting that the House of Representatives investigate what was going on at Hanford.

As he stood before the media in the Tri-Cities, all of this was in the back of Lorenzini's mind. So too were the firm assurances his team had given him. He trusted that Ruud's complaints were being addressed, that no serious problems had been uncovered, and that the auditor was more or less satisfied with the course of events. The *Seattle Times* had "grossly misinterpreted and in many cases misstated the audit findings," Lorenzini said. "We can assure the public that the plants are being operated in a very safe manner." Lorenzini's appearance was broadcast by all the Tri-Cities TV stations.

But, much as it may have reassured most viewers, it enraged Casey Ruud. He decided, at last, to go public with his complaints. He was moved to act when Lorenzini stared into the television cameras and said that Ruud had never recommended closing either the Plutonium-Uranium Extraction Facility or the Plutonium Finishing Plant.

"That's it. To hell with them," Ruud said to his wife as the two sat in their living room watching the news conference. "I can't live with this. I told them not to say that, and they did it anyway. But what do I do? If I go public, they could fire me tomorrow."

Ruud felt tortured by both his conscience and his commitment to his family. If he went public in his challenge to Rockwell, he would not go alone. His children and his wife would be dragged into this fight, whether they wanted it or not. Their friendships, their contacts in the community, even their financial security, would be placed at risk.

As Casey and Suzi talked about what might happen if he made his story public, they concluded that they would, at the very least, become social pariahs. Kennewick was a company town, and its citizens believed that the company was benevolent. Ruud's challenge would inevitably be viewed as a threat to the entire community. The entire family could expect to be shunned or even attacked by Hanford loyalists. The worst that could happen was that Casey would be fired and find himself unable to get new work because of his status as a malcontent.

Although both of these outcomes were painful to contemplate, they involved outside pressures. In the end, Casey and Suzi decided it would be better to face attacks from outside the family than the crisis of conscience that would come with backing down. "Let me ask you one question, Casey," Suzi said during their long deliberation. "Can you live with yourself if you do nothing?" Casey didn't have to answer.

Ruud felt compelled to call Eric Nalder and invite him to come the next day for an on-the-record interview. But he still felt uneasy about what he was going to do. He walked around his house, imagining foreclosure. He looked in on his sleeping children, and worried about the ways they might be ostracized once their father was known as an agitator. He even walked down the street to see his brother, John, who also worked at the Area. In the insular Hanford community, John would likely suffer for his brother's actions. He told Casey he would stand behind him, no matter what he decided.

Back at home, Ruud dialed the number for the *Seattle Times* and asked for Nalder.

"I'm ready," he told the reporter. "Let's do it."

The two men agreed to meet the following day. Then Nalder recommended that Ruud also call Jeffrey Hodges, staff member for Congressman Dingell's committee. Nalder explained that Ruud was about to become a whistle-blower and he was bound to suffer the consequences of a public challenge to Rockwell. He might be harassed by other workers or set up by his superiors to be fired. There might even be some physical danger. In Nalder's work with other whistle-blowers, some had come to interviews armed, for fear of being attacked by co-workers. Both men knew that although an actual physical attack was unlikely, Ruud was nevertheless in harm's way.

That night Ruud called Hodges at home. It was 1:30 A.M. in Washington, D.C., but Ruud needed to know that the committee was interested in his case. In the partisan politics that surrounded America's nuclear complex, the Democrat-led committee often posed as a critic of the Republican administration and protector of those who came forward with key information. In the interlocking relationship between Congress and DOE, the agency was dependent on the legislature for funding and for authorization to conduct programs such as the waste-isolation project. From day to day the Department of Energy managed the facilities as it saw fit. But powerful members of Congress could demand that someone like Casey Ruud be protected, and the DOE would make it so.

On the telephone, Ruud discovered that Hodges was indeed interested in what he knew. The congressional aide must already have begun to imagine how a disgruntled auditor who knew where the skeletons were buried at Hanford would serve a useful purpose. He told Ruud that the committee would fly him to Washington in a few weeks. That wasn't good enough for the auditor. Ruud was afraid that after two weeks of meetings with Rockwell people, his fire of indignation would be doused by fear and uncertainty. He insisted on meeting with the committee immediately. Though he couldn't guarantee it, Hodges promised to try to meet Ruud's demand.

The next morning Eric Nalder, accompanied by a *Seattle Times* photographer, again flew to the Tri-Cities; he rented a car and followed the directions he had received over the phone to Ruud's house. On the drive, Nalder once again worried that he was being followed. When he got to Ruud's neighborhood he parked the car a few houses away from the address and walked the rest of the way.

Nalder was surprised by the appearance of the man who answered his knock on the door. At first glance, Ruud looked even younger than his thirty-two years. He had a smooth, almost child-like face with an open, innocent expression. Nalder found it hard to believe that this grinning young man, who appeared at the door with his two-month-old son, Evan, on his shoulders, had spent the previous six months battling with Rockwell's top executives.

The two had barely gotten into their small talk—about running and skiing—when Nalder looked out a front window to see a couple of men in suits drive up in a drab-looking American-made car. As they got out of their car and walked up Ruud's driveway, Nalder became agitated. Quickly explaining that he thought these were Hanford security people, Nalder hid behind the draperies as Ruud answered the door and sent the two well-dressed young Mormon missionaries on their way. Embarrassed and amused, Nalder laughed at himself and then sat down on the sofa. For the next five hours he reviewed the documents with Ruud, who took care of little Even as the two men talked. Ruud was easy to interview. He spoke methodically, even pointing out the items Nalder should be sure to get down in his notebook.

In Nalder's article, which appeared the next day, Ruud attacked both his employer and the Department of Energy. He accused his bosses of lying about the audits—by saying no shutdowns were recommended—and he chastised Department of Energy officials for shirking their oversight responsibilities. Ruud had a down-home way of talking. He described himself as a "tiny squirrel" opposing a company that was like a "giant horse." And though he declared his support for nuclear technology, he said Hanford should be held to a high safety standard. "After all," he noted, "we are not making TVs or cars."

Of course, Nalder again seized the opportunity to present the audit findings in detail and fan public concern about Hanford. He didn't trust Rockwell's managers, and he was afraid that Hanford was out of control. The article also gave Ruud the chance to note, in public, that DOE oversight of Hanford was weak compared with the more adversarial Nuclear Regulatory Commission, which was in charge of commercial atomic facilities.

Department of Energy officials were thin-skinned about comparisons to the Nuclear Regulatory Commission. Since 1950, various members of Congress had complained that the AEC and later the DOE could not be effective as both operator and regulator of the weapons complex. Critics said it amounted to a classic case of the fox guarding the hen house, and they often suggested that the NRC could do a better job as overseer. With skillful politicking the agencies had managed to hold on to this power of self-regulation. But the fear of losing it was ever-present. Paul Lorenzini would later say that Hanford manager Mike Lawrence had often said that the department could never accept Congress handing oversight to the Nuclear Regulatory Commission or anyone else.

In the five days after Nalder's original story was published, Casey Ruud's audits became a major issue in Pacific Northwest politics. Members of Congress in both Oregon and Washington began to demand that both the House and the Senate investigate. Washington's governor, Booth Gardner—who wisecracked that the audits read like the script from a disaster movie—said that Rockwell's credibility would be restored only by an outside inspection. Senator Dan Evans went so far as to say that perhaps the government should be more decisive when it came to firing contractors.

On the day after he broke his silence, while the controversy continued to expand, Casey Ruud quietly slipped out of town. After writing a rubber check for some cash, he drove his battered old truck to the Tri-Cities airport and boarded a plane to Salt Lake City, where he would make his connection to Washington. Congressional aide Jeffrey Hodges had come through. The committee wanted Ruud's testimony and had agreed to bring him east immediately. As Ruud flew across the country, copies of his audits secure in his briefcase, he knew nothing of the events that were rapidly unfolding back home.

Hours after Ruud's story came out, the Department of Energy issued a press release that began with the following paragraph:

Michael J. Lawrence, Manager of the Department of Energy's Richland Operations, today directed officials of Rockwell Hanford Operation to immediately stop all plutonium processing and handling operations for which the firm is responsible at the Department's Hanford site near Richland, Washington.

According to the press release, Lawrence was responding not to the *Seattle Times* reports and the ensuing political furor, but to a violation of the procedures for preventing criticalities at the Plutonium Finishing Plant. Though this was the type of problem cited in Casey Ruud's audits, it was not actually one of Ruud's discoveries. This particular incident involved workers who bypassed certain safety valves as they rushed to ship plutonium solution through pipes in the plant. "In general, there was a lack of appropriate controls, reviews and approvals," the press release read, echoing the kind of language in Ruud's audits. But of course there was nothing in Lawrence's announcement referring to the Rockwell audit mess. At a press conference, Lawrence said the criticality violation was serious—"a number four" on a scale of one to five—and he said a team of experts would review the audits and produce a report within a matter of weeks. In the meantime, three-fourths of Rockwell's roughly $10-million management fee for Hanford would be withheld pending the results of the review team's work.

Paul Lorenzini heard about the shutdown order while he was visiting his own bosses at Rockwell headquarters in El Segundo, California, near Los Angeles. He had gone there to discuss the audit crisis and to work on the proposal for the lucrative consolidated DOE contract. The consolidated contract would mean an enormous increase in Rockwell's business at Hanford, and by winning it, Lorenzini would become much more important in the Rockwell hierarchy. When a call came in from Richland with the news of the federal government's stop-work order, Lorenzini knew that whatever lead Rockwell might have had in the race for the contract had disappeared.

Later, Lorenzini would remember that no one at headquarters had said much about the shutdown order. This may have been because Rockwell had so many other problems. The company's Rocky Flats operation was also racked by controversy, and then there was the ongoing investigation of the disastrous launch of the

*Challenger,* in which Rockwell had participated as a major contractor. Hanford's troubles must have seemed much less significant by comparison. And besides, they were being managed by Lorenzini, whom the company's top executives trusted.

As he flew back to the Tri-Cities in a Rockwell company jet, Lorenzini couldn't help thinking about how quickly his fortunes had changed. A week earlier he had been the most powerful executive in the Tri-Cities. Suddenly he was impotent, unable to control much of anything in the strange atomic city where he lived. Even his friend Mike Lawrence had abandoned him, choosing to announce the shutdown to the world without giving him advance warning. Lawrence and Lorenzini were not close friends, but they were friendly. Two men with a world of experience outside the Tri-Cities, they had both come to town to provide fresh leadership, and they had both succeeded. While Lawrence had opened the gates of Hanford to let in the public and rebuild trust, Lorenzini had been exceeding the goals set for him by the government. He had improved the safety and environmental performance of PFP and PUREX while setting all-time plutonium production records to satisfy the Reagan arms buildup. Indeed, Rockwell had just been awarded its $2.3-million management fee, an obvious sign that DOE approved of its operations. How bad could things be, he wondered.

But as he thought about Lawrence's decision to shut down the plants, Lorenzini realized that he hadn't responded strongly enough to Casey Ruud when he had the chance. Lawrence had often told Lorenzini that criticality procedures were a major issue. He now realized he should have suspended operations in order to show he was taking Ruud's concerns about criticality seriously. Lorenzini also realized that, in the end, Lawrence was not an ally. He had suspected this earlier, when he had tangled with Lawrence over a seemingly innocuous issue: Lorenzini had wanted to shift some funding to give his best workers merit raises. Lawrence, who had made a big show of announcing a 1.5-percent cap on all raises, refused to approve Lorenzini's plan, even though he knew that Rockwell was having trouble holding on to qualified technical people. When Lorenzini then suggested consolidating positions, and using the leftover money to give better raises, Lawrence still refused. It would have cost nothing, but Lawrence had stood firm so that he could appear to be a tough budgeter. The same sort of thing had happened with the Ruud audit flap. The way Lorenzini saw it, Lawrence had done what was best for himself, at the expense of their working relationship. "It was grandstanding for his bosses in Washington," Lorenzini would remark much later.

Back in the Tri-Cities, Lorenzini called his key managers together. "Hold your heads high," he told them. Lorenzini was angry that an auditor with two years of college had passed judgment on his team, and that DOE was buckling under the pressure. He still believed that Ruud had found nothing wrong with the actual engineering and operation of the plants. His main criticisms had to do with paperwork. That shouldn't be enough to shut them down. But with the politicians screaming, Lawrence had acted. There wasn't anyone out there trying to find things Rockwell was doing right, Lorenzini told his people. "Hold your heads high," he repeated.

The community seemed to react to the news in the same stiff-upper-lip way. The *Tri-City Herald*'s editorial writers urged that judgment of Rockwell be withheld. "We should be careful about using Rockwell's internal auditing procedure as a bludgeon to beat the company over the head," the paper said. On the same day the *Herald* published a poll showing that although others in the state opposed the atomic dump project, people around the Tri-Cities wanted the waste repository. But the support was not overwhelming—46 percent supporting the repository against 32 percent opposing it—and for the first time since Hanford was created, the state's politicians may have seen a crack in the region's historical support for the Area.

For generations, Washington's senators and representatives had used their political muscle to please the voters by keeping funding and jobs at Hanford high. To be pro-Hanford was to be pro–Washington State. Other states with big Department of Energy facilities had the same political dynamic. South Carolina, for example, could always count on its powerful senator, Strom Thurmond, to protect the Savannah River reactors. But in the fall of 1986, amid Rockwell's troubles and the nuclear waste dump controversy, this political formula began to change. In Washington State, Democratic Senate candidate Brock Adams, seeking to unseat Slade Gorton, decided to campaign against Hanford. Gorton, who had ridden into the Senate on Ronald Reagan's coattails in 1980, had been a champion of the Reagan administration and of Hanford. But in the fall campaign, even he ran TV commercials attacking DOE. As it became clear that most of the state feared Hanford, the two men competed to see who could be more critical of DOE. Adams, who had no loyalty to Ronald Reagan, won this competition easily. He called for DOE Secretary John Herrington to resign, and early in the wake of Chernobyl he had insisted that N Reactor be closed. In November, Adams would prevail by being the most anti-DOE candidate. For the first time Washington would send someone to the Senate who was not an unadulterated Hanford booster.

The *Tri-City Herald*'s poll on the atomic waste burial ground proposal and a front-page report on Hanford-bashing by the two Senate candidates greeted Rockwell executives who picked up their afternoon paper when they got home. That night, when many surely believed that things couldn't get much worse, Casey Ruud's face haunted their television screens. There he was, coming out of a rest room at the Rayburn House Office building on Capitol Hill. With Jeff Hodges at his side, he had a goofy smile on his face (on the other side of the door, Ruud had giggled and said, "We better check our zippers"), and declined to answer questions. Nevertheless, the reporters made it clear that Ruud was the focus of closed-door meetings with the Dingell committee. This former welder, with no engineering degree and the happy-go-lucky demeanor of a ballplayer who had just hit a home run, was speaking to power, and power was listening.

Ruud had stayed in the Watergate Hotel the night before. In the morning he had gone down to the lobby to ask for a cab. A man standing nearby invited him to share his limousine for the ride up Constitution Avenue to Capitol Hill. (Ruud guessed that he was an ambassador or someone else important.) On this, the first limousine ride in his life, Ruud was enthralled by views of the White House, the Washington Monument, and the Capitol. After having breakfast with Hodges in one of the House cafeterias, Ruud met for most of the day in a locked hearing room with a small group of congressmen and their aides. He went through the audits, explaining what he had found and offering his version of Rockwell's handling of the issues.

Ruud would later recall that Congressman Ron Wyden, a Democrat from Oregon, seemed most impressed by his criticism of the DOE management. Wyden had long been uneasy with an arrangement that had a single agency both producing plutonium and policing the safety and environmental effects of the production facilities. What Ruud was telling him, about lax procedures and slipshod record-keeping, would be political ammunition for an assault on the Department of Energy's management team.

Eventually Ruud caught on to the fact that the committee's interest was inspired in large part by partisan politics. Republican committee members and their aides routinely supported the Reagan administration, while Democrats such as Wyden were unrelenting in their criticism. Ruud was shocked to see how this division was played out in sometimes petty ways. Democrats would grow quiet when Republicans joined the conversation, but when the Republicans were called away for some other business, the Democrats would then become animated and critical of their colleagues. While this was politics as usual, it was all new and unnerving to Casey Ruud. Worse were the comments of a senior congressman he would later refer to only as "Representative Martini."

"This guy comes back from lunch and he is in the bag," Ruud explained long afterward. "He pulls me aside and says, 'Ya know, young man, let me explain where I'm at. I'm not pro-nuclear. I'm not antinuclear. As a politician, you decide which side you're going to get the most votes from, and that's the one that you pick.' "

It was at this point that Ruud announced that he needed to use the rest room. He and Hodges used a side door to elude the reporters camped outside the committee room, but they were spotted as they entered the rest room, which was down the hallway. Ruud and Hodges were trapped by the media horde, which waited for them outside. On television back home, Ruud came off as a kind of wise guy, mugging for the cameras and blurting, "No comment." But the smile covered his nervousness, and his surprise at the cameramen who were pushing each other aside just to get closer.

Ruud returned to the Tri-Cities late the following night. Suzi met him at the airport, with one child in a stroller and the others holding

her hands. As they walked through the baggage-claim area, a photographer from the *Tri-City Herald* suddenly appeared to take their
picture. Ruud, who felt he had crossed the line into the public
arena, was getting used to the paparazzi-style treatment. When a
*Herald* reporter then asked for a brief interview, he willingly answered questions. Yes, he had recommended shutdowns. No, he
didn't believe Rockwell's responses to his audits were adequate.
Yes, he believed the design system was still out of control.

Though Casey Ruud had emerged as a public figure—riding in
limousines and dodging newsmen at airports—life at his suburban
tract house was far from glamorous. Just as Tom Bailie was
shunned as a troublemaker by his neighbors in Franklin County,
Ruud and his family would be given the cold shoulder by their
friends and acquaintances. This was especially true of the parents
of the soccer players Casey Ruud coached. Most were Hanford
workers, after all, and Coach Ruud was threatening their liveli-
hoods. Not all of the parents felt this way; some even told Ruud he
was setting a good example for the children. But these were the
exceptions. Most just stopped talking to him. Suzi Ruud endured
a similar kind of isolation. Other mothers in the neighborhood were
just not interested in her. And then, of course, there were the
financial worries that came with her husband's risky public stand.
She was at once proud of him and terrified of the consequences to
come. There were still plenty of bills to pay, and the Ruud family
was dependent on Casey's income alone.

    That fall, money worries led Ruud to try to solve a problem with
overflowing toilets without a plumber's help. The sewer pipe running to his leach field needed to be replaced. With no extra cash,
and the prospect of losing his job looming large, Ruud had decided
to dig the four-foot-deep, eighty-foot-long trench himself and lay a
new pipe. Sometimes he had to work into the night, digging by
lantern light. It was on one of those nights, when he was waist-deep
in dirt and feeling more than a little sorry for himself, that he got
a call from Mike Lawrence. The manager of Hanford wanted him
to be part of the audit review team. Ruud didn't hesitate to say yes.

    The team of DOE reviewers and outside consultants was charged
with assessing the seriousness of Ruud's initial complaints and

Rockwell's response. Much of this work consisted of the team asking questions and Rockwell answering with written reports. Mike Karol, a young DOE administrator who directed the project, handed most of these reports on to Ruud. Convinced that his future at Hanford would be short, Ruud was no longer concerned about being diplomatic. In some cases he assented to the Rockwell version of events. In other instances he lost his patience and scrawled "Bullshit" across those pages of documentation that had not been verified by the department's own experts. This did not endear Ruud to the no-nonsense engineers who were part of this review team.

Ruud's reputation in the larger Hanford community grew worse as time wore on. This was made clear during an on-site inspection tour, which was part of the review team's work. Ruud entered an engineer's office and found a cartoon posted on the back of the door. The drawing showed a skeleton covered with cobwebs and seated at the controls of a workstation inside the Plutonium Finishing Plant. The caption read, "Well, you think it's okay if we start up now, Mr. Ruud?"

The cartoon was not the only evidence of the anger many Hanford workers felt toward Ruud. In their eyes, he had attacked not just Rockwell, but the people who worked in the Area. They resented seeing what they viewed as family business aired in the media. It made them look bad, and it frightened the outside world. Thousands of Hanford jobs—high-paying jobs at that—depended on public trust and continued government funding. Rockwell officials knew of several groups of workers who had discussed doing Ruud bodily harm. Though this never came about, management took it seriously enough to make sure that supervisors discouraged aggressive actions against Ruud. This did nothing to stem other forms of harassment, including chain-letter-style memos that attacked Ruud's character. In one, titled "Casey at the Bat," Ruud was depicted as a troublemaker who could cost Rockwell the consolidated contract. "Because of our boy Casey," the parody concluded, "mighty Rockwell might strike out." Another parody, called "The Legend of Casey Ruud," implied that Ruud was simply a destructive, evil man and that Congress had helped him defame Hanford. Inside Rockwell, a whistle-blower like Casey Ruud was a traitor.

Knowing that he would never again be trusted by the rank and file, Ruud committed himself to defending his audits and fighting those in DOE who would forgive some of Rockwell's shortcomings. He got into frequent scraps with federal overseers and consultants, many of whom came to agree with the people out in the Area who saw Ruud as an unnecessarily stubborn young man who alienated others. Their conclusions about Ruud may have had more to do with their need to defend themselves than with Ruud's actual behavior. But clearly he was as stubborn as the Hanford culture was hidebound.

Ultimately the review team's report conceded that the original audits had been done properly and that Rockwell should have shut down operations while the problems were fixed. But the team did not go far enough, in Ruud's mind, in their criticisms of the company. Ruud quietly refused to sign the report, but he didn't make a public fuss about his dissent. Instead he filed away his objections in his mind, understanding that someday Congress might ask him about the way the Department of Energy had responded to the audit scandal.

At the end of November 1986, Mike Lawrence announced that Rockwell suffered from a lack of discipline that was "unacceptable." He ordered the company to move immediately to improve its quality-assurance program and its commitment to safety. The review team's report not only confirmed Rudd's original audit, but noted additional problems. It referred to a "serious lack of overall SNM [special nuclear materials] control," and it chided Rockwell's slow response to the audit findings. Similar conclusions were reached on the design audit, and at several points in their report the investigators noted that Rockwell had failed to notify DOE of important problems.

This verdict could not have come at a worse time for Paul Lorenzini, who refrained from publicly challenging Lawrence's criticisms. He might have said that Rockwell had told DOE about the NQA-1 problem, and that John Baker had informally discussed Casey Ruud's audits with his DOE counterparts months before. He might even have noted that in a formal performance grading in July, the same DOE officials had rated Rockwell's operation as "excellent" because record production was achieved "while operating in a safe, secure, and environmentally sound manner." But Lorenzini still worked for DOE and Mike Lawrence, and he felt that he could not speak his mind. Through the autumn, while the fire of the Ruud controversy burned all around him, Lorenzini remained focused on Rockwell's lengthy proposal for the $4-billion consolidated Hanford contract.

The multi-year contract would guarantee the jobs of everyone on Mahogany Row. But beyond that, a victory in the competition for this prize would amount to nothing less than the resurrection of Paul Lorenzini. The Ruud affair had ruined Lorenzini's standing within the corporate community. Already besmirched by the *Challenger* disaster and problems at Rocky Flats, Rockwell's image was further damaged by the Hanford fiasco. At times Lorenzini felt abandoned by his bosses at company headquarters because they were not interested so much in solving Hanford's problems as in protecting the parent company's name. It was up to him to win the contract and redeem himself.

As he worked twelve- and sixteen-hour days on a proposal that totaled many hundreds of pages, Lorenzini was busily denying the certain fact that Rockwell was finished at Hanford. Though he still believed he had a chance, most of the residents of Mahogany Row had to know that Rockwell was out of the running. During this time Lorenzini was often puzzled by the way these people spoke to him. It was as if he suffered from some terrible illness. They treated him with such sympathy and kindness that Lorenzini couldn't stand it. He was annoyed, too, by the poster-wielding antinuclear protesters who had begun coming over from Seattle to march outside the Federal Building. Lorenzini would have to pass these people almost every day. He wasn't affected by their arguments, but he did resent their presence.

"Their message was 'You are here to fatten your pocketbook by doing something immoral,'" Lorenzini would later recall. "Well, we were doing what we did because the Congress said it was important, because the nation told us to do it. For them to take a position that we are doing something immoral, when it was a national program, was a little off base."

About two weeks after Mike Lawrence released the review committee report, Lorenzini took his completed proposal in hand and traveled to Washington, D.C., for the "dog and pony show" presentation of his contract bid. The pitch was made to a group led by Deputy Secretary of Energy Joseph Salgado. Lorenzini thought he had done well. He believed that Rockwell had developed a solid plan for administering the sprawling Hanford complex, repairing what needed to be repaired and resuming normal operations. But after the meeting, as he flew back to the Tri-Cities and replayed what had happened in his mind, Lorenzini knew he had lost. The clue was in a seemingly off-the-cuff remark Salgado had made during a question-and-answer period. "Of course," Salgado had said, "we expect contractors to keep us fully informed." The inference here was that Rockwell had failed to keep DOE fully informed in the past.

When the announcement came that the Westinghouse Corporation had won the contract, Lorenzini felt disappointed and angry. He was angry at Mike Lawrence, Eric Nalder, Karen Dorn Steele— all the people who he believed had willfully ignored half of the evidence in order to indict Rockwell. After work that day, Lorenzini and many of his top managers went to one of the bars in downtown Richland. They could all expect to lose their jobs in a few weeks, when Westinghouse took possession of Hanford. Ironically, this would have no effect on Casey Ruud and the thousands of other rank-and-file workers who stayed on no matter who had the contract. At the bar, Lorenzini and his comrades tended their wounds. In an unguarded moment, when he stood at the bar next to a Hanford worker, Lorenzini introduced himself and apologized for losing the contract. In the end, he blamed himself.

Lorenzini was most sorry for those executives he had made part of his team who would soon lose their jobs. Weeks later, after devoting much energy to helping the incoming Westinghouse executives understand their new home, Lorenzini cleaned out his personal office and prepared to depart. Rockwell had offered to take him in at some other corporate outpost, but Lorenzini refused the charity. Eventually he would find another job. But it would not be with Rockwell.

In the end, Lorenzini left Mahogany Row accompanied by his friend Clegg Crawford. Crawford admired Lorenzini and was grateful for the lessons he had learned at Hanford. "Paul taught me there was more than black and white, that life had shades of gray," he would say years later. But at the time he found it difficult to be philosophical. He and Lorenzini were both so disappointed and angry. They believed they had met all of DOE's goals—balancing safety and high production levels—only to be undone by a rebellious auditor and betrayed by the federal bureaucracy. After helping Lorenzini put a few last personal belongings into boxes, Crawford said good-bye to his friend. The men hugged each other and, for a moment, cried.

# WE ARE THE FUTURE

IF THERE WAS a turning point in Hanford engineer Mike Fox's life as a nuclear professional, it may have come in the 1976 explosion that turned Harold McCluskey into the "atomic man." McCluskey was working at a glove box in the Plutonium Finishing Plant when an explosion shattered the protective glass, and hundreds of contaminated shards flew into his body. Miraculously, the then-sixty-four-year-old McCluskey survived. And as far as Fox was concerned, it was a relatively minor accident with a happy ending, especially when one considered what might have happened. But although Fox took the explosion in stride, he was astounded by the uproar that followed. Every TV network in America reported the accident, and the people he supervised were deluged with calls from worried friends and relations. None of them seemed to know the first thing about atomic processes. They all thought a mushroom cloud had formed over Richland. Mike Fox felt annoyed.

Days after the accident, Fox bumped into a network film crew at the Tri-Cities airport and sardonically asked the cameraman if he had come to record scenes of death and destruction. The out-of-towner admitted that he had been disappointed by the lack of gore. Fox replied that he would have better luck if he had hung out with the state police and accompanied them to fatal accidents. He pointed out that car wrecks killed thousands each year, while the number of people who had been killed in nuclear accidents could be counted on two hands.

In this brief conversation, Michael Fox believed he discovered the depth of the public's nuclear ignorance. He also found his second calling. If Americans didn't know enough about atomic technology to understand and embrace it, Fox would educate them.

After putting together a slide show, he took to the road, speaking to every professional and civic group that would have him. He went before the brewmasters in Portland and college students in Seattle. Sometimes he carted around a Geiger counter and a set of Fiesta Ware dishes, which were decorated with radium paint and has long been banned. His demonstration of how much radiation existed in the everyday world of Fiesta Ware and luminous watch dials was a sure crowd pleaser. In time, Fox's presentation became most professional. By his own estimate, he answered nearly a thousand questions a year without notes and without ever failing to argue that nuclear energy was safe and essential to America's future.

"Like the typical scientist, I sweated bullets in those first appearances," he would later recall. "Would they like me? Will they be hostile? I was a nukie in a strange land. But time after time, people came around. I realized that C. P. Snow, the British physicist and writer, was right about the gulf of communication between 'techies' and the public. We can't expect a truck driver to spend his time in the library, and we cannot trust the media to do the communicating for us. Only we can convince the people."

Michael Fox was particularly well suited to his role as a nuclear advocate. A handsome man with silver gray hair and a bushy black mustache, he exuded confidence and sincerity. Born in 1936, Fox recalled a childhood dominated by World War II. His father had been a radar operator on the Washington coast, and Fox remembered well the fear and anger his family had felt during the war. As an adult, he was committed to Hanford and its Cold War mission. Fox knew the Soviet threat was real, and he believed that the only appropriate response could be fashioned in super-secret weapons plants. (Of course, he wouldn't say Hanford made weapons, per se. Instead he would say that Hanford made "materials" or a "product." The actual weapons were put together elsewhere.) Most important, Fox was not cowed by the controversy caused by the Three Mile Island accident. While the nuclear industry as a whole became defensive and even meek in the wake of Three Mile Island, Fox remained exuberant about nuclear technology. But like C. P. Snow, he believed that scientists were underappreciated. Fox thought the solution to this problem required that scientists ease public fear. But he was frustrated by the timidity of his peers, who fled from debate. He used to say that if a man-eating lion were set loose at a meeting of nuclear scientists, it would starve. "They take it, and they take it, and they take it from the other side. I'm not like that."

Ten years after the "atomic man" explosion, in the midst of the furor over the nineteen thousand pages of historical documents and Casey Ruud's complaints, Fox again waited for someone to lead the defense of nuclear technology. He waited as N Reactor was shut down in Chernobyl's wake and the restart date was pushed back further and further. He waited as production was halted at the Plutonium-Uranium Extraction Facility and the Plutonium Finishing Plant. But even as the Spokane and Seattle newspapers seemed to bear down on Hanford almost spitefully, no one came to the rescue. As Casey Ruud became a folk hero in some corners of the Northwest, Fox decided to act. He began with a photocopied flyer inviting people to attend a pro-Hanford meeting at the Holiday Inn in downtown Richland. The flyer, distributed at shopping centers by a half-dozen of Fox's like-minded friends, also announced the creation of a new force in the nuclear debate. It was called the Hanford Family.

"Family" was the perfect name for a group defending the Area. Indeed, those who worked at Hanford willingly subsumed a part of their identities, becoming members of an institution, a "family" that was bigger than any individual. These workers were bonded together, like a distinct tribe, because they could not speak freely with anyone from the outside. Just as important, the Tri-Cities' economy depended on Hanford as if it were an old family business. The Department of Energy and its contractors provided jobs, paid the bills, and even employed sons and daughters when they reached working age. Now under siege, it required that loyal family members come to its defense.

About fifty Rockwell employees, union officers, and local civic boosters answered the first call to arms at the Holiday Inn in the autumn of 1986. Mike Fox gave an inspirational talk in which he decried the "Hanford bashing" being done by the big-city papers to the east and west, and he lambasted politicians like Brock Adams who had suddenly turned on a benevolent federal institution that pumped $1 billion a year into Washington State's economy.

One of the few scientists who understood that he had been plunged into a political fight and not a scientific debate, Fox knew he must employ the same rhetorical techniques used by his opponents. He described those on the other side as "enemies," and recast their challenge as a threat not just to the nuclear industry but to the people of the Tri-Cities. HEAL and the others were not just antinuclear, they were anti–Tri-Cities. So too were the newspapers in Seattle and Spokane.

While this first meeting gave the Hanford Family members a chance to vent their anger and fear, the most important thing they did was to begin to organize. A scientific panel was reviewing the future of N Reactor, which had been closed after Chernobyl. Without it there would be no supply of plutonium for PUREX and the Plutonium Finishing Plant. If Hanford was to have a future as an atomic center, the Family would have to fight to save the reactor. They would also resolve to campaign for the waste repository. "But we have to learn to play their game," Fox told the small group of loyalists at that first meeting. "Read Saul Alinsky's book *Rules for Radicals,*" Fox advised the group. "It's like an instruction book for organizing." Ironically, Alinsky was a ferociously liberal social activist who would no doubt have been on the side of HEAL and its allies. But Fox urged the Family to adopt Alinsky's methods— grassroots organization, education, direct protest—because they worked.

With information drawn from Mike Fox's files, which included materials he had collected during years of pro-nuclear activism, the Hanford Family put together a long list of facts to counter the antinuclear attack. They had "risk assessment" figures that used fatality data to show that working at Hanford was safer than working in a sawmill or a mine, or even staying at home. They found studies that showed that Japanese survivors of the atom bomb actually had fewer of certain cancers than one might expect. And they argued that where excess cancers had been found near atomic facilities, people had also been exposed to cancer-causing chemicals. Who could say that radiation was the culprit? "Ninety-nine percent of carcinogens are naturally occurring," Fox would say. "But the antinuclear bastards select small samples. They pick a year when the cancer rate was low and a year that was high and say 'Aha!' But if you look at the entire scope of things, there's no effect. People have to be told this."

Through the winter of 1986–87 the Hanford Family met often to plan rallies and protests. One of these early meetings featured a rousing address by the curmudgeonly Dixie Lee Ray. A former governor of Washington, Ray had been the last chairperson of the old Atomic Energy Commission, before it was dissolved in 1975. No single American politician was more closely identified with the atomic cause than the seventy-two-year-old Ray. Donning a cap decorated with an atom symbol and the words "Proud of Hanford," she peered over half-frame reading glasses and told the members of the Family to fight on against the hated press and anti-nukers. (As governor, Ray had named her pet pigs after various reporters, and she considered the editors of the Seattle papers personal enemies.) She told the members of the Family to talk tough, as she had, because "there are enemies committed to the demise of nuclear power." In subsequent speeches in the Tri-Cities, Ray would describe the antinuclear side as "enemies of the U.S." because they would limit America's military strength.

Ray's appearance drew several hundred people who became active defenders of Hanford. But the biggest event of that first season of activities was a rally held on the Cable Bridge, a graceful span that crossed the Columbia River and connected Pasco and Kennewick. The organizers hoped to draw five thousand people to the demonstration. Posters went up all over the Tri-Cities, imploring people to turn out to defend Hanford and the community. "If this community has made even a small contribution to your life," the notice read, "now is the time to pay her back."

On a warm November Sunday just weeks after the shutdown of PFP and the Plutonium-Uranium Extraction Facility, more than two thousand people gathered on the Cable Bridge to wave placards and cheer for Hanford. The *Tri-City Herald* reported that one dog was decorated with a banner that read NUCLEAR POWER, MAN'S BEST FRIEND. The paper noted other signs that said IF YOU DON'T WORK AT HANFORD YOU'RE A SAFETY RISK and THE NUCLEAR INDUSTRY IS SAFER THAN FARMING AND LOGGING. Surrounded by the trappings of an old-fashioned, Main Street–style political rally, Mike

Fox stood on a flatbed truck provided by the Hanford unions and issued a call to arms.

"We've got a war ahead of us," Fox told the crowd. He said that the shutdowns of N Reactor, the Plutonium-Uranium Extraction Facility, and the Plutonium Finishing Plant proved that safety came first at the site. The fear-mongering critics were wrong. Other speakers, most of them union leaders and local politicians, spoke of the need to defend the Tri-Cities as a symbol of progress and prosperity. Quoted in the *Tri-City Herald,* Richland's city manager sounded a familiar theme: "We are the voice of energy. We are the voice of progress. We are the future."

The future was an immediate concern for the young mothers and fathers who came to the rally with their children perched on their shoulders or nestled into strollers. Their jobs and mortgages and college savings were all on the line in the battle over N Reactor and the other facilities. The reactor was expected to be restarted within a year following improvements recommended by the various experts who were asked to examine the plant after Chernobyl. The DOE's Roddis Commission had split on the question of a permanent shutdown, with four experts saying N Reactor should be refurbished and restarted and two recommending it be closed. The major problem with the reactor was loosening and swelling of the graphite blocks that made up its core. This problem had been anticipated by designers, who predicted a twenty-year life for N Reactor when it was opened in 1963.

The repairs to extend N's life would cost $50 million at a time when government deficits were well over $100 billion a year and the Reagan administration was struggling to contain runaway spending. The Secretary of Energy, John Herrington, a former lawyer and longtime Reagan loyalist, also had to consider proposals for costly upgrading throughout the far-flung weapons complex. The reactors at Savannah River would require hundreds of millions of dollars to fix. Facilities at Rocky Flats, Fernald, and other sites were also scheduled for expensive overhauls. Then there was the looming problem of pollution control. If the federal government was to begin cleaning up the messes it had made in all these places, billions of dollars would be needed every year for the foreseeable future.

All of these financial considerations formed the backdrop for the debate over N Reactor. In Washington, D.C., officials spent months considering whether the nuclear weapons program could get along without Hanford. As the deliberations over the future of Hanford and the entire weapons industry dragged on, DOE's public policy called for restarting not just the reactor, but all the facilities at Hanford. But anyone who knew anything about atomic politics understood that DOE's assurances were subject to change. After all, weapons production was vital to national security, and decisions about production were rarely made in full view of the public and America's Cold War enemies. Then there was the matter of Congress. At any moment the House or Senate could shut down Hanford by refusing to fund the improvements. Likewise, budgetary experts in the administration's Office of Management and Budget could choose to put the public's money somewhere else.

All of this uncertainty meant that places such as Hanford and Savannah River, which did essentially the same work, would have to compete for scarce funding or face permanent closure. While the young people who depended on Hanford paychecks saw this struggle as a battle for their futures, another generation in the Hanford Family considered this a battle over the past and their accomplishments. These first-generation Hanfordites, many of them retirees, would become the backbone of the defense against all the bashers. And of these, gray-haired Ruth Nelson, whose husband, Clayton, had been one of the men who helped build Hanford in 1943, would stand out as an energetic and tireless campaigner.

The Nelsons' story was one that could be claimed by any of the thousands of the settlers—they called themselves "pioneers"—who had created the atomic boomtown. The Nelsons could remember how hard it had been to leave friends and family behind in Texas in 1943 for this isolated, windswept outpost. "No one had any family, and we all griped about the dust," Mrs. Nelson, a wiry, blue-eyed woman would recall. "But we had each other. We all made friends, and we got along, creating a life for ourselves out of nothing." Thirty years later they lived in the same AEC-built house, an "R model," that they had moved into in 1956.

In the old days, no one had any doubt about the rightness of nuclear technology and Hanford's mission, especially after World War II ended in the blinding light of Hanford's exploding plutonium. Men like Clayton Nelson were proud of their work and hoped their sons would follow in their footsteps; they never expected that the nation would be anything but grateful for the dangerous work they performed. With the rising criticism of nuclear technology and Hanford in the 1980s, these men felt betrayed. The workers, especially those who were not decision-makers but simply employees who had done their duty, resented the suggestion that they had polluted the earth and endangered the lives of the people who lived nearby. After all, they lived here too.

When the Hanford Family began its work, Ruth Nelson and her friends found an outlet for their anger at the outsiders' attacks. They became regular volunteers at the Hanford Family office, a storefront donated by a local businessman. They answered the phone and ran the copying machines and sold "Proud of Hanford" T-shirts and caps. "We wanted to educate people about nuclear energy," explained Ruth Nelson. "We weren't the people who were always out front, with their names in the paper. But we helped put on the rallies and we answered the questions when people called on the phone."

Their efforts were quickly recognized by the local and national media. The spectacle of a large, pro-nuclear demonstration—at a time when huge antinuclear rallies were commonplace—was a man-bites-dog kind of event. The Cable Bridge rally was reported on network television and in newspapers around the world. A friend of Mike Fox read about it while she was visiting in Denmark. Fox found himself being interviewed on "Good Morning America." And William F. Buckley even came to the Tri-Cities and put him on his "Firing Line" program opposite Tom Bailie. Although Bailie had nothing to do with the Casey Ruud audits, he was the best living symbol of the Hanford threat. He and Karen Dorn Steele stood for the growing involvement of the public in the business of the nuclear arms industry. Fox, meanwhile, represented the human face of Hanford's past, a face that looked out onto the future with great anxiety.

But even as Fox and the Family assembled their defense of Hanford, the critics continued to attack. At the time of the Cable Bridge
rally, Reverend Bill Houff of HEAL came right to Richland to
criticize both Hanford and the national nuclear establishment. The
occasion was the annual convention of the Washington State Public
Health Association, which included county public health officers
and others concerned with community health issues. Rarely had
this group heard a more dramatic presentation. Houff began his
speech by recounting Dr. Herbert Cahn's failed attempt to distrib-
ute antidote tablets to area residents; these tablets could be taken
in the event of an unusual release of radioactive iodine. Higher
county officials had rejected this idea because it would reflect nega-
tively on Hanford and the nuclear establishment.

Houff framed this story in stark moral terms: "A dedicated
health professional found himself bullied by a minor bureaucrat."
He also placed it in the context of a long history of government
decisions that appeared to put nuclear interests ahead of public
health. Beginning in the 1950s, when U.S. Public Health Services
officers complained about radiation near the Nevada bomb-test
site, they were discouraged from warning those people who were in
harm's way. The same thing had happened when they discovered
grossly inflated leukemia rates downwind from the tests and high
levels of lung cancer in uranium miners. Time and again, national
security concerns overwhelmed worries about radiation exposure.
The main problems with Hanford and the entire atomic weapons
complex were not technical but moral, Houff insisted. Like Mike
Fox, Houff was influenced by C. P. Snow. But the Snow line he
quoted in Richland referred to the dangers of secret science: "It
takes a very strong head to keep secrets for years, and not go
slightly mad."

In the long prosecution of the Cold War, Houff argued, atomic
science had been infected by the madness of secrecy. "America's
military nuclear establishment is corrupted by the nearly absolute
power it wields," he declared, "And in its use of secrecy, the same
establishment first slips into deception and ultimately into the sort
of arrogance which mocks human dignity and trammels democratic
process." The DOE's power, used under the protection of government secrecy, had been effective against threats from both outside

and inside. The atomic community moved quickly to punish even its own when they dissented from established positions. The classic example of this heavy-handedness had involved J. Robert Oppenheimer. When he dared to oppose the arms race, the AEC revoked Oppenheimer's security clearance and announced an investigation of his ties to prewar Communists. In the end he was exonerated, but only after public humiliation and the destruction of his reputation. And though he was found innocent, Oppenheimer's security clearance—a scientist's ticket to the upper echelons of atomic weapons research—was never restored.

Reverend Houff traced this abusive power politics directly to the Atomic Energy Act of 1954. The act authorized the secret production of weapons by a government-run industry that would be exempt from public scrutiny and almost every local, state, and federal regulation. Under the Atomic Energy Act, Hanford and many other facilities routinely violated pollution and health standards, even the labor laws that governed every other industry in America. All of this was legalized by the act and justified by Congress and the White House in the name of national security.

Although the public health officers gathered in Richland could take some comfort in the way Houff described the almighty power of the men who ran Hanford, they did not escape his pastoral rage. He ultimately portrayed them as conspirators in an evil silence. These health officers had done little to warn the public of a risk they must have suspected. "My thoughts flash back," he said, "to the era of those good Germans who did as they were told and did not raise questions about mass moral outrages."

Inflammatory rhetoric, like the "good Germans" remark, wounded Mike Fox, the members of the Hanford Family, and even the children of the Tri-Cities. They were not ashamed that Hanford had served as an arsenal in the Cold War. They were proud of their past and angry at those who would find evil in a clean, wholesome community that had done so much for America. Such feelings were expressed in a variety of ways. PROUD OF HANFORD buttons and bumper stickers suddenly appeared all over the Tri-Cities. Pickets with signs that said SAVE N REACTOR lined the road to the Area almost every day. And letters to the editor of the *Herald* com-

plained about the "Hanford bashing" and evoked the Tri-Cities'
heroic past. "On our family trips back East," one letter writer
explained, "we have always held our heads high to tell everybody—
friends and relatives—that we're from the atomic capital of the
world, Richland, Tri-Cities, Washington."

The sense of outrage and concern was also expressed by elementary school children who wrote letters to President Reagan
and Energy Secretary Herrington, begging them to protect N
Reactor. High-schoolers from Richland and Kennewick com-
posed a declaration titled "In Defense of Our Parents." The idea
began in a religion class taught by a local judge at one of the area
Catholic churches. Students were pondering the Ten Command-
ments when they decided that Hanford's critics were "bearing
false witness" against their parents. Their statement said, "Our
parents . . . are more caring and loving for us than you give them
credit for. They fully know that the consequences of an unsafe
operation could well spell disaster for us, their children, because
we live closest to the operation. This family caring is a tradition
going well into the third generation." These pleas elicited some
sympathy within the administration, which was, after all, dominated by hawkish Cold Warriors who appreciated the job Hanford had done. Indeed, Herrington was so taken with the
wholesomeness of a picture, sent to him by some boosters, of the
Richland High cheerleaders in their mushroom-cloud sweaters,
that he hung it in his office.

While Mike Fox and other defenders of the atom may have
believed they could make their case on purely scientific grounds,
both sides in the Hanford debate were inclined to make emotional
appeals because, in the end, the issues were not scientific. This was
a struggle over politics, morality, and faith. Those who believed in
high technology, science, and an ever-expanding future felt compelled to protect Hanford's status as a center of nuclear activities.
While the critics saw Hanford as a center of deadly atomic weapons
production, these defenders, and even their children, referred to it
in sanitized terms such as "the operation" or "the Area." For them,
Hanford was not threatening or ominous but life-giving. And the
mere suggestion that it was run in an unsafe manner was an attack
on their character.

This was most evident on the few occasions when the two sides met face to face. In one particularly dramatic confrontation, a Hanford engineer named Wanda Munn appeared with Tim Connor of HEAL on a program aired by a TV station in Spokane. Munn, who looked like everyone's grandmother, was a feisty, intelligent debater who was comfortable in her role. She took the challenge from HEAL personally, and she defended Hanford and the Department of Energy's nuclear weapons program in personal terms. When Connor suggested there was something wrong with a system that allowed the Department of Energy to monitor its own environmental performance, Munn said he had attacked the integrity of the people of Hanford. When he then said that the Green Run and other secret transgressions revealed by Karen Dorn Steele reflected bad judgment, Munn responded as if he had said she and everyone else at Hanford were bad mothers and fathers. Would scientists who were mindful that their own children lived nearby do anything to harm the downwinders? she asked, then said, "I am not going to move from Richland or stop drinking water from the Columbia River downstream from Hanford."

These kinds of confrontations between Hanford boosters and outside critics escalated over the course of several months. From time to time antinuclear protesters from Seattle or Portland or Spokane would trek to the site and march around with signs. Sometimes they would climb over the Hanford fence and get arrested. In other cases they would bring their complaints to the park outside the Federal Building in downtown Richland. Often they were met with a counter-demonstration organized by the Hanford Family. The purpose of this strategy was to force the reporters who covered the anti-Hanford protests to present the other side. It worked. Thanks to the Hanford Family, most of the journalists drifted from one demonstration to the other and presented both views in their articles and broadcasts. And almost always these dispatches from the atomic city showed how the community had united against the antinuclear threat posed by outsiders. In this way the Hanford Family succeeded in capturing a share of the victim status that, as sociologist Michael Blain had documented, worked very well in grassroots campaigns against the atom. The Hanford Family could show it was being injured by the outsiders, and this made them more sympathetic figures.

The two groups that battled over Hanford—HEAL and the Hanford Family—were remarkably similar in several respects. Both viewed the other as powerful, threatening, and perhaps even sinister. Both sought to pose as the virtuous victims of an unreasonable opponent. And both denied the humanity of the other. In HEAL's case, there were those who easily threw names like "Nazi" at the people of Hanford. In the Family there were many who would call the people of HEAL "enemies" and "traitors." Of course, none of this was recognized by either side at the time. Like the combatants in any war, HEAL and the Hanford Family found it necessary to construct an image of the other side that made it possible for them to go on fighting.

During the Hanford Family's first year of struggle, it must have seemed that the enemy grew stronger and more threatening with every month. The Department of Energy was publicly committed to getting all the old facilities—the Plutonium-Uranium Extraction Facility, the Plutonium Finishing Plant, and N Reactor—back into full production, and there was still a chance that the nuclear waste dump would be funded. But as time passed, the projected start-up dates for the closed plants were pushed further and further into the future. In August 1987 the National Academy of Sciences, which had been asked by Energy Secretary Herrington to look at N Reactor, issued a fairly gloomy assessment. The report cast doubt on whether operators could prevent a Chernobyl-style explosion in the event of an emergency inside N Reactor. Documents eventually released by the federal government would show that the danger of a hydrogen accident at N Reactor had been known since 1966, but it had been ignored. For twenty years the government chose to forgo safety improvements to limit the hydrogen explosion risk. There was still time to make some improvements. But these fixes would push higher and higher the cost of making N Reactor safer.

Later in the year, congressional budget-makers hinted that N Reactor might be closed simply to save tax dollars. PUREX and PFP ran into similar problems as the new contractor, Westinghouse, struggled to refurbish the plants and retrain workers. Finally, in December of 1987, Congress chose to put the nation's nuclear dump not at Hanford, but in Nevada. In the end, it seemed, the objections voiced by Washington State's residents, and the technical problems cited by the dump proposal's critics, persuaded the politicians that the Hanford project simply wouldn't work. The loss of the waste-isolation project cost the Tri-Cities 1,200 jobs, billions of construction dollars, and the hope of a continuing atomic mission.

The dump-site decision cast a pall over the Tri-Cities' economy. To make matters worse, it was accompanied in April 1987 by a second release of secret Hanford documents—this one comprising twenty thousand pages—and a second round of media reports on the troubling history of the nuclear reservation. Though there was no scandal like the Green Run in this second batch of papers, there were additional revelations of radiation emissions.

Later in the year, Karen Dorn Steele also reported on the preliminary conclusions reached by Centers for Disease Control researchers who were looking into the radiation exposure of the downwinders. The CDC experts had concluded that the downwinders were quite possibly the most irradiated civilians in the United States. As many as twenty thousand children had been hit by high levels of radioactive iodine, Steele reported in the *Spokesman-Review*. The children would have taken in much of that contamination through milk produced by cows that had grazed in contaminated pastures. This exposure would greatly increase their chances of developing both benign and cancerous thyroid tumors.

The new revelations put Tom Bailie and the other enemies of Hanford in the spotlight once more. Bailie's face was again on TV screens all over America as he stood in his fields, the injured farmer accusing the mysterious nuclear plants across the river. Though Hanford's supporters may have thought that Bailie was enjoying his moments of fame, it was, in fact, difficult for him. He and his family had already lost friends and endured the criticisms of neighbors who thought he had pried into something better left alone. Bailie's wife, Linda, grew ever more impatient and angry about the publicity. The couple fought frequently over Tom's continued involvement in the cause. Linda had to worry about the reactions of friends in the Tri-Cities and neighbors in Franklin County. Most probably resented her husband's activism; they feared he was threatening the value of their lands and crops. And they let their resentment be known by turning a cold shoulder at the post office or looking away as they passed on country roads.

The pressure of the Hanford issue often dominated the mood of the Bailie home. Sometimes it would be expressed in a roundabout way. Linda might scold Tom for raiding the refrigerator at night. (Cursed with a chronic sweet tooth, he loved to eat spoonfuls of whipped cream.) At other times they would fight about money. All farm families must be careful with their finances. But this was especially true for the Bailies after local bankers withdrew their credit due to the Hanford issue. On the occasions when cash ran out, Tom and Linda would invariably argue about the many hours that Tom spent on the telephone talking to reporters and down-winders. Each of these calls took time away from productive work that could have improved the cash flow. Besides, all this Hanford activity cost Bailie as much as eight hundred dollars a month in telephone bills.

The phone calls became a major source of conflict between Linda and Tom. He just couldn't say no to any of the reporters, anti-nuclear activists, or downwinders who left messages. He gave extra attention to people who called to report that they had cancer or some other illness, and wanted to know if it had anything to do with Hanford. These calls came from all over the country. People would read a wire-service article about Bailie in their local paper, or see him on TV. Those who had once lived downwind from the nuclear reservation would find his telephone number and call for consolation or information. Bailie was more than willing to spend hours on the phone explaining what he knew and commiserating with the sick. Many of these people suffered from cancer or thyroid disease, which made them overweight and chronically fatigued. Everything in their lives, from sex to work, had been affected, and after years of suffering, they leaned heavily on Bailie for support. And he couldn't ever turn them down.

Bailie did this because he liked being famous and he enjoyed the contact with the people who called. The Hanford issue brought some of the world's most accomplished journalists to his door. Without Hanford, he would never have met Connie Chung or any of the others. Bailie also enjoyed the powerfully emotional conversations he had with other downwinders. A relative loner, Bailie had

had few close friends in Franklin County before the downwinder stories appeared. Afterwards he had none. And even his wife had become withdrawn. "There he goes, off to save the world," Linda would say as he left to meet a reporter at the café in Mesa, leaving the farm in her hands. Even though Sabro, the hired hand, was capable of running the farm, Linda had to assume extra responsibilities when her husband wasn't around. She would have to calve the cows when the time came, and talk to the impatient creditors—the fertilizer company, the power company, even the water authority—who called with increasing regularity.

With so much conflict at home, Bailie came to appreciate the conversations with people who called to say they were grateful for what he was doing and wanted to know more. Even as his own family became less and less supportive, he found that the outside world was increasingly curious about the downwinders. Over time, Bailie's interest in Hanford became an obsession. He could no more stop thinking about Hanford than he could stop the changing of the seasons in the Columbia Basin. He could not let go of his own anger and fear about what had happened in the past. This obsession was fueled by the memories of his childhood illnesses, by the sorrow he felt over his sterility, and by the shame he had suffered at the hands of schoolyard bullies. The feelings of inadequacy, instilled in him by children who had called him a runt and taunted him because he walked strangely and often looked sickly, colored the way Bailie thought about himself and reacted to events in his life. In Hanford he found an explanation for his illnesses and something to blame for the shortcomings he had felt as a little boy. Bailie's obsession with Hanford was, in part, an effort to rewrite his own life story in terms that made him feel better.

While Hanford provided a kind of therapy for Bailie, it consumed the energy and attention that might have been better spent on his family. When Linda or his children threw phone messages into the trash or "accidentally" erased the tape on the answering machine, Bailie knew it was because they were jealous of the time he lavished on the people they called "the nukies." Sometimes they would simply hang up the phone when an unfamiliar voice, calling long distance, asked for "Mr. Bailie." Bailie's wife and children had a right to feel resentful. There was no time when Bailie wouldn't answer a call from a downwinder or a reporter. He would make promises to cut back this activity, but he always broke them. In a matter of days he would once again be on the phone, late into the night, while Linda fell asleep upstairs. Of course, this arrangement suited them when they were fighting. On those nights, Bailie would settle into a chair in the living room and be awakened when his children got ready to leave for school the next morning. The children, from whom Bailie felt detached, even estranged, were just as critical of the nukies as their mother was.

Years later, Bailie would admit that his Hanford activities had exacted a price from his family and from the farm. He would recall working the fields after dark, with the lights of the tractor blazing, to make up for lost time. There were times when he even took naps in the closed cab of his tractor because he just didn't want to go inside the house and face his wife. And when Jill, his daughter from his first marriage, came to live with him, he didn't have the time or the presence of mind to help her with her teenage problems. She vividly remembers walking out into the field one night, hoping to join him in the tractor so she could talk about something that was bothering her. Bailie was cutting hay at the time. When he saw blond-haired Jill approach, he cut the engine and waited for her. She climbed up, happy that she finally had a chance to talk with him. But when they settled in together, she found her father was too consumed by Hanford to listen to what she had to say.

"I know it's hard on everybody," he told Jill at the time. "It's hard on me too. That's why I'm out here in the dark. But the worst of it, Jill, is I can't be sure I'm right. In my heart I think I am. But sometimes, in my mind, I've got doubts."

Jill listened patiently and told her father to follow his heart. She would have to do the same with her own problems because, she believed, her father just didn't have the time to help her.

Others also felt abandoned by Bailie. Once, in desperation, Linda wrote Tom a note asking him to understand her feelings and limit his public appearances. Bailie saved the letter to remind himself of the sacrifices his wife had made. On the outside he wrote the following recollection: "Linda wrote this to me after the biggest chewing-out I had received from her. I declined 'The Joan Rivers Show.' "

Of course, the outside world knew nothing of the strife the Hanford issue had caused inside the Bailie family. No one knew about the times Bailie turned down TV interviews. Instead, on the outside, he appeared to be at the head of a renewed media siege of the Tri-Cities. As 1987 wore on, criticism of Hanford dominated the nightly news programs and the daily papers. If it wasn't Bailie appearing on the nightly news, it was HEAL, or some member of Congress calling for an investigation.

At the time, in late 1987, Casey Ruud reappeared and reviewed all of Hanford's safety problems at public hearings conducted by the Dingell committee (formally, the Subcommittee on Oversight and Investigations.)

The hearings were held in a packed committee room on Capitol Hill. After the chairman banged his gavel, Ruud was one of the first witnesses to take a chair behind the long table set before the committee members, who posed their questions from their perches, high on an elevated dais. Beside Ruud sat James Simpkin, another Hanford inspector who had also raised safety concerns. Simpkin had complained that some dangerous equipment tests had been done in a high-radiation area at N Reactor, where he had been working. This violation of procedures had placed him and four others at risk of injury or death. In written reports he had complained of an "overall lack of concern for the safe operation of the plant." His criticisms had been practically ignored.

Under questioning from Washington State congressman Al Swift, Simpkin explained that two thousand pounds of water pressure had been sent into pipes that had been repaired. These pipes had not been surveyed first, as required, to make sure they could withstand the force. "If there was going to be a leak, that is where the leak would have been, and because of the high radiation and because of the high pressure, it could have been a serious accident."

"Could it have killed you?" the congressman asked.

"Yes, it could have, sir," he answered.

Simpkin also told the committee that the inspection system at Hanford was deficient. He said that inspectors who had falsified their resumés and flunked tests were nevertheless certified to work on the site. Worse, he said, were instances in which false data and misleading tests were used to prove that N Reactor was in good condition. Finally he recounted the ways that workers were allowed to circumvent regulations and receive excessive radiation exposure, and remain on the job.

Though Simpkin's testimony was quite dramatic, it was brief compared with the time the committee spent going through Casey Ruud's audits, from the burial grounds inspection done with co-worker Inez Austin through the nuclear materials control audit at the Plutonium Finishing Plant. The committee was most interested in Ruud's assessment of the overall inspection system at Hanford. He explained that in nearly all cases the DOE relied on the truthfulness of its contractors. If the contractors gave the agency reports saying everything was going well, the government routinely rewarded them with timely payment of their fees including bonuses for good performance.

As he answered the committee's questions, Ruud smiled as if he were enjoying the process. Behind him sat Hanford executives and federal managers, including Mike Lawrence. Before him were congressmen eager to make the Department of Energy look bad. In the middle, Ruud answered their questions in a matter-of-fact style. Yes, he had called for a shutdown of the Plutonium-Uranium Extraction Facility. No, the responses to his audits were not adequate. No, the Department of Energy was not up to the task of reviewing its own contractor's work. "Do you want me to expound on this?" he asked one congressman before offering his analysis of DOE's problems with inspections and audits.

"When the contractor writes in and says, 'These are the great things to achieve this award fee,' there was no one there to even determine whether or not they were telling the truth," he continued. "That is how the system works."

When Mike Lawrence was called to testify, he had to struggle against the perception of Hanford created by Casey Ruud. Under questioning, he had to admit that the DOE had just four inspectors on staff to monitor the seven thousand employees working on weapons programs. But this did not mean the department was in the dark about its own facilities, Lawrence insisted. "We look at the record which they generate," he said. "We check their information." Sitting next to Lawrence, Assistant Secretary of Energy

Mary Walker admitted the agency's problems and promised improvements.

The impression left by all of this was that of an agency, the Department of Energy, and a facility, Hanford, spinning dangerously out of control. To top it off, the committee members went to great length to praise Ruud and Simpkin as heroes, and to warn Lawrence to protect the men from reprisals. Simpkin had already been shifted to a less responsible position, and he felt that the demotion was related to his safety complaints. Committee chairman Dingell didn't want anything bad to happen to either man. "Is somebody going to be looking over their shoulders and try to do them hurt because they came in and testified before this subcommittee?" he asked.

"No, on the contrary," said Lawrence.

"How about that, Madame Secretary?" Dingell asked of Mary Walker.

"I think they ought to be given bonuses," she answered. "I think that people who are willing to stand up and question safety practices, under circumstances where it might be difficult for them, should be rewarded."

Ruud left the hearing feeling as if he was, indeed, the kind of hero the committee members had described. He was also relieved by Dingell's protectiveness. The chairman of the committee had made it clear that Ruud was not to be punished. He felt sure he could go home to Suzi and tell her his paycheck was safe. Though she would listen to his reassurances, and try to be confident about the committee's power, Suzi never fully believed they would protect her husband. At some point, she feared, the management at Hanford would exact a price for her husband's outspokenness. And while he was reluctant to face it, Casey Ruud often shared his wife's fear. He kept himself going by denying it.

While Ruud was encouraged by the congressional investigation and the ensuing publicity, the hearings only heightened the sense of foreboding and resentment in the Tri-Cities. This was especially true for those who worked on the nuclear reservation and felt the powerful attraction of atomic technology. Few of the more than fourteen thousand people who worked at the Area would say they actually made atomic weapons. Instead, they said they did paper-work, ran machines, repaired equipment, or performed scientific experiments. They had no qualms about the morality of performing these tasks. And in many cases the work was both intellectually and financially rewarding.

James Stoffels was typical of those who had followed a well-worn path to the rewards of a Hanford life. In 1962 he was recruited to come to Hanford by General Electric, which was then the site's major contractor. He had a degree in physics from Marquette University and no other job offers. But what made Hanford most attractive to him was its technical education program. Stoffels could earn the equivalent of a doctorate by taking short-term jobs all over the site. It was in one of these assignments, at the mass spectrometry lab, that Stoffels found his calling. With machines called spectrometers, the lab's technicians could use light to analyze the isotopes sent from the eight operating reactors. Stoffels, whose favorite childhood toy had been an Erector set, fell in love with this technology. He would make this his life's work, and even design new spectrometry equipment, which he built himself on precision lathes.

In the early years, controversy was unheard of at Hanford, and pride flowed through the site like the Columbia River. One of Stoffels's clearest memories of that era was the ceremony marking the start-up of N Reactor in 1963. President Kennedy came to dedicate the new machine, and Stoffels stood on the edge of the crowd watching the young President speak as American flags flapped in the breeze. A committed Cold Warrior, President Kennedy had overseen the continued buildup of the weapons facili-ties. Thirty years later, Stoffels could still feel the excitement, opti-mism, and pride that had filled the crowd as Kennedy described Hanford as the bulwark of America's defense and a laboratory for the technologies of the future. At that time, before the assassina-tions of the 1960s, the Vietnam quagmire, and the Watergate scan-dal, America seemed to be on a righteous path to a gleaming future. Hanford would pave the way, and Stoffels was thrilled to play a part.

Fresh out of college, Stoffels had worked intently on mastering the demands of his first job. While the tiny samples he tested were radioactive, the hazard was so slight that he didn't give much thought to the lethal characteristics of the "product." As far as he was concerned, he wasn't engaged in making poison, or atom bombs. A gentle, bookish man, Stoffels was a scientist who designed and operated exotic machines. He loved his job.

Stoffels also grew to love Richland, where he found big-city pleasures such as a symphony and an opera company in a small-town setting. He married and had children and was divorced. Through it all, the Catholic church was a mainstay in his life. And it was through the church, and liberal theologies developed in the 1960s and 1970s, that Stoffels's views began to change. No one teacher or writer was more influential than another. But over time, as he read peace-oriented works by various bishops and theologians, James Stoffels came to see a certain evil in the atomic arsenal. It wasn't that the people of the Tri-Cities were devilish warmongers; it was more the weapons themselves. He felt almost as though the bombs and missiles contained not just radioactive isotopes, but the elements of sin. Their very existence was a threat to peace. A similar view was held by the American Catholic bishops who, in the early 1980s, wrote and published a pastoral letter condemning the war machines of both East and West. Although the churches of the Tri-Cities could hardly be said to have embraced these teachings, liberal-minded Catholics such as Jim Stoffels considered these teachings a call to action.

Recognizing the sensibilities of his community, Stoffels did not mount a home-grown antinuclear campaign in the Tri-Cities. But one night in the summer of 1983, he and a handful of others gathered in a room at the Richland public library and held the first meeting of World Citizens for Peace. The organization's first actions included writing letters to the *Tri-City Herald,* letters that asked their fellow citizens to consider the morality of Hanford's operations. On August 6, 1983—the thirty-eighth anniversary of the Hiroshima bombing—they conducted a memorial service in the park opposite the Richland Federal Building. This became an annual event, but it never drew more than a few dozen participants. Those who were Hanford workers were careful to avoid being

identified as such. In the past, one person who attended an antinuclear protest had been fired for wearing his Hanford ID badge to
a political event.

The annual memorial services attracted little attention until the
Hanford Family was created. That year, when the small band of
peace advocates gathered across from the Federal Building, the
Family staged a counterdemonstration. Police strung yellow crime-
scene tape down the middle of the park to separate the groups. On
one end, World Citizens for Peace listened to songs and sermons
intended to mourn those killed in Japan and warn against the evils
of the bomb. At the other end of the park, several hundred men,
women, and children listened to rousing pro-nuclear speeches, ate
hot dogs, and waved signs and banners. A local conservative minister gave a pro-Hanford sermon, and Mike Fox and other leaders
also spoke. Among the dignitaries on hand was Harold McCluskey,
the famous "atomic man," who had reached the age of seventy-five.
It would be McCluskey's last appearance as a nuclear booster.
McCluskey, who was so hot he could set off a Geiger counter fifty
feet away, died of heart disease a week after the rally, which Hanford health experts said was unrelated to the 1976 accident that had
irradiated him.

Except for a passing pickup truck full of teenagers screaming
epithets at the peace service, the first encounter between the two
groups was remarkably calm. But as homegrown critics of the
nuclear industry, World Citizens for Peace represented something
dramatically new to the Tri-Cities. For the first time, people who
worked at Hanford—children of the Family, as it were—were challenging the economic and moral foundation of the community.


Sadly, for Mike Fox and the others, there was little they could do
to influence the future of the nuclear reservation. Although many
millions of dollars worth of repairs were done on the facilities, the
*Tri-City Herald* reported almost daily on the uncertain future of
plutonium production. On one day, local congressman Sid Morri-
son, a Republican, announced that President Reagan wanted to
restart N Reactor to supply the weapons buildup. A few days later,
congressional budget writers speculated about closing the reactor
to save money.

In its attempt to restart N Reactor, the Department of Energy was vexed by Northwest congressmen who made a show of demanding safety, and by the threat of a lawsuit drafted by the Natural Resources Defense Council and signed by six members of Congress and eleven other environmental organizations. The NRDC often sued the government to force its compliance with environmental laws. In this case the NRDC insisted that the agency publish an environmental impact statement before the reactor could be operated. An EIS would assess the effect of a reconditioned reactor on the air, water, and land. It would also contain information that might be used to oppose the reactor. The NRDC argued that federal law required this report. The Department of Energy agreed to prepare the environmental review, in large part to appease members of Congress and avoid the lawsuit. But the pressure did not abate. A few months later the environmentalists threatened a second lawsuit based on N Reactor's operating record. It turned out that the water the reactor discharged had exceeded temperature limits set by the Clean Water Act about twenty-five times per year for the previous five years. Water as hot as 130 degrees had reached the Columbia, threatening plant and animal life. (The eight old reactors that were all closed by 1970 had discharged 190-degree water.)

The pro-nuclear people of the Tri-Cities responded to the succession of conflicting reports about the future of N Reactor with symbolic displays of affection for the old reactor. It was as if the reactor were a person—perhaps a benevolent leader—who had been stricken by a grave illness. The Hanford Family tied yellow ribbons around trees to symbolize their hope for the rescue of the reactor and the 6,200 jobs related to its operation. The Family also collected eleven thousand signatures on a "Restart N" petition that was sent to the White House. Civic leaders proposed schemes for reviving Hanford's atomic production, including finishing the abandoned WPPSS reactor and using it to make weapons materials. But by January 1988 these alternatives had all been rejected by the DOE, and all that was left was the hope that N Reactor could be resuscitated. On a night when the temperature hovered around freezing, seven hundred people turned out for a candlelight vigil of support for the old reactor.

The vigil organizers brought out pro-nuclear speakers who made the usual points. Some complained that the federal government was betraying the Tri-Cities by capitulating to antinuclear forces and abandoning the Tri-Cities. Others worried out loud about where workers would find employment at the high rates of pay Hanford offered. No other employer in the lower Columbia Valley could pay high-school-educated workers the twelve-to-fifteen-dollar-an-hour rates common in the Area. Mike Fox told the crowd that Hanford's enemies—the press, certain politicians, and the people on the west side of the Cascades—were not grateful for the Cold War achievements of Hanford. "We're speaking English and not Russian tonight because of our involvement in all that," he said. Others said that without N Reactor, America would decline in military might and find itself in the same position of weakness that had made it difficult for the country to respond to the start of World War II.

The Hanford Family felt betrayed by a government that seemed to them to be bending to antinuclear fanatics while leaving the loyal Tri-Cities without a future. It had long been acknowledged that the region was dependent on Hanford, but too little had been done to diversify its economy. Now it seemed that the government was on the verge of summarily ending production. Hanford manager Mike Lawrence, once the friend of the Tri-Cities, had become an enemy in the eyes of many because he had failed to save the reactor. And the Reagan administration, once loved for its aggressive nuclear strategy, was now widely criticized. At the height of the struggle over N Reactor, when yellow ribbons fluttered everywhere, Kelso Gillenwater, publisher of the *Herald,* authored an article accusing the administration of ruthlessness and deceit. The people of the Tri-Cities, he wrote, have been "betrayed by their friends."

The betrayal felt by Gillenwater was completed on a cold February morning in 1988 when a flatbed truck was wheeled inside the gates of the N Reactor area. At two-thirty in the afternoon, workers were called into the yard. More than a thousand men and women, many in hard hats, stood in silence as Mike Lawrence climbed onto the flatbed and announced that N Reactor was dead. "That's not good news for you. That's not good news for me," he said. "But that was the decision that was made today."

The punch had already been telegraphed many times by politicians warning of the reactor's demise and by the DOE's compliant responses to environmentalists. If the Reagan administration had intended to restart N Reactor, it would never have bent so willingly to the threat of lawsuits from the Natural Resources Defense Council. Privately, government officials had earlier concluded that they could meet the weapons program's needs at Savannah River. Keenly aware of the money that could be saved by shutting down N Reactor, Secretary Herrington had decided to cut the government's losses and halt work at the Hanford reactor.

Though Hanford's workers had expected this news, it was still a shock. They stood in numb silence as Lawrence explained what would happen. Initially, life and work would go on as usual. A full contingent of employees would be required to mothball the plant and begin to decontaminate the area. With a stockpile of plutonium still on hand, it was likely that the Plutonium-Uranium Extraction Facility and the Plutonium Finishing Plant would be needed for a short time to finish processing the material. But once that job was completed, Lawrence told the crowd, Hanford's nuclear weapons work would end and more than 2,500 workers would lose their jobs. By the mid-1990s a total of 6,500 jobs would be eliminated. William Jacobi, the president of Westinghouse Hanford, which ran the facilities under the new consolidated contract, urged workers to make use of job-placement services and retraining programs that would be developed in the coming months.

The news of N Reactor's demise was so important that all of the region's TV stations broadcast live reports on developments all day long. The *Tri-City Herald* presented the news in its bleakest terms. In one article, the paper listed the wide-ranging disastrous effects predicted in a Battelle study of the Tri-Cities after the atom. Among the newspaper's dire predictions:

• Suicides, alcohol and drug abuse, child abuse, and divorce would all increase.

• Property values would fall.

• The population would decline by thirteen thousand, emptying schools and tax rolls.

• Half a billion dollars in salaries would evaporate, devastating local retailers and other businesses.

Although the Tri-Cities braced for an economic cataclysm, the fact was that Hanford would remain an active government facility for the foreseeable future. For one thing, Battelle's research labs and the Fast Flux Test Facility would continue their work. But, more important, Hanford needed to be cleaned up. There were 1,400 known radioactive waste sites in the Area. More than 170 temporary waste tanks, one-third of them leaking radioactive liquid, would have to be emptied and their contents—60 million gallons—would somehow have to be stabilized. A massive cleanup effort would be needed to prevent radioactive material from leaching into the Columbia River. With billions of cubic yards of known wastes, no place in the Western world had been more polluted by both radioactive and chemical contaminants.

As the Tri-Cities had struggled to save N Reactor, the State of Washington, the federal Environmental Protection Agency, and the Department of Energy had begun to negotiate the terms for the cleanup. In the next year they would complete their work and sign a "Tri-Party Agreement" governing the reclamation project. Hanford would be reborn as a center for ecological research, and thousands would be retrained, becoming environmental technicians. As Richland's city manager had said at the Cable Bridge rally, the Tri-Cities was "the future." But the future was not one of nuclear energy or high-technology weapons. Instead, the future would lie in the spoiled environment of the Hanford reservation and the challenge of restoring it. Hanford had created its destiny by spilling its wastes into the air, water, and ground. Cleaning it all up would create the largest federal public works program in history. There was a good chance that this project, and the government dole, a drug on which the Tri-Cities was so dependent, would go on for several decades.

Few in the community understood the importance of the environmental mission that Hanford might one day assume. It was possible that huge amounts of federal money would continue to pour into the Tri-Cities for decades to fund the environmental cleanup effort. But for most, the end of more than forty years of atomic production seemed like the end of the world. Westinghouse executives advised workers to make plans to find work in other industries, perhaps in other parts of the country. Housing sales plummeted, and construction of new homes was slowed. In the country-club neighborhoods where large subdivisions had been laid out, the bare skeletons of abandoned house frames bore quiet testimony to the community's economic fears.

No one was more discouraged by the sudden loss of N Reactor than Michael Fox. But unlike others, who focused on the technical aspects of the decision and therefore couldn't understand what had happened, Fox was able to explain events in political terms. "DOE is in a tough spot politically," he would explain to others. "They have to implement congressional will. When people in Congress say N Reactor is a threat to the Northwest, or the waste dump is a threat, it's not in your interest, if you are the Secretary of Energy, to say, "You've got it all wrong, sir.""

Even if they could understand the defeat, Mike Fox and others who backed the Hanford Family were angry and frustrated. These feelings would be vented in a series of events that could only have taken place in an atomic community like the Tri-Cities. It all began at the time of the N Reactor decision, when a school board member wondered aloud whether the mushroom cloud was an appropriate symbol for the athletic teams of Richland High. Before 1945, the school's teams had been dubbed the Beavers, but in the midst of the celebration at the end of World War II, they were renamed the Bombers and the cloud became their icon. When it was suggested that the symbol was in bad taste, and the *Tri-City Herald* agreed, a minor public uproar ensued. If they couldn't hang on to their atomic facilities, at least the people of Richland could keep their symbol. The high-school principal put the matter to a vote, and a great majority of students and faculty voted to keep the cloud.

The cloud of controversy would not disappear, either. As members of the Tri-Cities community stood to defend the mushroom cloud, the press again descended on their community. People all over the world soon learned of the Tri-Cities and their struggle to save both their symbol and a way of life that was based on the most horrible weapons imaginable. While those who worked to keep the cloud truly believed it was an emblem of "peace through strength," few outsiders could understand how such a symbol could be embraced so affectionately. The difference between the Tri-Cities and the rest of the world was that the people here had been so fully involved with nuclear bombs that for them these weapons had acquired a different meaning. Indeed, in the Tri-Cities the nuclear weapons complex symbolized wealth and abundance, not death and destruction. The rest of the world was terrified by plutonium and atomic weapons; the Tri-Cities owed its very existence to them. Everything good—the graceful parks beside the Columbia River, the excellent schools, the shopping malls—came from Hanford and the bomb.

Though the vote at the high school resolved the matter of which symbol would be painted on the sign in front of the school, people on both sides remained resentful and angry. Jim Stoffels and the members of World Citizens for Peace did not want to let go of the issue. They believed that if they could get people to examine this symbol and its meaning more closely, they could help people envision a future without nuclear arms. With this in mind, Stoffels invited a group of *hibakusha*—Japanese survivors of nuclear war to visit the Tri-Cities.

The *hibakusha* had campaigned for nuclear disarmament since the early 1950s, when the first group from Hiroshima visited American and Soviet UN delegations in Geneva and called for an end to nuclear bomb tests. Similarly, Western peace activists had often visited Nagasaki and Hiroshima to dramatize their pleas for disarmament. In 1987, Holocaust survivor and Nobel Peace Prize winner Elie Wiesel had gone to Hiroshima on a much-publicized pilgrimage. After laying a wreath at a memorial to A-bomb victims, Wiesel had said, "What worries me is maybe I have not seen the past, and what I have seen is the future." Any public event involving the *hibakusha* carried obvious emotional power. James Stoffels hoped that this power could challenge the Tri-Cities' affection for nuclear technology.

In June of 1988, when the *hibakusha* came to visit Richland, local students still sported PROUD TO BE A BOMBER lapel buttons, and Hanford Family leaders were eager to counter every antinuclear statement with a powerful response. Indeed, before the delegation of old men and women arrived, one leader of the Family wrote a letter to the *Herald* condemning their visit. Noting that he was the son of World War II veteran, Cliff Groff offered a concise version of the traditional defense of President Truman's decision to use the bomb. Recalling the loss of life inflicted on America by Japanese forces at Pearl Harbor, Wake Island, Bataan, and Tarawa, Groff wrote, "I'm sure that families who face the loss of their jobs and home will really find it delightful that this group plans to rub their faces in it again." His hostility to the visitors was shared by many.

Into this environment came the busload of Japanese led by two Hiroshima survivors, Hiroshi Hara, a fifty-seven-year-old male florist from Hiroshima, and Sakae Ito, a gray-haired seventy-seven-year-old woman peace activist. The stated purpose of the visit was to promote understanding between the Tri-Cities and the Japanese and perhaps to begin a friendship. The delegation was to tour the city, drive through the nuclear reservation, and meet with townspeople at the high school and at the public library.

It was not the best moment for resurrecting the feelings of the World War II era. The people of the Tri-Cities already felt as if they were under attack. They had just suffered the loss of their atomic industry. Now another group of outsiders wanted to take away their symbol of a proud past. When she heard the Japanese were in town, Ruth Nelson rushed to meet them at Richland High School. Because school had been let out, the crowd in the classroom was small. Just a few teachers and principal Gus Nash listened while the Japanese, seated at a long table, spoke before several TV crews and reporters. Mrs. Nelson slipped into the room and stood against the wall.

The handwritten notes from Hiroshi Hara's opening statement, which he read at the high school on a warm spring afternoon, suggest that he had come in peace. "I want to know your feelings and ideas. What way do you think is best to make and keep the twenty-first century a peaceful era for all humanity?" he asked.

But having seen the enormous painting of a mushroom cloud on a sign outside the school, Hara had to struggle to contain his anger. "It was a great shock to me to know that 1,085 students among 1,300 students in your school supported the mushroom cloud in the vote," he said through an translator. He showed a collection of children's pictures depicting the suffering of A-bomb survivors, and he tried to explain how an understanding of Hiroshima's experience might prevent the future use of nuclear weapons. Those who knew the *hibakusha* story, he reasoned, would never celebrate the image of an atomic explosion. "I ask you to replace this symbol with another one. Back in Hiroshima I have a little flower shop. My wife and I sell flowers to the people in the neighborhood. Every flower is beautiful, including the flowers imported from abroad. I think that feeling in us that enjoys beautiful things is the same. . . . Please come to Hiroshima if you can," he said. "We wait for your visit. I believe that your visit will unite our hearts, our hearts that hope for a peaceful world."

With his measured tone and gentle words, Hara had avoided a confrontation. Mrs. Ito was not so successful in restraining her anger. Standing there in the mushroom cloud high school, which she had read about in the Japanese press, she grew flushed with anger, asked who the principal of the school might be, and then began lecturing in Japanese. An interpreter explained that Mrs. Ito regarded the cloud as a symbol of Richland's shame, and that the school was probably teaching "military-type thinking."

The old Japanese woman directed her remarks at Principal Nash, who listened politely for about half an hour. He explained repeatedly that here the mushroom cloud was considered a sign of peace and strength, and that the community had voted to keep it. But Mrs. Ito continued complaining, jabbing her index finger in Nash's direction. She spoke like a mother disciplining her child. Soon, Nash could take no more.

"I'm not going to change the symbol," he said firmly. "I stand behind it. We did not start the war, and that should end it." Nash then turned and walked out of the room to the sound of a few hands clapping furiously. Later Ruth Nelson would recall that she had "blistered" her hands by applauding so hard.

That night the Japanese found another forum at the Richland public library. Again Ruth Nelson was in the audience. This meeting was no more harmonious. Already angry about the recent criticisms of Hanford, many of the people of the Tri-Cities could not abide a delegation of Japanese peace advocates reminding them of the dark side of the atomic project. When they were given the chance to respond to the antinuclear statements of the *hibakusha,* the locals reminded them of every atrocity and outrage committed by the Japanese military in World War II. Japan started the war. Hanford ended it. And they were proud of this.

"I'd like to ask why people who don't like the logo don't see it as I see it—as something that stopped the greater slaughter of Americans and Japanese," said one older woman who was quoted in the *Tri-City Herald.* "I see that symbol as a reminder not to buy Japanese products, not to buy Toyotas from the friendly people who also brought you Pearl Harbor."

This remark was greeted with loud applause. But on one side of the room, one man sat in conspicuous silence. It was Tom Bailie. He had driven into Richland to see the *hibakusha* for himself. He felt embarrassed by the angry response of the local people who had come to the talk, and he felt some affection for the Japanese. He wondered if he, and the other downwinders, weren't also victims of the bomb, if they weren't American *hibakusha.*

Bailie wanted to speak in defense of the Japanese, but he couldn't get up the nerve. And soon he lost the opportunity. Chastened by the sharp reaction, the Japanese quickly tried to reach some agreement with their hosts and leave. One of the visitors, a high school teacher, explained that he taught his students that the Japanese leaders had been trying to prolong the war, in the face of inevitable defeat, at the time the first bomb was dropped. "As for the responsibility of Japan starting the war," he added, "I feel very responsible. That's why I'm involved in the peace movement, so there won't be any more of them."

The next day, the *hibakusha* took their bus to a landing upriver from the Hanford reservation. They climbed into some rubber rafts and floated down the Columbia River, past the hulking abandoned graphite reactors, past N Reactor and the WPPSS facility. Along the way, a guide described the facilities they passed, and some of the pollution that had been left behind by Hanford's operations. When the group landed on the Franklin County side of the river, Tom Bailie was waiting to meet them. The night before, he had met the trip's organizers and offered to narrate a brief tour of the county.

As an old bus carried the group up and down country roads, Bailie stood in the front and spoke through an interpreter. He pointed out the abandoned radar base and missile defense station that had once guarded Hanford, and a little fenced-in monitoring station that operated on a patch of grass on a nearby roadside. Bailie showed the Japanese the irrigation system that drew water from the river and delivered it to his farm. He took them down the "death mile" shown in Mrs. Andrewjeski's map, and, as he had for Karen Dorn Steele, he recalled the illnesses that had struck each household.

There was a certain power in the monotonous way that Bailie talked about the "death mile" residents. He would say a name, and then utter "died of cancer" or "thyroid" or "lost a baby." He didn't have to say that he believed these illnesses were connected to Hanford. He knew that in their minds, the *hibakusha* were making the connection for themselves. As he looked at the Japanese, and the local peace activists, he couldn't help but notice that they were stunned by what he was saying. Some actually had their mouths open.

At the end of the tour, Bailie directed the bus driver to the Mesa café. When they arrived, one of the farmers inside jokingly asked, "Are they here to buy the town?" But little more was said about the miniature invasion. After all, the regulars at the café were accustomed to Bailie bringing TV crews and reporters in. This was little different.

For more than an hour the *hibakusha* and their hosts feasted on hamburgers, french fries, soft drinks, and beer. Bailie would long remember how delighted the Japanese were when they discovered that beer cost only one dollar a bottle. He would also remember the emotional farewells as they finally got onto the bus for a ride to their hotel. Each of them made a point of hugging Bailie, and many had to speak to him. Some apologized for the "stupid Japanese leaders" who had prolonged the great war. Mrs. Ito grabbed Bailie and held on tight. Then she said to him the words he had hoped someone from his own government would say: "We are sorry for what Hanford has done to you."

After they were gone, their bus leaving a cloud of diesel fumes and dust in the air, Bailie stood in the café parking lot for a moment. Part of him felt like a traitor to his country. The Japanese had been the enemy in World War II, and they were a modern economic rival. But Bailie also felt, more strongly, a sense of kinship with the *hibakusha*. Unlike so many of his neighbors, they shared his fear and anger. His meeting with them had been one of the few times when he had been able to talk about Hanford and trust that he had been understood. As they drove away, he began to miss them.

# THE DOMINO EFFECT

IN EARLY 1988, after Hanford's N Reactor was laid to rest and the people of the Tri-Cities were plunged into mourning, yet another reporter came to meet Tom Bailie. They found each other at the Mesa café, the warm home-away-from-home where Bailie conducted his "downwinder" work a safe distance from his bemused wife. (By this time he had given up promising to cut back on his activism. Instead he tried to do it in secret whenever possible.) After coffee, the farmer took Keith Schneider of *The New York Times* on a tour of Franklin County that included all the local farmers' café hangouts and the "death mile" along Glade Road. The metallic winter sky, frozen fields, and gusty winds helped create a melancholy mood. As he drove, Bailie explained that of 108 residents along the "death mile," twenty-four had gotten cancer. Another seven children had been born with birth defects or had died as infants.

As he always did, Bailie traveled slowly past each house, named its owners, and reeled off a medical history. At one house he mentioned a rash of thyroid illness and a granddaughter born without eyes. Farther down the road lived a couple who had adopted all their children after eight miscarriages. Next was the Bailie homestead. Here he recalled his own illnesses, the tumors removed from his sisters, his father, and his uncles, and the cancer that had claimed two grandparents. The toll continued as he drove: two children born without hip bones; a couple both sick with cancer; a farm wife who had killed her baby and herself one year after her husband died of cancer. Bailie introduced Schneider to many of his neighbors, who told him of stillbirths and tumors. Some lifted their chins to show him their scars from thyroid surgery. When he was finished, Bailie stood on a ridge overlooking the atomic reservation and damned the government bureaucrats at Hanford and in Washington, D.C., who had injured his community and lied about it for decades.

Schneider, a thirty-year-old man with dark hair and eyes, was astounded by the anecdotes about sick and dying people. Although activists and renegade scientists had always spoken of the theoretical possibility that nuclear plants could hurt their neighbors, he had never seen an actual community where so many real people could ask, with powerful justification, if their illnesses were caused by radiation from an atomic facility. The stories of simple farmers and a fearsome technology contained an almost mythic power. Schneider intended to combine an account of their human struggle with the facts of Hanford's past and reveal an industry and a government run amok. The reporter had learned to be suspicious of both the government and the nuclear establishment during one of his first big assignments—covering the Three Mile Island accident for a local paper in Pennsylvania. He would long remember the way a couple of big-time journalists had forced utility and government spokesmen conducting a news conference to admit that a major emergency was taking place. Just twenty-two years old at the time, Schneider had watched the journalists and thought, "I want to be like them."

Even though he was excited by the downwinder story, Schneider didn't rush it into print. He had a larger picture to paint, a vision in which Hanford was just part of a national problem. Months before, Schneider had gone down into the mine shafts and inspected the Department of Energy's Waste Isolation Pilot Project in New Mexico. He had been impressed by how deep the mine was, and how the sky appeared like a speck of light from the bottom of the shaft. But once underground, he had found that storage areas that were supposed to stay dry for centuries had begun to leak. He wrote an article describing the waste project's problems and challenging the government's assertions that the project was proceeding smoothly. That piece was followed by another, on the effort of Idaho citizens' groups who wanted to stop construction of a Department of Energy laser facility. By the time Schneider had arrived in Mesa to see Tom Bailie, he had recognized a pattern: everywhere, it seemed, local citizens were standing up against the DOE. The agency had been unable to build a new, working weapons plant for twenty years, and criticism of the old facilities was snowballing.

Weeks and then months passed without anything about the Franklin County farmers appearing in *The New York Times.* Eventually, Tom Bailie even forgot that Schneider had come to visit. As time passed, other journalists came to town and Bailie took them on the same tour. Gradually the interview process and the ramble through the countryside became a rote exercise, repeated and repeated, like some kind of religious ritual. Bailie would tell his story of illness and death and suspicion as he pointed out the pertinent landmarks: the house where, as a boy, he had seen the soldiers in the dust, the radiation monitoring station where he had played as a teenager, the farms where the "demon lambs" had been born. At the end of each tour he drove his visitors to the bluff that overlooked the river, the Hanford Reservation, and the hulking reactor buildings. Bailie would speak of the sense of betrayal he felt. Then he would sit silent, waiting for the emotional impact of the tour to settle on his guests. The journalists would depart and Bailie would feel let down, depressed. When the cameras were on and the notebooks were out, he felt alive. When they were gone, he missed the attention. Sometimes he wondered if he was becoming addicted to it.

As Bailie continued to share his personal story, providing the human-interest angle of the Hanford saga, Schneider and several colleagues in the *Times'*s Washington bureau grappled with some larger issues. They understood that Hanford was just the most urgent example of a growing crisis affecting the entire federal atomic-bomb-making complex. At each location—Hanford, Fernald, Rocky Flats, Savannah River, and others—local activists were gathering data on radiation releases, investigating accidents, and trying to determine what harm the local people may have suffered. But these citizens generally worked in isolation. The activists in South Carolina had no contact with their peers in Washington State or Idaho. Indeed, the team at the *Times*—Schneider, Matthew Wald, Michael Gordon, Kenneth Noble, and others— were among the few outsiders who connected the troubles at all these locations and began to suspect that the entire network of weapons factories was on the brink of collapse. But this problem was not widely understood. Even within the Department of Energy there were many people, right up to Secretary Herrington's level, who did not fully grasp the true condition of the nuclear weapons industry.

John S. Herrington had known remarkably little about atomic weapons before he took office. In fact, before he came to Washington to work in the Reagan White House, Herrington hadn't even known that nuclear weapons were the Department of Energy's main business. Herrington, like most Americans, had associated the Department of Energy with electric power, oil, and the development of exotic energy sources like solar cells and high-tech windmills. But these programs, which received a great deal of publicity, accounted for only one-third of the department's spending. The rest of the money—more than $20 billion a year, including the Pentagon's contribution—went into atomic weapons. "The DOE was a marvelous cover for all sorts of secret programs," Herrington would later recall. "You would be amazed if I could tell you it all."

As he entered the world of top-secret bombs and science-fiction-like technology, Herrington often reflected on the nature of his work. When he thought about it, he had to conclude that he was sitting atop an enormous and insane enterprise. "Defense expenditures are nuts," he would explain. "And MAD [the long-standing Mutual Assured Destruction strategy] is insane." But it was an insanity that he believed was inescapable. Like his President, he thought that nuclear strength was essential to deter Soviet aggression.

Even as he was taken aback by the moral and psychological implications of his new job, Herrington was also drawn to the gee-whiz quality of the instruments his agency fashioned. Once he had been amazed when technicians showed him a nuclear weapon small enough to fit in a briefcase. On another occasion he and President Reagan had spent some time marveling at a mock-up of a nuclear warhead that had been brought into the White House and set on the conference table in the Cabinet Room. The technology and the enormous scope of the nuclear weapons program never ceased to astound the secretary. Herrington liked to impress people with the observation that the government's nuclear research and production sites constituted the single largest industrial program in the United States. With more than 150,000 workers and $24 billion in real estate and equipment, the complex would have rested near the top of the Fortune 500, were it a corporation.

Given its size, it was all the more remarkable that the atomic production effort had gone virtually unnoticed for so long. This obscurity was a legacy of the Manhattan Project. During World War II, plutonium production and the manufacture of weapons had been scattered across many different sites, separated from one another by hundreds or thousands of miles, to shield the process from enemy attacks. No attack against a single facility could disable the entire production program. At the same time, atomic physicists were invited into the fold of the national security community. The long-standing international network of atomic researchers was disbanded in the war years. Ideas were no longer shared across oceans and criticized in public. As part of government policy, the high reaches of nuclear science became a secret, state-dominated discipline.

In peacetime these policies continued and conveniently served to hide the development and production of weapons from public view. Thus many of the people who lived near the Feed Materials Production Center in Fernald, Ohio, which made uranium fuel, thought it produced agricultural products. The checkerboard sign on one of the buildings, which resembled the logo of the Ralston Purina Company, cultivated this misconception. In Texas, many who lived near the Pantex facility, which assembled warheads, thought it made electronic parts. And of course there were people in the Northwest who thought the PUREX plant at Hanford made bleach.

Important scientific and technical concerns—whether they had to do with the environment or public health—were also hidden from view. Only approved experts could work in the highest reaches of nuclear-weapons-related science, and all of their work, whether in fission or epidemiology, was government-funded. Once their studies were done, they were entrapped by censors who classified their work top secret. Even the scientists in one branch of the Department of Energy had difficulty getting information from those in another area.

The entrenched culture of secrecy affected everyone in the DOE bureaucracy, including Secretary Herrington, who found that the secrecy made it difficult for him to assess the condition of the plants that were his responsibility. When Herrington, a California lawyer and former campaign advance man for Ronald Reagan, took office in 1985, he knew that many Department of Energy sites were beset by pollution problems. Senator John Glenn of Ohio had already helped expose a history of radiation releases at the Fernald plant, and the department was busy mapping the chemical and nuclear wastes it had dumped across the country. But it wasn't until he heard of a low-level official named Bob Tiller that Herrington began to understand that the bomb-factory complex was running out of time.

Tiller, an angular Western native who liked cowboy boots and big belt buckles, had worked at the Idaho National Engineering Laboratories before transferring to the Department of Energy's headquarters. When the new secretary took office, Tiller came to the executive suite in the Forrestal Building, the agency's nondescript headquarters on Constitution Avenue, near the Smithsonian complex. He requested an appointment with Herrington's key deputy, Joseph Salgado. Another California lawyer, and a former Oakland city police officer, Salgado was a longtime ally whom Herrington had brought to Washington to manage the day-to-day operations of the agency. Single and singleminded, the dark-haired, sad-eyed Salgado dedicated himself to his work in an almost monkish way. It was natural for him to welcome Tiller into his office. He always had time for someone interested in adding to his understanding of his job. Years later, Salgado would vividly recall what Tiller had to say.

"He really came to warn us," Salgado recalled. "He sat on the sofa in my office and I sat beside him. He told me, 'You've got to address these environmental and safety problems. They are serious enough that there could be a real disaster at any of a number of sites.' "

Tiller informed Salgado of the existence of a report on the department's reactors that had been done in response to the Three Mile Island accident. A similar study—known as the Kemeny Commission report—had been made of the Three Mile Island plant and commercial nuclear power stations in general; it had recommended a series of changes in safety practices and regulation, which the government had embraced. Conducted at the same time, the Department of Energy study, which had never received publicity, was known as the Crawford Report, because it had been directed by John W. Crawford, a "nuclear navy" veteran who had been assistant secretary of energy.

Completed just as the Carter administration was leaving office and the Reagan people were taking over, the Crawford Report had received scant attention. By the time Salgado saw it, it had been collecting dust for more than five years. But its findings were anything but stale. On the very first page, the report announced that "significant deficiencies exist in DOE's reactor safety management activities" and that "many of the 'TMI lessons learned' have not been adequately addressed or applied in DOE reactor programs."

Specifically, Crawford and his panel of experts had found that changes in the Department of Energy's management scheme had eroded its ability to protect public health and safety. They cited weak leadership by Washington and a growing gap between the secretary's office and reactor safety organizations. The report noted that the secretary's office lacked the expertise to assess safety reports and had little contact with inspectors in the field.

A typical example of this problem—which was really a matter of bad management—involved the setting of safety and training standards. Although the Department of Energy had told its contractors that they must follow standards set by the Nuclear Regulatory Commission, the people running the reactors were unaware of the NRC's various requirements for training and responses to emergencies. NRC rules were distributed haphazardly, according to the Crawford group. Even after Three Mile Island, important documents covering health and safety had not been sent to the people who ran the Department of Energy's reactors. Ultimately, the report found, "no safety requirements appeared to be mandatory for DOE reactor contractors."

One of the reasons for this lapse was that over the years the department's local site managers had been ceded great power, and each had taken a different approach to safety. In many cases they had abdicated their authority, believing that the contractors who ran the plants should be responsible for public health and worker safety. According to the report, one result of this policy was that "serious shortcomings" had developed "in most training programs at DOE reactor sites." Finally, the Crawford group noted that quality-assurance programs at federal facilities were inconsistent and often inadequate; field offices either didn't understand the QA process or lacked the expertise to oversee contractors. (All of this would have greater meaning to Salgado when he later attended congressional hearings on Casey Ruud's audits and government management problems at Hanford and other sites.)

The lack of consistent management had led to a series of practical problems. One glaring example involved access to reactor control rooms. Utilities with commercial reactors set stringent limits on who may enter a control room and always establish strict rules for the behavior of operators. At most Department of Energy facilities, the Crawford group found, there were no formal rules for control-room conduct or access. Except at one reactor, there were no rules governing how long an operator could stay on duty, or how many days an operator could work without relief. The committee also found that reports on Unusual Occurrences were often misleading, incorrect, and incomplete. It was frequently impossible for some-one in the department's headquarters to understand reports on accidents or mishaps at the various sites. In many cases, UOs were not reported at all.

After scanning the Crawford report, Salgado feared that in many ways no one at the Department of Energy—either at the headquar-ters level or in the field office—was minding the store. The Reagan administration's budget cuts, which Herrington had accepted, had reduced the number of federal safety inspectors to the point where they couldn't get out from under their paperwork and into the field. Contractors such as the Rockwell Hanford Corporation had been given carte blanche to run the facilities as they saw fit, as long as they met production goals. At this time, 1985, those goals were set high. To satisfy President Reagan's buildup, the Department of Defense had demanded record output from plants like the Pluto-nium-Uranium Extraction Facility and the Plutonium Finishing

Plant. These goals were being met. But as Salgado found when he began asking questions, the mundane chore of overseeing environmental and safety concerns had been given a low priority.

In 1985 Herrington and Salgado tried to improve the government's oversight of safety and ecological issues. For years these jobs had been handled within the office that also guided production at the bomb-related facilities. To correct this obvious conflict of interest, they created a new post of Assistant Secretary of Environment, Safety and Health, and gave it to yet another Californian, attorney Mary Walker. They also set aside nearly $38 million for the new assistant secretary's work.

With Walker and Salgado in place, Herrington confronted the entrenched insider bureaucracy in the department with his own team and his own priorities. For the next two years the insiders and the outsiders struggled quietly over the future of the atomic weapons complex. Herrington wanted to know the extent of the mess the department would have to clean up, so he asked Walker to survey every site and report back on what was known about pollution problems. At the same time he requested safety appraisals of every key facility. This concern had been piqued, in part, by a tour Herrington had made of one of the department's Savannah River nuclear reactors. There he had happened to notice that the lens on a control-room warning light was green, rather than the usual red. When he asked about this, he was told that maintenance workers had run out of red lenses and that "everybody knew" about the mix-up, so it wasn't a problem. Herrington did not find this response reassuring.

The more Herrington learned about the condition of the plants and the enormous environmental problems at many of the sites, the more convinced he became that the future of many of these facilities was limited. Because they had been given short shrift for so long—especially during the Vietnam War era, when conventional weapons were a priority—the atom bomb plants were sorely outdated and poorly maintained. Herrington's worries were only confirmed by the revelations about the Green Run and other radiation releases contained in the nineteen thousand pages released by Mike Lawrence at Hanford early in 1986. Lawrence had acted on his own, and Herrington had been surprised by the contents of the documents. He had been unaware of Hanford's history and, contrary to what many of the downwinders thought, he sympathized with them and supported the continued release of previously classified information. More than the career officials in the agency, Herrington could see that the era of secrecy was fast coming to a close. He knew that the Department of Energy would somehow have to be transformed into a more open agency, and that environmental restoration could become its biggest mission, but he faced an uphill fight within his own department. And he accepted that it would be a long, slow process.

All this began to change in the predawn hours of April 26, 1986, when Herrington was awakened by a call from the National Security Council staff. U.S. spy satellites had detected a major explosion at a Soviet nuclear installation in the Ukraine. Herrington was to prepare to speak with the President. Reagan called moments later. He asked Herrington to draft a cable offering American assistance to Soviet authorities. Reagan also wanted Herrington to prepare an immediate assessment of the accident and the threat it posed to the environment. It would be almost a day before the public came to understand what had happened at Chernobyl. But it would take only hours for Herrington to learn of the extent of the damage and the long-term implications for the worldwide nuclear industry.

Herrington believed that a similar accident was unlikely to occur in the United States, even at Hanford's N Reactor, because it had redundant safety features that were missing at Chernobyl. Nevertheless, he couldn't dismiss the concerns expressed by the national media and critics in the Northwest. But rather than try to cover up the problems with N Reactor, he used the questions raised by Chernobyl to justify a more aggressive safety review of the entire atomic complex. He appointed the Roddis group and accelerated the reactor safety review begun by Mary Walker's office. Chernobyl, as it turned out, helped Herrington begin to overcome the secrecy and the production-oriented mindset within the department.

"Chernobyl broke the log jam," Herrington would say later. "Everything we had started to do in terms of safety and the environment was speeded up." Salgado would put it more bluntly: "We had been trying to open the box very slowly. Then, kaboom!"

Herrington and his aides had to race to keep up with events after Chernobyl. They were not surprised by the decline and fall of the Plutonium-Uranium Extraction Facility and the Plutonium Finishing Plant. After all, their own internal reviews of the weapons industry showed that the whole complex was riddled with similar problems. In June a preliminary report on Fernald had identified staggering pollution problems. Thousands of tons of radioactive waste had been released into the environment, and it wasn't clear that the plant could ever be fixed to work safely. In November of 1986 Herrington ordered that power levels of the Savannah River reactors be cut in half when it was discovered that operators were unable to back their emergency response plans with adequate data. The next spring, three small reactors at Oak Ridge, Tennessee, were shut down owing to quality-assurance deficiencies.

For the Department of Energy, the events of 1986 and 1987 amounted to a slow-motion crisis. One by one, environmental audits revealed massive pollution and, one by one, safety problems forced the closing of facilities. Finally, at the beginning of 1988, N Reactor was closed. Herrington was reviled by many in the Tri-Cities, who considered him detached and uncaring. But the secretary, who had sentimentally hung a picture of the Richland High School cheerleaders in his executive conference room, was aware of the pain his decision would cause. He was also confident that the Tri-Cities' suffering would be brief and that environmental restoration would bring another boom to the atomic boomtowns.

Like the people in the Tri-Cities, many of the career officials who worked in the Forrestal Building were appalled by the criticisms in the press, opposed Herrington's actions, and were dismayed by the way the secrets of the past had been laid bare. But the worse things got, the more naked the agency's history became, the more open Herrington and Salgado became. As political appointees whose tenure would last only as long as Ronald Reagan occupied the White House, they had no long-term interest in protecting the dirty secrets of the bureaucracy. They also had no allegiance to the past. They weren't around when the Green Run decisions were made, and they did not feel compelled to paper over the mistakes of their predecessors. As Salgado saw it, the government had wrongly pursued its Cold War atomic weapons strategy with the same secrecy and high-handed attitude that had propelled the Manhattan Project. What had worked during World War II—a time of acute national emergency—had mutated over the course of forty years. In the dark shadow of secrecy, the agency had grown unresponsive to the public and almost impossible to control. "The department had failed to establish public confidence," Herrington would say later. "That was our major problem." In order to recover public trust, Salgado and Herrington tried to override the secretiveness that had come to permeate the agency.

Their more open attitude was on vivid display on May 11, 1988, when, once again, Hanford auditor Casey Ruud came to Washington to appear before the Dingell committee in the same hearing room of the Rayburn House Office Building. In general, the committee wanted to review progress in the Department of Energy's safety program. Six months earlier, Ruud and his fellow auditors James Simkin and Mark Hermanson had described the problems they had found at Hanford. Other whistle-blowers from DOE's Savannah River nuclear reservation had outlined serious safety deficiencies there, including an inadequate fire-protection program. The water supply at the South Carolina site was so poor that crews would have had trouble extinguishing a serious fire in the reactor buildings.

Hanford's problems, especially those identified by Casey Ruud, had been confirmed by a Department of Energy headquarters review. And rather than argue defensively when the committee reminded him that little progress had been made toward correcting the trouble, Salgado accepted responsibility. While Mike Lawrence and the Westinghouse executives looked on, he apologized over and over again. "This is a very disturbing hearing to myself, and to Secretary Herrington," he declared. "It's disturbing because it calls into question the commitment of the secretary and this department to environment, safety, and health." Salgado went on to explain that spending for these areas had more than doubled, but the department's performance was still lacking. "It is my personal opinion," he added, "that we did fail, as a department, to take some responsibilities. I admit that."

All of this surely grated on the ears of the lifelong federal officials who sat in the hearing room. But Salgado didn't care about the scraped egos of veteran managers; he saw the hearing as an opportunity to score some points for the Herrington team—the outsiders—whose reforms were resisted by the bureaucracy.

Though the hearing was intended to review the department's progress on safety issues, Salgado wasn't the only one who used the forum to send a message to his opponents. After enumerating the safety concerns, Congressman Dingell spent more than an hour asking pointed questions about the way Hanford contractors had treated Casey Ruud. When the Westinghouse Corporation took over operation of Hanford from Rockwell in 1987, it inherited the rank-and-file workers and middle-level managers who had been dealing with Ruud all along. Despite the congressman's warnings, Ruud had been fired by Westinghouse soon after his first appearance before the subcommittee. Westinghouse could justify this by claiming that the loss of the nuclear waste dump project and N Reactor had forced them to lay off hundreds. Ruud complained, however, that he was singled out while other auditors were protected. He also claimed that Westinghouse managers had told him he was, in effect, being punished for being a whistle-blower.

Sitting high in his chairman's seat, Congressman Dingell looked down at the witness table, where Salgado and the Westinghouse executives sat, and reviewed what had happened to Ruud. He described how Ruud had been shuffled from one assignment to another, how he had been invited to apply for an auditor's slot and then rejected. He even quoted Ruud's complaints about Westinghouse managers who had told him, point-blank, that he would be punished for having squealed to the Dingell committee.

By the time he had finished, Dingell had worked himself into a fury. "We have here a very bad situation, not one that the committee can easily tolerate," he said sternly. "I guess the big question is, What is the company going to do about this?"

Under Dingell's glare, Salgado readily admitted his agency had "failed" in the whistle-blower case. And the Westinghouse managers fell over themselves promising a review of what had happened to Ruud. Over and over again, they insisted that the famous auditor had not been a victim of retribution. Layoffs were required by the loss of key projects. Some workers had to go. It just happened that Ruud was included.

Of course, in the fuss raised by the congressman and the defense put up by the contractor, nothing specific was said about the personal price that had been paid by Casey Ruud and his family. Ruud, jobless, sat in the back of the hearing room. And as he listened to the jousting, he realized that his concerns were being lost in the personal power struggle between the chairman and the executives. Dingell had promised to protect him and the other whistle-blowers. The Department of Energy had agreed, at least officially, that the whistle blowers were exemplary employees who should not suffer for their integrity. But back at Hanford, where the nuclear community still exercised its own form of justice, Ruud had gotten what many co-workers believed he deserved. The House committee had been ignored and, aside from complaining, there was nothing Dingell could do.

Listening with half an ear, Casey Ruud reviewed in his mind the events of the preceding months. As various facilities had been shut down and programs ended, everyone at Hanford knew that layoffs were coming. During the winter, Ruud had scoured the Area, looking for a secure job. But every time he'd heard of an opening and raced to apply, he had been told that he was too late. The last chance had come in December 1988, when his brother, John, phoned to tell him of two openings for auditors to work on the decommissioning of N Reactor. Minutes later, when he called the man doing the hiring, Ruud had been told the jobs were suddenly filled. The next month he was among the few hundred workers, out of nearly fourteen thousand, who were fired.

These memories troubled Ruud. He was also disturbed when he thought about how his stubborn response to the powers who ran Hanford had affected his family. His wife had been afraid all along. Suzi was worried that as her husband gained notoriety, her family would be ostracized. She feared that the *Seattle Times* and the Dingell committee had used her husband and would not protect him. All along she had believed that Casey would eventually lose his job, and that in a one-industry town he would have no chance of finding work. She worried about being evicted from the sprawling split-level home that offered her both financial and emotional security. Time and again Casey had said that Eric Nalder, or the committee, would protect him. Westinghouse couldn't get rid of him, he insisted. Then they did.

In the time since, Suzi's worst fears had begun to come true. Neighbors were no longer friendly. And when the phone rang, it was a sure bet that it was a bill collector, not a friend. Meanwhile, even members of her own family found it difficult to offer support. With her children listening in, Suzi's brother, who worked for the Hanford Patrol (the private police force for the complex), had confessed that he didn't want to be seen with Casey in downtown Richland. At the same time, Casey felt that whenever he saw his own brother, John, who also worked in the Area, he was more likely to receive criticism than comfort.

After the firing, the Ruuds became increasingly isolated, and in this isolation it was even easier for them to feel frightened and angry. When Suzi gave birth to their fifth child, Samantha, on April 19, it was difficult for the Ruuds to avoid thinking that here was yet another responsibility. At times, when Suzi cried late at night and Casey descended into a dark mood of self-recrimination, it seemed that their marriage would not survive his war with Hanford. Suzi would tell Casey he had ruined their life together. He felt alone and abandoned. He sold his small motorboat to raise cash. He even investigated selling the house. But with Hanford's troubles, the local real-estate market had become so depressed that even if they had sold, the Ruuds wouldn't have been able to repay their mortgage.

Somehow, through all the struggle and self-doubt, Casey and Suzi Ruud stayed together. They were just as stubborn about preserving their life together as Casey had been about his audits. They always thought of their children, and tried to maintain a normal family life. And they also thought of their enemies at Hanford. A divorce would mean that they had won, and the Ruuds refused to give them that victory.

All of this ran through Casey Ruud's mind as he watched Congressman Dingell close the hearing. He listened to the committee chairman and the chief of Westinghouse Hanford, William Jacobi, begin to make amends. Congressman Dingell said he wanted to have a good relationship with the Westinghouse team, and he advised Jacobi to review the company's performance in the Ruud affair. "I understand your message, Mr. Chairman," Jacobi answered. The hearing was then adjourned.

In the days after that hearing, Westinghouse offered Casey Ruud a low-level job training employees in safe work habits. (He would derisively describe this job as "how-to-climb-a-ladder instructor.") Ruud tentatively accepted the offer, but notified Westinghouse that he would not waive his right to sue the company for harassment. He believed he had been laid off because he had gone to Congress with his original audit problems; he suspected he could make a case against the company. This warning was too much for the Westinghouse managers. They withdrew the job offer.

Over the course of the summer, Ruud applied for work at every Hanford contractor and subcontractor. None would have him. In the fall he took a job with an oil company, selling lubricating oil and hydraulic fluid door-to-door, to farmers and other small businesses. Franklin County was part of his territory. Ruud would drive his little yellow Mountain Oil Company truck more than two hundred miles a day, trying to sell them Mountain Oil. He even wandered up Tom Bailie's driveway a few times, hoping to make a sale. But Bailie was never around when Ruud came to call, and the whistle-blower and the downwinder never actually met.

During this time, Ruud did take legal action against his former employer. He filed a complaint with the Department of Labor, charging harassment; he also threatened Westinghouse with a lawsuit. The Labor Department concluded that Ruud had been harassed, and the lawsuit was settled out of court, with Ruud receiving an amount roughly equal to two years' pay. As a condition of the agreement, the exact settlement price would be kept secret. By the end of 1988 it appeared that Casey Ruud's fight with Hanford was over. He had enough money to take his time looking for a job, and he turned his attention to his wife and his children. He bought himself an expensive set of new golf clubs and tried, for the first time in years, to relax.

Although the Ruud case was over, Hanford's troubles with whistle-blowers did not end so easily. In the following months, other Hanford workers who had safety complaints filed labor harassment charges similar to Ruud's. Most notable was tank-farm worker Edwin Bricker, who went to the press with complaints about fires left unreported, control-room operators who abandoned their posts, and slipshod handling of plutonium. Bricker charged that

Rockwell, and later Westinghouse, had waged a quiet campaign to justify firing him. Bricker was required to see company psychologists, and was assigned to such jobs as picking up cigarette butts. Though he was loudly criticized by other workers, he too would ultimately be exonerated. An investigation by the Department of Labor uncovered a plan by executives—it was called "Special Item: Mole"—for getting rid of Bricker by "subtly recruiting employees to report on him." The department concluded that Rockwell and Westinghouse managers had engaged in "hostilities" against Bricker. It was clear that the Area was still ruled by a code that punished those who took safety concerns outside the family.

While the Dingell hearings and the resolution of Casey Ruud's fight with Westinghouse took Hanford off the nation's front pages, the Department of Energy was just beginning to come to grips with the larger crisis affecting weapons production. Concerned that they were getting predigested, half-accurate reports from their site managers, Salgado and Herrington hired an outside expert to provide them with detailed assessments of all of the department's atomic reactors. A former navy engineer, forty-four-year-old Richard Starostecki had an impeccable pro-defense, pro-nuclear record. The son of Polish immigrants, both of whom had served in an exile army organized by the British during World War II, Starostecki had been raised on anticommunist politics and was a sharp-taloned hawk. He had attended Annapolis, served aboard nuclear submarines, and even taught in the navy's nuclear power school. As a civilian he had worked for the old Atomic Energy Commission and then the Nuclear Regulatory Commission. There he had overseen the construction and operation of thirty different commercial reactors.

Though he believed nuclear technology was safe, and that atomic weapons were necessary, Starostecki had been involved in the Three Mile Island crisis, and he had seen, firsthand, the importance of maintaining public trust. This attitude was reinforced by his long involvement in the contentious debate over construction of the Seabrook atomic power plant in New Hampshire: he had learned in the kitchens of local townspeople that ordinary citizens had legitimate doubts about nuclear power and that they would use whatever means necessary to hold up a project if they believed they weren't getting straight answers. Given all the information, Starostecki believed, the public would make the right choices. Most of the time, he thought, they would support nuclear technology.

When Starostecki was brought to the Forrestal Building, Salgado told him he was concerned about the safety of government nuclear facilities. He was especially worried that the reactors were not being operated as well as the commercial plants regulated by the NRC. "He told me, 'I don't know if these machines are safe. I want you to find out,'" Starostecki said later. "I immediately found out that no one in headquarters in Washington understood what I was talking about when I discussed reactor operations and safety. They just didn't have the technical expertise to judge what they heard. And what they did tell me was based on old NRC stuff, much of which I had written."

Starting in early 1988, Starostecki assembled a small staff and began to visit atomic-weapons-making sites to make his own assessments of facilities and workers. He began at Savannah River, where he requested an extensive tour of the three operating reactors. Savannah River's production reactors made plutonium and tritium; the latter is an atomic element that boosts the explosive power of a warhead and reduces the amount of plutonium required. Tritium has a relatively short half-life, however, so a steady supply was needed to maintain weapons.

As he traveled the site, guided by local Department of Energy officials, Starostecki was startled to see that many of them had never met their counterparts at Du Pont, the contractor that had operated the site since the 1950s. The Department of Energy maintained offices in the nearby town of Aiken, but it seemed to Starostecki that the federal officials might as well have been a thousand miles away, for all they knew about what went on behind the gates. Starostecki was also troubled by restrictions his hosts placed on his movements. They prevented him from going down certain hallways in reactor buildings, and they made it difficult for him to stop and talk at length with employees.

To circumvent his handlers, Starostecki went back to the site late one night to talk with people on the midnight shift. Because his security clearance was one of the highest, he was able to wave his plastic badge, pass through the reservation gates, and enter the control room of one of the reactors. Once inside, he was shocked to find that none of the operators possessed basic knowledge of nuclear physics. When Starostecki posed hypothetical problems—about loss of cooling water or sudden energy surges—the control-room operators would have to turn to their manuals and try to figure out how to respond. He found that the "as built" plans for the plant, which should show where every piece of equipment was located, were out of date. The operators had not been adequately trained and certified for their jobs. And equipment had not been maintained.

Starostecki spent two hours in the control room. When they relaxed, the operators confessed that they didn't much like their work. Many were former truck drivers and custodians who wanted their old jobs back. They said that they had not been required to take a test to start work. They admitted that they didn't know what went on inside the reactor core. And they weren't quite sure of the function of the control rods, which moderated the power of the atomic reaction.

Though some of what he heard was startling, Starostecki believed that none of what he found constituted an immediate danger. The facilities he inspected seemed to be functioning relatively well, and he was not aware of any recent incidents or accidents. But the atmosphere in the control room was a problem. In thirty years with the NRC, Starostecki had never seen such ill-trained operators. Even if a commercial plant did have inexperienced operators, they would be helped by the highly sophisticated monitoring devices and computerized controls that were used in every modern facility. Already highly sophisticated, the control rooms in privately run nuclear plants had been substantially improved since Three Mile Island. But at Savannah River, Du Pont operated old, one-of-a-kind reactors with a minimum of monitoring devices and controls. Here the operators had to know much more about atomic physics and theory if they were going to solve unexpected problems. All of this was presented in the "out-briefing" at the end of Starostecki's tour. He would later recall that local Department of Energy staff "didn't want to hang around and listen. And those that did took the side of the contractor."

After Savannah River, Starostecki went to Rocky Flats, near

Denver, Colorado, where the Department of Energy fashioned plutonium into parts for nuclear weapons. Like Hanford, the Rocky
Flats site had been polluted by decades of dirty operations. It was
also the facility that public health officer Carl Johnson had blamed
for excess illness in the surrounding area. Pollution at Rocky Flats
would one day become the subject of a criminal investigation. But
on his visit, Starostecki was intending to look only at the procedures followed by employees who worked with radioactive materials. He found workers performing risky assignments without
protective clothing or adequate inspections to determine whether
they had become contaminated. They would then go straight into
the lunch room, perhaps carrying radioactive particles on their
hands or clothes, and share a meal with scores of co-workers. The
same workers failed to follow standard practice for disposing of
contaminated rags and dangerous industrial solvents.

Starostecki's inspection tour also included Hanford, where he
paid special attention to the crews in charge of N Reactor. Since N
Reactor was to be mothballed, Starostecki was surprised to find a
superior crew. The Hanford group was better trained and more
safety-conscious than the workers he saw at the other sites. Though
it lacked a containment building, N Reactor was also better maintained and seemed to have more modern controls. But it was also
evident why it could not be restarted. Over decades of operation,
the graphite core had expanded to the point where it was about to
press against the ceiling. (This expansion was natural, an expected
result of the reactor's operation.) Rebuilding N Reactor would
have cost nearly as much as constructing a brand-new facility.

Though he was encouraged by what he had seen at the Hanford
reactor, Starostecki found problems inside the Plutonium-Uranium
Extraction Facility and the Plutonium Finishing Plant. On a late-
night tour he saw scores of people working hard at doing nothing.
"They were sitting around with no real work to do," Starostecki
recalled later. "There were Kentucky Fried Chicken boxes and
Sunday funnies tossed into low-level radioactive waste barrels. And
everybody was just standing around. I got the feeling that there
were a lot of people there, but nobody was really working."

After his nationwide tour of the nuclear weapons complex,
Starostecki returned to Washington with grave news for the Secre-

tary of Energy. The complex was in bad shape and deteriorating quickly. It would take many billions of dollars to repair and rebuild. Workers needed to be retrained, and clear standards had to be established for the safe operation of reactors and other plants. Most important, he argued, the mentality of many DOE officials had to be changed. Hidebound and production-oriented, the site managers and their corporate operators failed to meet industry standards for facilities that could cause enormous damage if they experienced a major accident. These local managers and operators considered headquarters a nuisance. Worse, they had developed their own avenues to political power—friendly members of Congress, administration officials, big-time party contributors—whom they could use to bypass the Forrestal Building and go right to Congress or the White House to get what they wanted. Starostecki did not trust the quasi-independent "shoguns" who ran the field offices to provide timely reports to the secretary when things went wrong inside their distant domains. He requested that headquarters establish a network of independent health and safety monitors who would report directly to the Forrestal Building. Starostecki got what he wanted; over the next several months his monitors were sent to new offices from Richland to Savannah River. These safety and environmental experts became Starostecki's surrogates, sniffing and probing for the kind of information that the local bureaucracy might conceal.

It was one of these moles who notified Washington of a small, unexpected power surge in a Savannah River reactor. P Reactor had been placed back into service following a maintenance shutdown in August 1988. The sudden two-percent jump in power was not deemed a significant event; the operators continued to increase reactor output. Even though the incident was small, Starostecki found the reaction of the contractor, Du Pont, a serious problem. He believed the company should have shut down the plant until it could explain what had happened. Otherwise it couldn't be certain that the surge was innocuous. But rather than immediately cease operations, the men in the control room had proceeded to bring the reactor to high power. Then the company had waited more than a full day, continuing to run the machine, before informing the Department of Energy of the surge. The control operators did not seem to understand the reactor well enough to develop a theory about why the surge had happened. And Du Pont's higher-ups couldn't provide what Starostecki thought was a reasonable explanation.

Starostecki's man in Savannah River pressed his investigation of the power surge until he came upon a historic document—a nineteen-page memo outlining three decades' worth of incidents and accidents at the site's five reactors. The accidents included the partial melting of fuel in one reactor and two incidents that involved the loss of core cooling water. During a fourth event, operators had barely been able to get control of a chain reaction that had increased in power at ten times the normal rate. This near meltdown had taken place in 1960, yet no record of it could be found at the Forrestal Building. Indeed, no one in the department's Washington office seemed to be aware that any of these incidents had ever taken place. As far as Starostecki could determine, they had all been kept secret by a contractor and local federal overseers who were powers unto themselves.

The nineteen-page memorandum and the daily monitor's reports sent to Washington made Starostecki's back stiffen. Like Casey Ruud, he came from the commercial nuclear industry, where NRC standards and public scrutiny had made safety the highest priority. By the middle of August he was locked in a battle with Du Pont and the Savannah River DOE people. At one point a team of inspectors recommended shutting down the reactor and requiring the operators to write new procedures for handling unexpected events. When the people at the site resisted, this decision was put off, and the plant continued to run. A day later, Du Pont voluntarily moved up the date for a planned shutdown, turned off the reactor, and began to study the safety concerns raised by Starostecki's team.

During all this debate, Starostecki's local inspector continued to tour Savannah River and find an almost endless number of safety and environmental problems. On a single day he noted a dozen different problems, from propane tanks stored in the emergency cooling system pump room at P Reactor to lax management of a waste dump. The technicians at the dump, where radioactive waste was to be carefully buried, failed to check the radiation levels of shipments sent in, even though shippers had frequently violated the standards set for materials going into the trenches. On another day the monitor observed operations at a waste-tank farm and witnessed fourteen violations of procedures. The workers didn't seem to be aware of the radiation hazards in their assignments; they left blank spaces on the paperwork where supervisors' signatures were required, and didn't sample the air to determine the level of contamination in their work area.

Gradually, Starostecki concluded that though the technical problems at Savannah River were relatively minor, he had significant concerns about the people running the facilities and their local federal overseers. In a memo to his superiors he noted that Du Pont's operators couldn't see that they had done anything wrong, though they had continued to power up the reactor after the unexpected surge. "They didn't care," Starostecki wrote. At the same time, the local DOE office lacked the expertise to oversee Du Pont. The government workers, he wrote, in many cases are "neutral or defends their contractor." In technical and politically careful language, Starostecki described a system in which the local managers and their contractor were pitted against the safety officer who reported to headquarters. He argued that the pressure to produce nuclear materials often overwhelmed safety concerns.

The confrontations between Starostecki's group and the Du Pont officials were complex and contentious. Du Pont had already chosen not to renew its contract, and would leave Savannah River within six months, after thirty-seven years. But Starostecki's criticisms surely stung those who could remember that it was Du Pont that had constructed Fermi's first reactor in Chicago, at a time when no one knew what a reactor even looked like. And it was Du Pont that had made the world's first high-power production reactors at Hanford during the war. Later the company had accepted President Truman's request that it build and run Savannah River. As in the Hanford contract, Du Pont had asked to be paid only the cost of the operation, plus one dollar. This proud history, deeply felt by Du Pont people, was being cast in a different light by those who complained of shoddy management and a careless attitude toward safety and the environment.

As they received reports on Savannah River and other sites, Herrington and Salgado could feel the pace of change within the nuclear complex quicken. Salgado, who likened the agency to a huge ocean liner that could only be turned very slowly, realized that the ship was more like a sleek sailboat that was fast coming about. He knew that once P Reactor was shut down, like Hanford's N unit, it might never be turned back on. In the midst of a renewed Cold War buildup, the nation was running out of nuclear production capacity, and as more and more problems were identified across the country, the Department of Energy's environmental crisis was deepening. It was already clear that more than $100 billion would be needed to clean up the mess, and both Herrington and Salgado knew that the agency would have to increase its credibility to justify such outlays. His days as an Oakland cop, and later as a county prosecutor, had convinced Salgado that government agencies could gain political credibility only by telling the truth, and *all* the truth. This was how a new African-American police chief in Oakland had won the public's trust in the 1960s and prevented race riots. This was how Salgado and Herrington hoped to handle the agency's problems as they inevitably came to the public's attention.

They got the chance to try out this strategy in October 1988 as Congress and the press—led by the *New York Times* team—brought the department's problems out into the open. On the first day of the month, Salgado and Starostecki were among six DOE officials who testified at a joint hearing of the Senate Governmental Affairs Committee and the House Government Operations Subcommittee on Environment, Energy and Natural Resources. The joint committee, led by Senator John Glenn of Ohio, had already begun to explore the many pollution problems at Fernald and other sites. Likewise, the House subcommittee had launched a separate investigation into the management of the plants.

The nineteen-page memo and the reports from Starostecki's field monitor were presented at the start of the hearing. Salgado and the others admitted that Savannah River was in serious trouble. They also acknowledged that the department had been kept in the dark about the thirty serious incidents—including the near meltdown—at the South Carolina site. They even revealed that although Du

Pont had provided documents on some of the problems, it appeared that others had been destroyed. They didn't have to say the words to make people think that a coverup had occurred.

Like the release of Hanford's secret history, the revelations about Savannah River's past made front-page news. They also were a jumping-off point for both Congress and the press. Keith Schneider and his colleagues had spent much of the previous year touring the nation's weapons complex and preparing a series of articles about its troubles. In the first week of October they published six pieces on Savannah River, most of them focusing on the material in the nineteen-page memo. As they reported the debate between Department of Energy headquarters and Du Pont executives, it became clear that Du Pont had informed DOE's Aiken, South Carolina, office of the incidents. And it appeared that it was the local federal office that had decided to keep the information from reaching Washington. Glenn Seaborg, the Nobel Prize–winning atomic pioneer who had headed the old AEC for many years, told Schneider he had never been informed of the mishaps at Savannah River. He and other old hands hypothesized that the secrecy practiced during the Manhattan Project had mutated in a way that eventually enveloped even the supposed leaders of the Cold War effort. Somehow, midlevel officials had come to believe that they should keep their bosses in the dark on some issues. Other present-day officials quoted in Schneider's articles complained that Secretary Herrington was meeting resistance in breaking down the culture of secrecy in the agency.

Schneider's investigation was aided by a steady stream of documents that arrived at his office almost daily from an anonymous source. The reporter worked around the clock, stitching the reports and internal memos into articles that shed a harsh light on the management of the entire weapons-making complex. The documents, which also illuminated Herrington's battle to get control of his own agency, could have come only from high officials in department headquarters. But they arrived with no sender's name, and though he suspected they came from Herrington's office, Schneider never inquired. "I believed that Herrington, Salgado, and Starostecki were at war with their own agency," Schneider would later recall. The reporter also believed that Herrington and his aides used the press to counter the strong political alliances that local site managers had formed with their states' congressional delegations. By supplying Schneider with information, headquarters people ensured that the public debate on the future of various facilities would be framed on their terms.

One of the most important documents provided to Schneider was a confidential Department of Energy study of the shoddy performance of the Savannah River plants. It showed that the reactors there had been shut down unexpectedly an average of nine to twelve times each year for the previous two decades; this was twice the rate for commercial power plants. The study noted that operator error and equipment failure—bad seals, broken generators, deteriorated parts—had caused the majority of the forced shutdowns. During one of the worst incidents, a reactor was nearly destroyed when a foreman moved to shut off the flow of cooling water. The error was corrected by a supervisor, but a secret report on the incident noted that "one trained man stood between us and disaster."

As the month of October 1988 wore on, the negative publicity grew. On October 11 the Department of Energy ordered the shutdown of the key parts of the Rocky Flats warhead-component factory because of an incident in which three workers had been exposed to plutonium. The technicians, employees of Rockwell International, had mistakenly walked into an unmarked room where contaminated equipment was being cleaned. (Later it would be revealed that the government was actually responding to a pattern of serious incidents and deficiencies that, according to one inspector, left "no margin for safety.") Days after the closure, area residents booed and heckled the plant manager who appeared at a crowded public meeting to outline the problems. They demanded that he "tell the truth" and screamed, "Shut it down!"

In the case of Rocky Flats, Starostecki was again a leading figure in the news reports. He answered calls for more than a dozen interviews, and in each one he admitted that the weapons-making industry was riddled with problems. Old reactors and factories that couldn't meet modern standards had been pressed beyond their reasonable lives, he noted. At the same time he warned that the production-oriented culture of the agency was overriding safety concerns. Starostecki made this point in a most dramatic way, declaring that "there are currently some senior managers with the Department with an attitude toward production reactor safety which, on the face, seems to be similar to that which existed in the space program prior to the *Challenger* accident." Ironically, weeks after Starostecki wrote this memo, the crew of the space shuttle *Discovery,* on the first shuttle mission since the 1986 *Challenger* disaster, conducted a memorial service in space for the seven lost astronauts.

The *Challenger* comparison would seem reasonable only days later, when yet another crisis struck the department, this one involving the Feed Materials Production Center in Fernald, Ohio, just outside Cincinnati. Documents released by another congressional committee proved that the government had long been aware of chronic radiation leaks at the plant. Federal officials admitted that the government had known for twenty years that thousands of tons of uranium waste were being released secretly into the environment, exposing thousands of workers and neighboring residents to potentially lethal radiation. The documents also showed that the government was aware that even under "normal" operating conditions the plant would pollute the local air and water supplies. Former Fernald managers testified that the plant had not been upgraded in the 1970s because it was believed it would soon close. With the Reagan buildup, however, production and pollution increased.

The public condemnations of federal authorities reached a new level with the Fernald hearing. One Ohio congressman, Democrat Thomas Luken, charged DOE with waging "a kind of chemical warfare" against his state's people. "And most important of all," he said, "it now admits it sat on its hands and did nothing to fix these serious and potentially life-threatening problems."

Rather than defend the agency, officials sat silently as members of Congress and environmental experts from Ohio attacked and attacked. By their silence, they admitted that the government was responsible for what had happened. A few weeks earlier the agency had quietly declared itself to be responsible and sought to absolve the Fernald contractor, a company called National Lead of Ohio, from financial responsibility for the wastes. With local citizens filing a lawsuit seeking $300 million in damages, agency lawyers filed papers informing the court that the government, not the company, was responsible for the pollution. Documents presented to the judge confirmed that for thirty years NLO had repeatedly warned against the use of waste pits at Fernald, and that the Department of Energy had failed to provide money the company requested for waste treatment until 1986. These public admissions would have been enough to force the shutdown of facilities at Fernald. But this was unnecessary, because days earlier the plant had been closed by a workers' strike. The employees at NLO had walked out demanding, among other things, safer conditions.

Poised with many months' worth of research and interviews, the team from *The New York Times* supplemented their month of news reports on the demise of the atomic facilities with poignant features on the communities affected. A front-page article on the people living near Fernald revealed the fear and anger of local residents who were convinced they had been poisoned. The most moving passages told the story of a steelworker named Charles Zinser, whose family had consumed vegetables from a rented plot near the plant. One of his sons had leukemia. Another had had his lower leg amputated because of bone cancer. Zinser had asked scientists to test plants from the garden and tissues from the boy's leg. Both contained uranium at ten times normal levels.

Other Fernald neighbors spoke of clusters of cancer cases that had begun to appear in the 1960s, and orchards that had died for no apparent reason. In another article, accompanied by a front-page picture of Tom Bailie standing with his hands on his hips in front of a Hanford reactor, the downwinders of Franklin County told their stories of illness and betrayal. "We don't appreciate being contaminated," Bailie said in the piece, written by Keith Schneider, "and we don't appreciate being lied to."

With shutdowns at Rocky Flats, Savannah River, Fernald, and Hanford, the key facilities in the weapons complex were falling like dominoes. The loss of all of its reactors meant the U.S. government could not make new weapons material. And with Rocky Flats closed, the DOE couldn't even finish working with the raw materials it had on hand. Even the Waste Isolation Pilot Project in New Mexico was in trouble. Its opening had been put off indefinitely as technicians tried to figure out a way to stop the unexpected leaks.

Legal challenges from local opponents of the project threatened to keep it closed forever. Meanwhile, tons of radioactive waste continued to pile up in temporary holding tanks and burial grounds at Hanford, Savannah River, and other sites.

With all this bad news, many of the career DOE officials who inhabited the Forrestal Building became grim-faced and defensive. The old, longtime Cold Warriors were concerned about maintaining the nuclear arsenal and defensive about the mistakes that might have been made. Many refused to speak to the press, and they openly expressed their anger about the documents being leaked to reporters. They argued that the negative publicity was hurting the agency and damaging the nation's strategic weapons program. At the same time they feared that the media barrage would hurt Vice-President George Bush's campaign for president. Though this fear was reasonable, and Salgado briefed campaign officials on his agency's problems, Democratic nominee Michael Dukakis never made an issue out of the problems in the bomb complex. All along, Herrington and Salgado had figured that they could limit the political damage caused by the crisis by being as open as possible. They also believed that they would have to confess all of the department's problems, if they were to persuade Congress to provide the huge amounts of money necessary to take care of environmental problems and rebuild the bomb-making system.

Herrington was determined to change the direction of the bureaucracy. He wanted to prepare the agency to operate in a more open way and accept a new mission—environmental restoration—that would consume more resources than weapons production did. He also faced mounting public pressure, including a threat by Washington and Oregon Indian tribes who threatened to sue if more information was not made available. The tribes, the downwinders, and environmental activists remained impatient with the government's slow response to their demands, but Herrington moved more quickly than many in his agency thought was prudent. In the midst of the torrent of revelations about mismanagement, he approved a series of health-related studies that promised to settle important questions about what had happened at Hanford. He agreed to end more than a decade of official stonewalling and let outside researchers—such as Alice Stewart, the British pioneer in radiation health research—examine Thomas Mancuso's controversial data on the health of Hanford workers. He also approved a $15-million study of Hanford's radiation releases, which would attempt to estimate how much radiation reached individuals living downwind. The Hanford Environmental Dose Reconstruction Project would be performed by Battelle Memorial Institute, a scientific consulting firm that had been working for Hanford since the 1960s. This close relationship raised eyebrows among critics of Hanford. To counter the inevitable charge that Battelle and the department would bias the project, Herrington appointed an independent panel to oversee the work.

The Dose Reconstruction Project was important because it would eventually provide enough information for scientists to estimate reasonably how much contamination had reached specific individuals. In theory, this meant that Tom Bailie could contact the researchers, describe where he had lived and his lifestyle, and receive a reasonable estimate of the dose of radiation he had received. Some people, such as the Indians who fished the river daily, or children who consumed milk from cows that grazed in pastures across from the nuclear facilities, might have been highly irradiated. Others, depending on wind patterns and living habits, may have received only a small dose.

While the Dose Reconstruction Project was of great interest to the downwinders, it became more significant when Congress approved funding for a companion survey of thyroid illness among the downwind population. (The study was approved after intense lobbying by HEAL and over the objections of the Department of Energy.) The thyroid research, to be conducted by the Centers for Disease Control, would also break new ground. Thousands of people who were exposed to radioactive iodine from Hanford as children—experts guessed that more than twenty thousand could have received a dangerous dose—would be examined for thyroid problems. Then researchers could use the findings of the Dose Reconstruction Project to estimate the exposure of each person. Any finding of excess thyroid disease linked to the levels of childhood exposure would have to implicate Hanford. It would also tip the scales in the ongoing debate over the health hazards from other radiation sources, including commercial nuclear plants.

It was obvious that Herrington's efforts to open up the atomic agency's past and turn it toward a new environmental mission would have long-term implications. One of the effects of this strategy, he hoped, would be steady improvement in the department's public image, which had been damaged by the years of secrecy and then the shocking revelations. But Herrington would never see the results of this policy. Indeed, he and Salgado knew they would leave office in a few months as the new president, whether it was George Bush or Michael Dukakis, put his own people in charge of the agency. This might have made it all the easier for Herrington to admit the problems in the arms complex. After all, he wouldn't have to fix what was wrong.

In 1988 President Bush nominated James Watkins, a retired admiral from the nuclear navy, to take over the Department of Energy. Watkins would be the first energy secretary with extensive experience with atomic technology. But Herrington worried whether Watkins had the political savvy to manage the agency under increased public scrutiny. New federal pollution laws meant that the Environmental Protection Agency and state governments would have access to the sites and power to regulate emissions and cleanup. At Hanford alone, 440 billion gallons of low-level radioactive waste had been dumped into shallow pits. Another 60 million gallons of high-level waste were waiting in tanks, many of which had begun to leak. Other facilities had similar problems. Savannah River, for example, had its own leaking tanks and continued to generate 180,000 gallons of radioactive waste per day. Every expert who considered the task of cleaning up the entire nuclear complex estimated it would require decades and cost well over $200 billion. But cleanup was only one of the challenges facing DOE. Somehow the new secretary would have to find the money to build new weapons-making facilities to supply the American arsenal. This would take billions more dollars. Finally, there was the matter of the civilians and workers who may have been damaged by the old plants. As a lawyer, Herrington anticipated a series of lawsuits that the government might have to settle at enormous cost. Herrington worried that the Bush team did not grasp the size of the problems it faced at Hanford, Savannah River, Rocky Flats, Fernald, and many other energy sites.

During the transition period, as Reaganites turned over their offices to Bush people, Herrington was visited by Richard Darman, who would become director of the Office of Management and Budget. Like the head accountant in a corporation, the OMB director tracks spending and tries to control it; the OMB also influences policy as it determines which programs deserve money and which ones do not. Once he was ushered past the conference room, and the picture of Richland Bomber cheerleaders, Darman settled into a chair in the secretary's office and asked Herrington for some straight answers about DOE's problems. It was clear that the aging bomb complex was all but dead. A new production reactor would be needed to fuel the atomic arsenal, and the waste-disposal controversy remained unresolved. But beyond the need for facilities, Darman wanted to know just how much it would cost to meet existing laws and standards for environmental restoration.

"Well, just how bad is this thing?" Darman asked, according to Herrington. "How much is it going to cost?"

"Dick," the secretary answered, "it's going to take everything you've got."

# ATOMIC HARVEST

BEFORE SHE BEGAN to speak, Judith Jurji smiled softly and leaned on the lectern that separated her from the hundred or so people who sat in a large classroom at Gonzaga University in Spokane. She was forty-three years old, with dark, wavy hair, delicate features, and a complexion so pale that she had an almost glowing, translucent appearance. Her skin had mysteriously lost its pigment years before. At the time, doctors couldn't say why it had happened, and Jurji had simply accepted it. On this day she wore a colorful long skirt and sweater and stood confidently at the front of the classroom. Behind her a cheery message was written in chalk on the blackboard: "Welcome Hanford Downwinders!"

In May of 1989, the Hanford Education Action League gathered people who considered themselves possible victims of Hanford's radiation. Since 1986 more than five hundred current and former residents of the area near the nuclear reservation had contacted the organization to ask for help. HEAL's political activists, who did not consider themselves downwinder advocates, brought them together to see if they could promote their own cause. As Jurji spoke and others responded, the assembly, called the Downwinder Gathering, took on the aura of a support group meeting, with participants telling their stories, voicing their fears, and receiving consolation.

The daughter of a Hanford pipe fitter, Jurji had moved to Pasco with her family in 1950, when she was four years old. She had eaten vegetables from a large family garden and drunk local milk, two of the surest ways to take in high concentrations of radioactive iodine 131. Of course, at the time, no one in the Tri-Cities would have known that there was anything wrong with the milk or the vegeta-

264

bles. "What we were really worried about were the Russians taking over," Jurji recalled. "Most of the workers were like my father—ex-military. They accepted the secrecy and the military order. We watched anticommunist films in school, and it seemed like everyone was a John Bircher. And everyone, including my father, said Hanford was safe. We all believed it."

Jurji thought her childhood had been relatively normal, though she had often been too tired to play and instead lost herself in books. She had left the Tri-Cities after graduating from high school and had never gone back. But at college she had continued to struggle with the same malaise she had felt as a girl. She experienced bouts of amnesia, and often was so fatigued that walking across a room felt like climbing a steep hill. Her skin turned pale and she stopped dreaming. After earning her degree she married a University of Washington professor, settled into a little yellow cottage on a hillside in Seattle, and began a career as an art teacher. But she was still sick. They would discover that Judith was unable to conceive a child, but except for this loss, they lived a relatively contented life.

It was not until 1987, when another ghostly pale woman, this one bearing a scar on her neck, enrolled in one of her art classes, that Jurji would learn the truth about Hanford and thyroid disease. By this time her bouts of fatigue were so profound that Jurji often found it too tiring to stand. She feared she had heart disease or some other serious illness. But her doctor couldn't find anything. "Little did I know," she told her fellow downwinders in Spokane, "that my freaked-out pituitary gland was working feverishly overtime trying to flog the radiation-damaged thyroid gland to get the hell back to work."

That autumn, in a casual conversation, Jurji and the wan-looking student realized that they had both grown up in Pasco and attended the Captain Gray elementary school. The student mentioned that the scar on her neck was from an operation she had had to remove her cancerous thyroid gland. She blamed the cancer on the Hanford releases, and advised Jurji to get a thyroid examination. Despite all the media accounts of the Green Run revelations, Jurji had never heard of Hanford's troubled history. Alarmed, she rushed to her doctor and was soon diagnosed with hypothyroidism—her thyroid was almost inactive—and given medication. In a matter of weeks her vitality, her memory, and her dreams began to return. Eventually five other members of her family, all of whom had lived in the Tri-Cities in the 1950s, were also diagnosed with thyroid problems. One of these relatives, an uncle, found out too late. Decades of untreated hypothyroidism had led to complications that eventually killed him. "The bomb that was detonated in Japan just weeks after my birth," Jurji told the Downwinder Gathering, "is still destroying me and my family."

Knowing that they had been in harm's way and suspecting they had been injured, Jurji and the other downwinders were left wondering what to do next. Several had contacted lawyers to inquire about suing the government or the contractors. They had some reason to hope for restitution. A few months after the Downwinder Gathering, the Department of Energy agreed to pay $73 million to settle a class-action suit filed by residents near the Fernald, Ohio, atomic weapons materials factory. The money would be used to pay for epidemiological studies and lifetime medical checkups for the residents. In 1987 the Department of Energy had made a similar arrangement with citizens of the Marshall Islands, where thyroid problems had cropped up in surprising numbers after a series of atmospheric atomic bomb tests. In this case the government paid the victims $150 million.

While many of the Hanford downwinders believed that a lawsuit was justified, they wanted more than just money. Before yielding to others who would tell their stories, Jurji suggested a possible course of action. First and foremost, she said, the downwinders deserved the truth about what the government had done to them. They were entitled to all the documents that would reveal their level of exposure, and to health studies to determine the extent of radiation-related illnesses caused by Hanford. Once all this information was made public, she suggested, the victims of the atomic-bomb complex should receive an apology and compensation. "All victims of the mismanagement of nuclear plants whose health has been damaged should be given full financial compensation and free lifetime medical care," she declared.

Jurji's downwinder platform seemed so ambitious and unattainable that it was not the subject of much serious discussion at the

Downwinder Gathering. But later that day, over dinner at the same Patsy Clark's Mansion where Tom Bailie and Karen Dorn Steele had met years before, a handful of downwinders began to organize a group to pursue Jurji's goals. It would be called the Hanford Downwinder Coalition. With the help of HEAL, June Casey, who was one of the original coalition organizers, mailed a questionnaire to nearly five hundred potential members. About 150 replied. Half of those reported that they had children with birth defects; forty-two reported cancer; another forty-three said they had thyroid problems. By the end of the year these people would make up the new Hanford Downwinders Coalition. The coalition would bind a diaspora of people who had once lived downwind but had been scattered around the country and the world. It would also offer some hope to those who, like Judith Jurji and June Casey, had lost faith in the government's ability to do right by its citizens.

"I remember that someone from the Centers for Disease Control attended the Downwinder Gathering," Casey explained later, "but a lot of us just didn't trust him." The CDC representative had announced that the agency intended to trace the effects of Hanford's emissions on public health. Because 80 percent of the radiation had been in the form of iodine 131, and I-131 was known to cause thyroid disease, the health study would focus primarily on thyroid problems in the downwinder population. Though a number of downwinders rushed to tell him of their own health problems, he couldn't promise they would be part of the study. He needed to find a more representative sample of downwinders who had lived in certain places at certain times. "Of course, when they heard this, people were up in arms," June Casey remembered. "They thought they were being ignored. Although I didn't say it, because I hate to embarrass the employees, I didn't have any faith in the study either. CDC is a government agency, and all I could think was 'Is this going to be another coverup?' "

If there was to be a coverup, it would have to be orchestrated by the government epidemiologist, whom June Casey had seen in Spokane. At the time, A. James Ruttenber, M.D., was the leading expert in radiation and health in the entire CDC bureaucracy. He had become interested in the subject as a medical student at Emory

University in Atlanta, where he had held a summer job working for
Glyn Caldwell, a pioneer in the study of soldiers who had been
exposed to atomic-bomb blasts. Caldwell, then a CDC scientist,
had surveyed one percent of the atomic veterans and found about
three times the expected rate of leukemia. For decades the Veterans
Administration had denied medical benefits to veterans who could
not prove their exposure to fallout had caused specific cancers. The
VA had also pointed out that even when these old soldiers could
show they had been exposed to radiation while in the service, they
could not prove how much radiation they had received. Without a
good estimate of their doses, individuals seeking benefits had trouble arguing that their illnesses—usually cancer—were service-re-
lated. Caldwell's study had advanced the veterans' cause, but
because their radiation dose levels were uncertain, many questions
remained.

Ruttenber was well aware of the scientific problems that had
made the veterans' case so difficult to resolve. The same uncertain-
ties had hindered lawsuits filed by civilians, such as the Utah sheepherders, who had been affected by fallout. One could argue that
they had been harmed, but how could an individual's claim be
resolved without a good estimate of his or her radiation exposure?
The controversy over low-level radiation and health would remain
until someone could study a large group of people who had been
exposed to a well-established range of radiation levels over a known
period. Only then might scientists begin to reach more precise conclusions about the true hazards of long-term, low-level
exposure.

Along with the scientific problems, Ruttenber was also troubled
by the politics of radiation health research. He knew that many
citizens no longer trusted the government to provide honest information. In his opinion this mistrust was well placed. After all,
research on these issues had always been clouded by the fact that
most of it was funded by the same agencies—the Atomic Energy
Commission and later the Department of Energy—that operated
major atomic facilities. It was difficult for outsiders to accept that
the nuclear agencies would do aggressive and unbiased research,
especially when the results might threaten their own operations.
This conflict of interest appeared in stark relief during the Mancuso

controversy, when DOE cut off funding just as it appeared that the professor from Pittsburgh would connect excess cancers in the work force to low-level radiation at Hanford. In the late 1980s public skepticism reached new heights when, after forty years of reassuring the nation that all was well with the nuclear bomb complex, the government had been forced to confess it had hidden enormous problems.

In the case of Hanford, Ruttenber saw a chance to get around both the general mistrust and the problem of measuring radiation doses in the communities beyond the atomic reservation's border. Hanford was awash in reports on its environmental impact. From the very beginning, scientists had monitored the air, water, and soil as well as the gases going up the smokestacks at its facilities. All this data could be used to reconstruct the actual emissions and their effects on people. Much of this work was already being done by the $15-million Hanford Environmental Dose Reconstruction Project, already begun by the Department of Energy. Ruttenber quickly negotiated with the Dose Reconstruction Project leaders to make sure that its findings would dovetail with the health study. Together the Dose Reconstruction Project and the thyroid survey might be able to make a very strong case for cause and effect.

The steering panel for the dose study was chaired by a widely respected, independent-minded physicist named John Till. Under his guidance, Battelle collected thousands of Hanford documents. These included reports from radiation monitoring stations; plutonium production records; analyses of water, soil, and vegetation taken from area farms; weather reports; census data; and much more. The Battelle scientists also conducted historical research on the lifestyles of downwinders. With all this information, they could then estimate the exposure of any person living near the reservation.

The Dose Reconstruction Project and the CDC health study were complicated by the fact that Hanford had been emitting many different kinds of radiation over a span of forty-five years. To make the job manageable, both groups would focus primarily on the most prevalent pollutant, radioactive iodine 131, and the period of time—the mid-1940s—when the largest releases were made. (In 1945 alone, as Colonel Matthias rushed to meet the Manhattan

Project's goals, the site emitted 555,000 curies of I-131. From 1945 to 1947, the year Tom Bailie was born, emissions totaled 685,000 curies. The largest single release was the Green Run, which was 11,000 curies. By comparison, the Three Mile Island accident involved about 15 curies.) Iodine 131 was a perfect subject for Ruttenber's health study because more was known about its effects on the human body than about practically any other form of radioactivity. The body treats I-131 like ordinary iodine, sending it straight to the thyroid, which regulates metabolism. Once inside the body, radioactive iodine could disrupt thyroid functioning, causing benign growths and cancer. In the normal population, only one in ten thousand people develop thyroid disease. If Ruttenber found a large excess of thyroid disease among downwinders born in the mid-1940s, he could connect it to Hanford's huge I-131 emissions.

At about this time, other researchers were suggesting connections between low-level radiation and cancer. A paper published in the August 1990 issue of the *Journal of the American Medical Association* described elevated risks of leukemia among people living downwind from the Nevada test site. Other studies showed high leukemia rates among employees of DOE's facilities at Oak Ridge and Savannah River. High occurrences of brain cancer had been associated with Rocky Flats. Citizens of Los Alamos had been alarmed by reports of excess brain cancers among neighbors of the New Mexico atomic lab. And rampant thyroid disease had been documented among children who lived near Chernobyl when Reactor Number 4 blew up.

Through 1989 and early 1990, as the Hanford dose estimate work was under way, Ruttenber began to design a pilot thyroid survey. The first phase of his study would focus on people who were born close to the reservation between 1942 and 1946. Ruttenber was confident these people could be found through a search of public records—such as drivers' license registries and marriage certificates—and old friends and classmates who remained in the area. And once they were found, the CDC would take a thorough medical history and give each person a comprehensive physical exam, including tests for thyroid disease. This would be the first such large-scale, retrospective study involving comprehensive medical exams and sophisticated dose estimates.

The actual work on the thyroid study would not be done by CDC staff. In the Reagan and Bush administrations, the CDC had moved away from doing its own projects, choosing instead to hire other institutions, such as universities and research hospitals, to perform the research. This contracting was intended to save money. It also shielded the agency from direct criticism. If a study was flawed, the contractor would be blamed. In this instance, the Fred Hutchinson Cancer Research Center in Seattle won the contract and provided the staff to do the actual work. Finding himself separated from the substance of the research, Ruttenber resigned from CDC and accepted a teaching position at the University of Colorado medical school. But the studies went on, and he was confident that together, the Dose Reconstruction Project and the thyroid investigation would combine to yield some of the answers the downwinders deserved.

The first answers came from a surprising source. On July 11, 1990, little more than a year after the Downwinder Gathering, Energy Secretary Adm. James D. Watkins appeared at a press conference at the Forrestal Building in Washington. Reading from a prepared statement, Watkins announced that the Battelle research had already produced a disturbing conclusion: the U.S. government's nuclear weapons complex had exposed thousands of innocent civilians to perilous levels of radiation. Watkins said that some of Hanford's neighbors had been hit by radiation equal to thousands of chest X rays. This dose was enough to make thousands of people sick, Watkins conceded. It may even have caused a number of them to develop cancer. Watkins said that the details of this silent human disaster would be provided the following day, when the Technical Steering Panel released a preliminary report: Phase 1 of the Dose Reconstruction Project.

There was no small personal irony in Watkins's statement. As a young officer he had been a protégé of Adm. Hyman Rickover, the father of the nuclear navy. Watkins could recall going to sea with Rickover and listening to his boss explain why he had always refused to link the navy's nuclear-powered submarine program to the Atomic Energy Commission's safety standards. In Rickover's mind, the AEC was too lax when it came to safety. He predicted that a disaster would occur in one of the facilities under its supervision. Now, more than twenty years later, Rickover's prediction was coming true, and it was falling to Watkins to handle the mess. In his brief statement, Watkins reversed a government position that had been maintained since the Manhattan Project. For the first time a U.S. official admitted that the bomb-making complex had created a secret health hazard that threatened thousands of innocent civilian neighbors. He did not elaborate on the morality of what had happened. Nor did he discuss who was to blame.

"It came about at a time when we knew little about the effects of radiation," he explained. "As years went along, we got a little smarter." Watkins also stressed that the serious mistakes were all in the past, saying that Hanford's past level of emissions did not relate "to what's going on today."

While major radiation releases may have been confined to the past, Watkins's agency was slowly being consumed by present-day scandals. The admiral had begun his term of office declaring that the bomb complex would be quickly rehabilitated and that many of its facilities—including the three production reactors at Savannah River—would soon return to service. But by the summer of 1990 it was clear that this would be technically impossible. The Savannah River units were so old and run-down that the department could salvage just one operating reactor, and it would not be restarted until 1992. Hanford and Fernald would never operate again, and Rocky Flats faced the same dark future. In fact, Rocky Flats became the subject of a grand jury criminal investigation of illegal dumping that included contamination of the grounds with plutonium, and the poisoning of local drinking water. Eventually the contractor, Rockwell, would pay $18.5 million to settle out of court. But members of the grand jury would charge that the Justice Department had made a sweetheart deal with the contractor, which allowed individuals to escape felony trial.

Plagued by breakdowns and scandal, DOE was practically forced out of the atomic weapons business, and it was fast becoming the largest environmental cleanup operation in the world. (Final cost estimates ranged from $200 billion to $1 trillion.) Although all of this distressed the Cold War patriots who warned of "unilateral disarmament" caused by the breakdown of the weapons factories,

the nation could be consoled by the geopolitical developments of
the late 1980s and early 1990s. After spending the equivalent of one
trillion U.S. dollars in the arms race with the United States, the
Soviet Union was disintegrating and the global nuclear menace was
receding. It was being destroyed not by bombs, but by economic
collapse and by the idea of freedom. In 1989, Communist governments were toppled in Poland and Czechoslovakia, and the Berlin
Wall fell as a reform government took control of East Germany. By
1990, freedom movements were threatening to break up the USSR.
Soviet leader Mikhail Gorbachev, who had already signed a treaty
banning short- and medium-range nuclear missiles from Europe,
unilaterally began to cut the Soviet military. Gorbachev, who
would win the Nobel Peace Prize in 1990, was clearly leading his
country out of the Cold War and Communist repression. But he
didn't move fast enough for those who had begun to demand basic
human freedoms and national self-determination. In the Baltics,
the Ukraine, and the Muslim south, regions that had been incorporated into the Soviet Union itself, the movement toward independence grew inexorable.

Many, including President Bush, seemed unable to grasp the
reality of the freedom movements. Bush, who expressed fears about
the pace of revolution and reform in Eastern Europe, worried
openly about the control of the Soviet nuclear arsenal. He hesitated
before recognizing the Baltics when they declared their independence, and he visited the Ukraine to counsel activists to slow their
rush to freedom. It was as if the president and his advisers had
become so accustomed to the Cold War paradigm, so addicted to
having a nuclear enemy, that they could not comprehend the significance of the change taking place.

Bush's halting response to change was understandable. For generations American politicians of both parties had defined themselves in part against the Russian threat. The president had his
"finger on the button." Like God, he could unleash an unimagina-
bly destructive force with a single order. This reality had controlled
the foreign-policy posture of every postwar president. The country
required a constant demonstration of presidential strength and
resolve. In response, Democrat John F. Kennedy had tripled the
country's nuclear arsenal in three years. Twenty years later, Repub-

lican Ronald Reagan had determinedly escalated the arms race against what he termed the "evil empire." All along, the Soviets had cooperated by behaving like a belligerent enemy for Republicans and Democrats alike. But then, quite suddenly, the fearsome "other" was reduced to an impoverished, fragmenting, disarming former superpower, and the old dynamic was shattered. Gorbachev had abandoned the arms race. And the justification for a huge nuclear arms industry disappeared.

In the summer of 1991 the freedom movement led by the new Russian leader, Boris Yeltsin, would face down a Communist coup. And one by one, states that had once been part of the Soviet Union would declare their independence. In December the USSR would be replaced formally by the Commonwealth of Independent States. Many analysts feared what might happen to the former Soviet military's nuclear weapons. But the new countries announced they were willing to negotiate steady reductions in their strategic forces.

Perhaps no one in America would be more affected by the sea change in geopolitics than the people who ran the Department of Energy. The department's bureaucrats and technicians had effi-ciently produced the best nuclear weapons, even if they had ignored the problems of public health and the environment for fifty years. Now, under Watkins, their new mission would be to repair the damage done by their scientific warfare. The studies of Hanford's impact on health and the environment, and research at other atomic facilities, were part of the government's attempt to identify the ravaged landscape and locate the human casualties of the Cold War. As Admiral Watkins acknowledged in July 1990, the govern-ment had a duty to "go back and find out what happened to these people."

On the day following Admiral Watkins's announcement, Technical Steering Panel Chairman Till appeared at a press conference in Richland and revealed the detailed results of Phase 1 of the Dose Reconstruction Project. The most shocking news in the report was that some babies living near Hanford could have received as much radiation as children who had been caught in Chernobyl's cloud.

These children would have lived directly east of Hanford, in places such as Mesa, in the mid-1940s, and they would have taken in radioactive iodine in the milk that came from family cows. These few children could have ingested as much as 2,900 rads, compared with 1,500 estimated for Chernobyl children. (A single rad is equal to the radiation in a dozen typical chest X rays.) Till noted that previous research had found that a dose of just 9 rads was enough to raise the risk of cancer.

The Phase 1 report also showed that between 1944 and 1947, about 13,500 people—out of 270,000 living in ten counties surrounding the reservation—had received at least 33 rads of exposure from Hanford. He described this amount as "significant" in terms of public health. Thirty-three rads is ten times the amount of radiation exposure a typical American receives—mostly from natural sources—each year.

The TSP's findings were contained in a little blue booklet that Till distributed to the reporters and others at the Hanford House hotel. Much of the report focused on radioactive iodine 131 and the "milk pathway." As the authors noted, "Iodine 131 was released to the air, carried by wind, deposited on plants and eaten by animals and people. . . . The iodine 131 eaten by cows enters the milk that the cow produces. When humans drink milk, the iodine in the milk collects in the thyroid." The report showed that more than a dozen commercial dairy farms had operated in the area hit by the largest amounts of Hanford's I-131. Children who drank milk from these dairies would have been affected by the milk pathway. Those who consumed milk directly from family cows would have taken in the most radioactive iodine. This is because I-131 has a half-life of just eight days, meaning it loses half of its radioactive potency in that time. Children are more vulnerable to the effects of I-131 because their thyroids are small and still growing.

To help downwinders figure out, in rough terms, how much radioactive iodine they had received, the TSP report included a list of milk-related questions. After answering each question, one could locate his or her exposure group on a chart that was also part of the report. Someone who drank milk from a family cow that grazed on a pasture in the downwind area, and was an infant between 1944 and 1947, fell into the top dose group. These people, about 1,400 in all, could have received as much as 2,900 rads from milk and vegetables during the mid-1940s. This meant that Tom Bailie and his childhood friends were probably among those who had received the maximum dose. The quarter-million others living in the ten-county area at the time had also been hit by I-131, but in widely ranging amounts.

Though the Phase 1 report may have startled some, it revealed only a small part of Hanford's polluting past: the airborne radioactive iodine releases of the mid-1940s. The experts knew that over the decades, people living near Hanford had been hit with many other, more lethal radionuclides such as ruthenium, americium, neptunium, and even plutonium. Anyone who drank river water or ate local fish could have taken in these contaminants. Indians, many of whom consumed large amounts of fish, and traditionally ate almost every part of the animal, must have been especially vulnerable. None of this was included in the first report. Likewise, the TSP had done no work on the substantial iodine releases that had occurred after the 1940s. They had not yet considered, for example, that in 1947 a Hanford health officer had estimated that two processing plants were sending more than 7 billion radioactive particles into the air each month. These "hot" particles were more dangerous than short-lived iodine; they could remain lethal for eons and were known to cause cancer in human beings. Information about all these releases was to be included in subsequent phases of the TSP's work. But a final report, including all of this data, was not likely to appear before 1995.

Tom Bailie found out that he was one of the most irradiated people on earth by listening to the radio in the cab of his tractor. In the years since he had first voiced his fears about Hanford, Bailie had come to find comfort among the antinuclear activists whom he once dismissed as extreme. He had grown comfortable, too, in challenging the government with nothing more than his own suspicions. Still, as he heard the news one sunny July afternoon in 1990—heard that he had been right all along—Bailie was shocked. Strange as it would have seemed to neighbors who called him "glow-in-the-dark Tom," Bailie did not want to be right. He did not want to consider himself a victim of Hanford. He did not want to believe that in the frenzy of the arms race, the government had decided that he and his neighbors and their farms could be secretly endangered. As the truth washed over him, Bailie stopped the tractor and turned off the radio. Alone, as he had been through most of the Hanford battle, he sat listening to the rhythm of the motor. And then he started to cry. Deep, uncontrollable sobs shook his body. When he was finished, he still couldn't think clearly about what had happened. The crying was the only thing that made sense to him at all.

In the next week, Bailie pulled himself together for the reporters and the TV crews who once again made their way to Mesa, to tell the nuclear-age parable of Hanford and the downwinders. But this time he didn't want to leave the telling to others. Working on a legal pad, he wrote a brief essay that was eventually published in *The New York Times* and several other papers. In this piece, Bailie described growing up in an isolated community where deformed animals, stillborn babies, and Geiger-counter-wielding soldiers were all part of the landscape. He observed that while the world had condemned the Soviets for keeping Chernobyl a secret for three days, the United States had been silent about Hanford for forty years. Even after the truth began to emerge, he noted, "We have been put off by politicians—except for a brave few—until we victims become a popular issue. . . . Who the hell do these people in the nuclear gang think they are?" he asked in the kind of plain language rarely seen on editorial pages.

This sense of moral outrage was shared by other downwinders and by the people of HEAL. In Spokane, Jim Thomas, the young researcher who had immersed himself in the documents released by Mike Lawrence, had continued to press the government for more information. By 1990 the declassified reports and memoranda churned up by Thomas and others had grown to more than sixty thousand pages. Insatiably curious about events such as the Green Run, Thomas was not satisfied when Admiral Watkins explained that the downwinders had been irradiated and the earth had been contaminated because the people in charge didn't know better. They *did* know better.

The documents contained ample evidence that government officials had long known about the dangers Hanford posed. The scientists and managers at Hanford were worried about radiation even when B Reactor began to operate in 1944. They tried to set limits on radiation exposure. But during the Manhattan Project and the early years of the Cold War, these standards were routinely ignored when demands for plutonium were high. As occurred at the time of the Casey Ruud audits, production pressure had often over-whelmed safety concerns. In 1947, Hanford officials had chosen to ignore health officers who suggested workers be given respirators to protect them from airborne radioactive particles. This idea was rejected because it would be bad for worker morale. In 1949, and again in 1951, health advisers urged the government to conduct cancer studies of Hanford workers and to warn those employees who had received a radiation dose above accepted limits. The gov-ernment did not act on those suggestions. Instead of warning work-ers that radiation could cause cancer years into the future, the AEC simply chose to inform departing employees that everything possi-ble had been done to safeguard their health.

Reports from other AEC facilities proved that the government had been aware of the danger posed by the excessive radiation created by the atomic-bomb project. Since the beginning of the Manhattan Project, officials had worried about both workers and innocent bystanders. During the Trinity test of 1945, when the very first atomic bomb was exploded in the New Mexico desert, they noted "potentially a very dangerous hazard" to the local popula-tion. The pattern of deceiving the public began with the Trinity test as well. Even though scientists knew that a small community was being blanketed by fallout, no warning was issued. Later, in 1951, the vice-chairman of an AEC health panel told the commission, "Cancer is a specific industrial hazard of the atomic energy busi-ness." But it would be more than a decade before the AEC would begin to study worker health in earnest.

While the declassified material contained many references to worker health, the papers also made it obvious that Hanford's operators had been willing to exceed the limits for radiation sent off the site. During the winter of 1945–46, *after* World War II was won, grazing animals outside the fenceline received radiation doses that were one thousand times what was deemed safe. At the same time, "hot" particles were found in downtown Richland. Three years later, at the time of the infamous Green Run experiment, Hanford's chief health officer, Herbert Parker, noted that again "range animals were heavily overexposed." Parker, who would be the primary authority on Hanford's health hazards, warned that farmers' livestock had been subjected to "unjustifiable overexposure with no arrangements for compensation."

Other documents showed that from 1945 to 1951, samples of vegetation from as far away as Spokane, 125 miles to the northeast, showed radiation levels exceeding what was considered safe. At one time in 1945, the I-131 levels on plants in the Tri-Cities were found to be between forty-five and seventy times the level believed safe. Of course, the public was never told of these problems. Indeed, throughout this time, federal officials assured local residents that Hanford's emissions were so slight as to be "innocuous."

HEAL made most of this historical information available in its publications, but little of it found its way to the general public. There were just too many facts for the media to present them in proper perspective and for the public to digest. Nevertheless, many of them bear repeating:

• Writing about hot-particle problems in 1948, health officer Parker had warned that the possibility "of injury developing ten to fifteen years from now poses a serious problem."

• After the 1949 Green Run, Parker advised plant managers that the health division at Hanford would oppose another experiment because the first had produced radiation releases "close enough to significant levels."

• In 1951, Hanford scientists observed that hot particles were still being emitted from processing facilities and remained "a very serious health problem."

• In 1954, Hanford scientists warned that increases in the power levels of the reactors would raise radioactive pollution in the Columbia to levels that might require a fishing ban. On six different occasions—the last in 1964—radiation levels in fish exceeded the point at which Parker considered a ban appropriate, but no action was taken.

• Also in 1954, Parker documented ruthenium releases that had left hot particles every six hundred feet in fields of grain across the river. If breathed into the lungs, perhaps by a farmer turning the soil, one particle could produce a dose of 60 rems per hour.

• In early 1955, radiation levels on vegetation found in Ritzville, 75 miles away, exceeded Hanford's health standards. No public warning was issued.

These revelations suggested that, contrary to Admiral Watkins's assertions, the officials who ran Hanford knew that the countryside, livestock, and people as far away as Spokane had been pelted with excessive amounts of radiation and that human health could be affected. Parker's reports leave no doubt about whether they understood the health effects of this pollution. They knew that the Columbia River and its fish were contaminated, that farmers' crops were laced with radiation, and that the poison could find its way to human beings.

Along with the documents describing the health hazards, Jim Thomas found repeated references to the public-relations concerns of the Hanford operators. When confronted with an off-site radiation problem, they held to their commitment to Cold War secrecy, even when it meant that citizens could be harmed. This penchant for secrecy reached bizarre proportions in the case of Hanford worker Ernest Johnson, which Jim Thomas discovered in his documents and Karen Dorn Steele revealed to the public in the *Spokesman-Review*. Johnson had died at home in 1952 after falling ill on the job. Though he had not been sick previously, his wife, Marie, had noticed he was lethargic in the weeks leading up to his death. When the funeral home director discovered strange marks on Johnson's body, he called the medical department at General Electric, the contractor running the site at the time. GE arranged for an autopsy, which concluded that Johnson had died of a ruptured aorta. The autopsy report ignored the marks on the body, and Marie Johnson was not satisfied. When Ernest's co-workers told her he had been exposed to excess radiation before his death, she arranged a second autopsy. This doctor declared that the marks were radiation burns, and that they had contributed to Johnson's death. Using this information, the widow applied for worker's compensation benefits. Hanford officials pressured the doctor to change his findings, but he refused. They finally arranged for a third physician, one with longtime connections to Hanford, to write a third autopsy report. This report dismissed radiation as a contributor to Johnson's death. It was used to deny Mrs. Johnson's claim for benefits and to preserve the public impression that Hanford was safe.

With their research, Jim Thomas and Karen Dorn Steele revealed many of the ways Hanford had affected its unwitting neighbors. But they could not explain how this could happen in a democratic society. Reverend Bill Houff would eventually suggest that the atomic deception had been practiced by "nuclear technocrats" who became so accustomed to presenting a sanitized version of reality to the public that "they inevitably ended up deceiving themselves as well." The way Houff saw it, forty years of secrecy, justified by the Cold War state of emergency, had overwhelmed the democratic values that normally restrained the government from harming its own.

But in the light of new research, some experts have come to argue that the justification for the secrecy, and for the Cold War itself, is no longer certain. Classified material released in the past decade casts doubt even on President Truman's decision to proceed with dropping atomic bombs. Many historians now argue that Japan was signaling its intention to surrender well before the bombs were dropped. Even at that time, some officers involved in the bombing said that the war would have been over in two weeks without the use of atomic weapons. Fifty years later, Stanley Goldberg, biographer of Gen. Leslie Groves, who had led the Manhattan Project for the Pentagon, suggested that part of the reason that the bombs had been dropped on Japan was that so much time, money, and effort had gone into their development. If no weapon had been used, the $2-billion project could have become a political scandal. At the same time there was evidence that U.S. officials, contemplating postwar competition with the Soviet Union, wanted to demonstrate America's awesome military advantage. By dropping the A-bombs on Japan, Truman immediately established the United States as the sole superpower in the period immediately after the war.

As the Manhattan Project and the bombings of Hiroshima and

Nagasaki have been called into question, so too have the claims of Cold War advocates been reconsidered. The statements of former Soviet leaders and documents released in the 1990s, after the disintegration of the Soviet Union, seem to show that in the early Cold War years, Americans frequently overstated the Russian threat. It now appears that in the 1940s and 1950s, when Hanford worked overtime and did most of its polluting, America enjoyed an overwhelming nuclear advantage. Of course, U.S. strategists could not be sure of the size and potency of the enemy force, and so they assumed the worst. At the same time, the Soviets feared American superiority and raced as fast as they could to build more weapons. Fear was matched against fear, and foreign policy was turned into pure military competition.

All of this seems to suggest that the atomic-bomb technology, once born, took on a life of its own, first insisting that it be used and then insisting on growth and development. It wasn't the technology, however, but the political leaders on both sides of the Atlantic who prosecuted the Cold War. Soon after the most terrible war in history, American leaders responded to a nuclear-armed Soviet foe that seemed bent on subjugating the world. They spent more than $1 trillion and risked the health of thousands of Americans in the race to amass ever more powerful weapons. Because all of this took place in secret, and the real facts of the arms race were also secret, citizens were effectively shut out of the decision-making. They played no direct role in deciding the size of the nuclear complex, the number of weapons needed, or the margin of safety that would be acceptable for those living near places like Hanford.

The TSP Phase 1 report, and Admiral Watkins's statement, pointed to the terrible legacy of this secrecy. People like Tom Bailie and Judith Jurji would draw a straight line from Hanford to their own health problems. But their conclusions were not scientific. That kind of assessment could be attempted only by the researchers at the Fred Hutchinson Cancer Research Center, who would conduct the Hanford thyroid study for the Centers for Disease Control.

One of the doctors who would conduct the study was Bruce Amundson, M.D., a general practitioner from Spokane who had long questioned Hanford's claims of safe operations. Amundson had helped train medical students in family practice at the University of Washington. Over the years he had noticed what he thought were excessive amounts of radiation-related illnesses in the region, but he had never been able to prove cause and effect. He also suspected that doctors in the Tri-Cities had become so much a part of the nuclear culture that they couldn't see the problem.

Amundson had visited with farm families in Franklin County soon after the documents revealing Hanford's emissions had been made public. When they told him about the clouds of dust they would create as they broke the sod cover on new fields, Amundson could easily imagine that the plows had also stirred up whatever Hanford had deposited on the land. As the son of dryland wheat farmers in Minnesota, he had been covered in dust more than a few times as a boy. "Then, when they told me their health histories— cancers, premature heart disease, lost pregnancies, birth defects—I was very moved," he would recall later. "I think any doctor would have had significant concerns about what had happened."

Eager as Amundson was to get to work, he could not move the bureaucracy any faster than it wanted to move. It would take more than a year for various agencies to approve the protocol for the research and free up the money to do the work. The researchers would then have to locate and examine more than two thousand people born downwind of Hanford between 1942 and 1947. They would perform thorough exams, including blood tests, ultrasound inspections of the thyroid, and biopsies if nodules were found. Results would be long in coming. As late as the end of 1992, the project was still not fully under way, and the only certain thing was that it would take years for the study to produce a final report.

As Amundson and his colleagues struggled to begin examining the health of Hanford's neighbors, two comprehensive studies on radiation and health among workers at the site were begun. One research project, coordinated by a Portland-based veterans' advocate named Walter Cummins, focused on the soldiers who had served in military detachments at Hanford in the 1950s. Cummins had been contacted by vets who said they had come down with cancer and other radiogenic diseases after being exposed to Hanford's emissions. Good health records were available through the

Veterans Administration, which agreed to cooperate. But as late as 1993, Cummins and his associates were still having trouble getting access to the information.

The other broad-based review of Hanford workers' health proceeded much more quickly under the direction of Alice Stewart, the famous British expert on radiation and health. In July 1990, the Department of Energy gave Stewart computer tapes bearing the health records of 35,000 people who had worked at Hanford. These tapes contained the same records that Dr. Thomas Mancuso of the University of Pittsburgh had been using when his research contract was canceled just as it seemed he would announce that even those Hanford workers exposed to low doses of radiation had suffered excess cancer.

By the end of 1992, Dr. Stewart issued preliminary findings that confirmed Mancuso's work and challenged generations of government assurances about the safety of radiation. Among those workers who had received only low doses, she reported, two hundred could be expected to die from radiation-induced cancer. By arguing a connection between low-level radiation and cancer, Stewart once again challenged the established wisdom in health physics, which held that low doses were practically harmless. Stewart, by this time eighty-six years old, would once again be in the position of standing against a torrent of opposition. But then, she was accustomed to the pressure. After all, when she had first suggested the dangers X rays posed to the development of fetuses, she had been widely criticized. It took many years, but doctors everywhere are now virtually unanimous in their agreement that unborn children be protected from all forms of radiation. It was possible, given Stewart's track record, that her work on the Hanford data would eventually lead to more stringent restrictions on radiation exposure for everyone, from technicians in nuclear power plants to employees of hospital radiology departments.

Though the legacy of Hanford included off-site emissions and serious public health risks, these were not the only problems wrought by forty-five years of operations. Inside the fences, Hanford had become perhaps the most polluted industrial site in the nation. The State of Washington, the Department of Energy, and the federal

Environmental Protection Agency had agreed on a plan for cleaning up the Area that would cost more than $1 billion a year for the
indefinite future. At first, much of the money would be spent deter-
mining exactly what had been dumped where on the 560-square-
mile reservation. Some of the dumping had been impromptu, and
the locations had been obscured by drifting sands. Researchers
brought old-timers and retirees out to the site to have them show
where unmarked dumping spots were located. They also combed
documents for notations about waste disposal. Eventually, more
than 1,400 individual dump sites would be found. Both the volume
and the toxicity of what they contained was astounding. More than
440 billion gallons of chemical and radioactive liquid waste had
been poured into the ground. Besides the by-products of plutonium
production, these wastes contained enough actual plutonium to
build two dozen nuclear weapons. In some places, so much plutonium was present that it was theoretically possible for a spontaneous criticality to occur. In other places, the concentrations of
uranium equaled those of some of the world's richest mines. And
below the soil, 230 square miles of groundwater had been polluted.
The groundwater tended to flow toward and into the Columbia
River. By 1990 the radioactive element strontium 90 was leaking
into the river from the groundwater near N Reactor. There were
other locations where tritium and uranium were discovered to be
seeping into the river.

Here again, there was ample evidence that federal officials had
deliberately ignored or concealed serious problems. In the era of
secrecy—from 1943 to the mid-1980s—Hanford's public environmental reports simply omitted problems such as steel tanks that
were leaking highly radioactive waste into the water table. At one
juncture, Hanford officials chose to reclassify plutonium-laden
waste, making it disappear on paper while it remained in the
ground. In other cases, when rabbits and coyotes spread radioactivity in their droppings, or chemicals from waste pits leached into
the groundwater, the size and severity of the problems were obscured by vague scientific language. It wasn't until the DOE began
to seek funding for environmental restoration that the truth about
Hanford's many ecological problems began to be revealed.

Perhaps the most challenging waste problems bubbled inside the

177 steel waste tanks—some dating back to the Manhattan Project—that were buried in the ground near various processing facilities. More than 60 million gallons of highly radioactive sludge had been deposited in these tanks over the years. Sixty-seven of them were known "leakers," and pools of radioactive liquid had descended beneath them toward the water table. In the long term, the Department of Energy intended to pump out the tanks and encapsulate the waste in glass, which would then be buried in a permanent repository. This plan would take years to implement. The department needed time to design and build a $2-billion "glassification" plant. In the meantime, twenty-eight new double-shelled tanks were constructed to replace some of the leaky ones. Wastes were shifted from tank to tank in an effort to minimize leaking.

The tanks did not generate much public interest until the fall of 1989, when it was revealed that twenty-two tanks contained a potentially explosive chemical, ferrocyanide, that had been mixed in with the wastes in the 1950s. Scientists working with HEAL raised the possibility that a stray spark could ignite the chemical, and Hanford officials admitted it was possible. A few months later, Hanford manager Mike Lawrence held a press conference to announce that another twenty tanks had the potential to explode and scatter deadly contaminants over a wide area. These problem tanks were generating dangerous amounts of hydrogen, which, under pressure, could be explosive. Hanford contractors had been aware of the hydrogen problem for more than a decade, and had tried to relieve the gas pressure. But they kept the danger secret. Lawrence broke this silence after a team from department headquarters criticized the handling of the problem. This team was in contact with HEAL, and Lawrence no doubt knew the hydrogen issue would come out one way or another. By coming forward, he was able to at least offer his reassurances and argue that the public was not at risk.

Lawrence and lower-level Hanford officials said the actual risk of a tank explosion was small—about the same as the chance of a gasoline truck blowing up on the highway. However, Lawrence had to admit that an explosion was possible. "I can't sit here and say it's not going to happen," he said. The idea of such an explosion—and the discharge of up to half a million gallons of deadly nuclear waste—was frightening to people who lived nearby. A similar tank had exploded in the Soviet Union in 1957, scattering radiation over an area the size of Rhode Island and forcing ten thousand people to flee. After the Soviet disaster, hundreds reportedly died of radiation sickness. No such accident has occurred in the United States, but in 1965, at Hanford, the gas pressure inside one tank had caused a fifty-foot-high geyser of radioactive material to erupt. As a stopgap response, monitoring of the tanks was increased, water was added to some to cool their contents, and DOE stepped up research on the best methods for emptying all of the tanks. (This work took on increased importance after the April 1993 explosion of a similar waste tank in Russia. The explosion spread radioactive contamination over an area of more than five miles.)

News of the exploding-tank danger alarmed people throughout the Northwest, and state officials complained that they had not been informed of the problem, as required by the Tri-Party cleanup agreement. Washington Governor Booth Gardner wrote to Energy Secretary Watkins, warning that secrecy and sudden press conferences on long-hidden dangers were "deadly to the credibility of the Department of Energy." He added, "We need to heighten the sensitivity of Hanford staff and contractors to health and safety concerns. The alternative is to leave the public perpetually alarmed."

Even in the Tri-Cities, people were shocked to learn that Hanford threatened them with present-day hazards. (Until this time, the dangers, like the Green Run release, all seemed to be in the past.) But those Hanfordites who worked at the tank farms were not surprised to learn of the explosion threat. As reporter Chris Sivula noted in an article in the *Tri-Cities Herald*, troubled tanks were so well known that one—Number 105A—was the subject of a song parody. Sivula published the lyrics, which had been found on a bulletin board in Richland. Written to the tune of "Sweet Betsy from Pike," the song began,

> *Do you remember Tank 105A?*
> *She bulged and she leaked and she stirred up a fray.*
> *Good to the last drop, she drained her cup,*
> *Got the coyotes, the sagebrush, and the sand*
> *dunes crapped up.*

The tank hazards were just some of the many problems that slowed the progress of the Hanford cleanup. In September 1990, for example, Westinghouse discovered a leak of radioactive water at a processing facility called B Plant. It was estimated that the irradiated water had been flowing undetected into the soil for more than a year. Throughout the site, old plants that had been shut down continued to leak radiation, and even operating laboratories poured more wastes into the soil because alternative disposal systems had still not been developed.

As the scope of the environmental problems became known, the deadlines set in the Tri-Party agreement for completing aspects of the cleanup were revised, and then revised again. Westinghouse was given a series of extensions to try to figure out how to proceed. In the meantime, employment at Hanford soared. Though very little cleanup work was being accomplished, the site's budget topped $1 billion, the work force went over sixteen thousand, and the Tri-Cities boomed once more. Between 1989 and 1992, in the midst of a national recession, housing prices in the Tri-Cities rose 50 percent and employment went up 18 percent. New hotels and shopping centers and subdivisions once again bloomed in the desert. The dire predictions of domestic violence and economic collapse voiced at the time of N Reactor's demise were forgotten. And a new billboard at the entrance to the Hanford Site proclaimed the reservation's new environmental mission with a fuzzy picture of children picking wildflowers and the slogan, "It's the Nature of Our Business."

Similar transitions were taking place throughout the federal nuclear weapons complex. At Fernald, nuclear workers became environmental technicians, and engineers turned their attention to cleanup technology. The same was true at Rocky Flats. Pantex, which had long been the major weapons assembly point, became a "disassembly" plant, the main facility for taking apart weapons no longer needed. And at Savannah River, employment doubled to 24,000 and spending went over $2 billion as the site grappled with its own waste-tank problem and its own contaminated soil and water.

Although the Department of Energy seemed to embrace environmentalism, it did not escape controversy. At many facilities, critics of the Department of Energy and its contractors complained that too little cleanup was being accomplished with the billions spent. In 1992, Leo Duffy, the Department of Energy's chief environmental cleanup official, admitted to *U.S. News and World Report* that only 60 percent (in some cases as little as 25 percent) of the money allocated was actually spent on environmental restoration. The rest—$2 billion a year—was lost to waste and corruption.

At Hanford, tales of mismanagement and waste were abundant. As office space and parking lots were built at breakneck speed, the glassification plant fell far behind schedule. Workers complained that they wandered aimlessly around the site as huge sums of money were being spent studying ways to dispose of wastes. Others joked about how the Tri-Cities had enjoyed forty years of federal bounty as a nuclear producer and, in the process, had created forty more years of work by fouling the environment. They joked, but they appreciated all the high-paying jobs created by the environmental mission. By 1991 it seemed that anyone could find work at Hanford, even someone like the infamous Casey Ruud.

In the time since he had been laid off and then settled his legal complaints with Westinghouse, Ruud had been on a cross-country career odyssey. In the summer of 1990, with all the doors in the Tri-Cities closed, he followed fellow whistle-blower Jim Simpkin all the way to Savannah River, where a small subcontractor, working for Westinghouse, took both men in, giving them low-level assignments as safety specialists. Ruud put his house in Kennewick up for sale and moved Suzi and his children to South Carolina. They hated leaving their old home, but accepted that South Carolina was where Casey could earn a living, and tried to adjust. They didn't have to try for long. The Westinghouse executives who ran Savannah River soon discovered that the Hanford whistle-blowers were in their midst. The two men were ordered to turn in their security badges and were escorted to the site gate. Without a badge, Ruud couldn't perform his job, so he resigned.

In January 1991 he again packed everything he owned into a U-Haul truck. He took his family back to the Tri-Cities, where they were able to move back into his old house, because it had not sold. Soon after he got back to Kennewick, the Department of Ecology hired Ruud to help monitor the Department of Energy and Westinghouse as they tried to comply with the cleanup agreement. Two years after he was laid off and the Dingell committee abandoned his cause, Ruud was right back where he had started, auditing environmental and safety problems at Hanford. This time, however, he was not vulnerable to the inside politics of the contractor. Armed with the State of Washington's authority to oversee the entire site restoration project, Ruud was free to scour the site for pollution problems and shoddy work.

Assigned mainly to the waste-disposal area, Ruud quickly discovered that some of the most dangerous leaking tanks had inadequate or broken monitoring devices. Ruud also found that yet another tank—the sixty-seventh—had started to leak. And he identified problems with the waste-disposal system at a laboratory used to analyze samples taken from the waste tanks; it seemed it was prone to overflowing and spilling high-level radioactive sludge. These problems were typical of the conditions at the site. Almost eight years after Mike Lawrence promised a conscientious cleanup, little progress had been made toward disposing of the high-level tank wastes, cleaning up the soil, or stopping the migration of pollution toward the groundwater and the Columbia River.

Though he was employed to hold the contractor to the letter of the cleanup agreement, Ruud was one of many experts who doubted that Hanford could, or even should, be returned to a near-natural state. As late as 1992, scientists at Hanford still had no confirmed methods for disposing of the vast majority of the wastes. Even if it was technically possible to get every square foot of the site clean, it was not clear that this would be worth the money. As actual cleanup began, the state and federal governments would continue to haggle over how clean was clean enough.

On a warm fall day in 1992, Ruud drove a state truck around the site, pointing out some of the biggest contamination problems. At the tank farms, the Plutonium-Uranium Extraction Facility, and other locations he noted the high levels of radioactive wastes and the huge volumes of chemicals that had saturated the earth. Three billion metric tons of soil and groundwater had been contaminated, he explained. He said this would make a pile as big as a football field two hundred miles high. In just two cribs—ditches where liquid wastes had been pumped—an estimated 8,900 pounds of uranium were mixed into the dirt.

At the tank farms—a flat expanse of fenced-in earth where steel tanks were buried underground—Ruud noted that the technicians on site still didn't know exactly what was inside the containers. Crews had been unable to meet the deadlines in the Tri-Party agreement for drawing samples and analyzing their composition.

The pace of the cleanup was frustratingly slow, and new problems were discovered almost every month. In the fall of 1992, for example, DOE and Westinghouse revealed the existence of 500,000 steel barrels of plutonium-laced wastes that were buried at various locations in the desert. Later, in the spring of 1993, the public learned of an internal DOE report warning that "the likelihood of a disaster is high" at Hanford and other atomic weapons facilities. The document, written by outgoing Bush administration officials, said that contractors "are failing to adequately protect workers, the public, and the environment." It revealed several recent accidents within the system, including an incident in which two workers were contaminated by plutonium at Hanford.

As the internal report and the regular discovery of new waste problems showed, Hanford was a mess. On the site, many workers expressed frustration and anger. Casey Ruud, however, was happy in his work. The state job provided him and his family with financial security, and he took some pleasure in the fact that he had returned to Hanford in a key role. "They didn't beat me," he would say. "I'm back, and I feel I was destined to be here doing this."

In 1992, Ruud's family tried to return to a normal routine. He resumed coaching. The older children went back to their schools. Evan, the youngest son, stopped having the nightmares that had plagued him when they went to South Carolina. Little Samantha, who was just three, seemed unaffected by the moving around. Within a few months of coming back to Kennewick, she couldn't remember ever having left. But while the children all seemed to ease back into their normal lives, Casey and Suzi never quite recovered from the tumult of his conflict with Hanford. In early 1993 they separated, and began divorce proceedings. (The Ruuds would remain together, in one way, as joint litigants in a lawsuit they filed in 1993 against Westinghouse and many of its top executives. In the suit, they charged the executives with harassment and a conspiracy that led to Casey losing his jobs at Hanford and Savannah River. In a particularly aggressive strategy, the Ruuds' lawyers cited federal anti-racketeering laws, alleging that the conspiracy against the Ruuds involved interstate mail fraud. As of April 1993, Westinghouse had refused to negotiate a settlement and had objected to Ruud's accusations.)

While the outcome of the lawsuit, and the future of the Ruuds' relationship, were uncertain, Casey's future at Hanford was secure. Hanford had a mandate to pioneer environmental technologies in the same way that it had pioneered nuclear production. This would be a long-term job because, even as late as 1993, the government's scientists were not sure how to dispose of most of the mess. They could dig up contaminated soil, or pump liquids from the tanks, but they didn't have proven techniques for turning it into something harmless. Indeed, many of the attempts to deal with the waste at other sites had failed. At Rocky Flats, for example, DOE had tried to stabilize a pond full of liquids by adding concrete, which they hoped would trap the toxic materials. But the concrete never set, so they were left with the added problem of disposing of many tons of hazardous waste mixed with unhardened concrete.

The wastes left behind by the nuclear-arms complex were unlike anything humankind had created before. This meant that hundreds of millions of dollars' worth of research would be done at Hanford just to invent disposal technologies. Once invented, they could be used throughout the world. In Russia, for example, the environmental problems caused by the old Soviet nuclear-weapons complex were even greater. At a site called Chelyabinsk, officials bent on matching American arms production had poured millions of curies of radioactive waste into the environment. Excess cancer had been well documented in nearby farming communities, and the pools of waste were larger and more concentrated than anything in the United States. Any practical cleanup technology invented at Hanford could conceivably be used at Chelyabinsk and at countless other places where radioactive and toxic chemicals had contaminated soil and water. This huge market for ecological technology, coupled with the size of the Hanford restoration project, promised a bright economic future for the Tri-Cities.

The future was not so clear for the downwinders. By 1993 more than four thousand individuals had signed as plaintiffs in a $100-million federal lawsuit against the companies that had served as prime contractors over the years: among the defendants named were Du Pont, General Electric, and Rockwell. All of the plaintiffs suffered from one or many radiation-related illnesses, ranging from lymphatic cancer to thyroid disease. The judge hearing the case rejected every attempt to have it dismissed, so it appeared that, short of a massive financial settlement, the case would go to court. But it would be 1995, at the earliest, before a trial would begin. And even then there was no guarantee that the downwinders would prevail. Indeed, many of them believed that they would have better luck seeking a one-time payment of reparations from Congress, like the settlement received by the Marshall Islanders.

Of course the lawsuit, and any appeal to Congress, would be affected by the findings of the Dose Reconstruction Project and the thyroid study, which were years away from completion. More than seven years after Tom Bailie and Karen Dorn Steele began asking questions, the downwinders had some answers. They knew that they had been subjected to routine and intentional radiation releases. They also knew that the government had chosen not to warn them, even when the danger was obvious. But there would be no resolution of their grievances until all the studies were done and the government either made amends or turned them down.

While they waited, the downwinders of Franklin County returned to the habits of their lives, the cycle of planting and harvesting, the pleasures and challenges of life in rural America. The reporters stopped coming to the Mesa café, and Tom Bailie was able to put more time into his farm, and coax more profit from it. He expanded the cattle business with his cousin Manton, and he started growing some unusual crops—cottonwood trees for paper companies and exotic hot peppers for Korean buyers. Bailie's experiences with the Hanford issue had expanded his sense of the world and his place in it. He now thought nothing of flying to the Far East to pursue new business. But whenever he drove past the old house where he had lived as a boy, or caught sight of the reactors from the top of a ridge on his side of the Columbia, Bailie felt the sadness and rage that Hanford evoked. In the fall of 1991 this sadness all but consumed him when he learned that Leon Andrewjeski had died. Leon and Juanita Andrewjeski had been the first to share Bailie's suspicions about Hanford. They had recorded their neighbors' cancers and heart ailments on the "death map," and had shown it to Karen Dorn Steele on her first visit to the county.

The Andrewjeskis were typical downwinders. They had come in the 1950s, staked out a farm, and raised a family. Juanita had had three miscarriages, but hadn't associated them with Hanford until much later. At the end, Leon died of heart disease, which could not be linked directly to Hanford. He was seventy-one years old, after all. Still, after she found him dead on the bathroom floor in their farmhouse, Juanita couldn't help suspecting that Hanford had contributed to his long illness and his death.

Leon Andrewjeski's funeral was conducted at the little Catholic church on Glade Road in Eltopia. A young woman played a guitar and sang. The priest, who came from nearby Othello to perform the service, kept it simple, the way Leon would have liked it. As the hundred-odd mourners left the church for the cemetery, a cold rain began to fall. The casket was loaded onto a wagon, which was hitched to a team of six huge gray and black Percheron draft horses owned by the Andrewjeskis' oldest son, Robert. A car couldn't navigate the rutted path that led through the entrance of the rustic cemetery where Mr. Andrewjeski would be buried, so the horses were used to carry him to the grave.

Tom Bailie met the funeral procession as it was entering the graveyard. It was a weedy patch of earth about two hundred feet deep and four hundred feet wide, flanked by stubbly cornfields that had recently been harvested. The cemetery had been purposefully left in a natural state. In the spring, wildflowers bloomed between the ornate old headstones from the turn of the century and the shiny granite markers from more recent times. On this cold, wet October day, the ground was matted with long grasses and thistle. A few plastic blooms decorated some of the graves.

As the horse-drawn wagon and then the mourners filed in, Bailie leaned against a fence by the entrance. He stayed there during the brief burial service, keeping a distance between himself and the others. At one point he caught Juanita Andrewjeski's eye, and she gazed back, to acknowledge his presence. But Bailie didn't move any closer. He hung back, because he couldn't be sure that the other mourners wanted him to be there. Many people in the county still avoided him because they didn't want to talk about Hanford. Here, especially, he didn't want to make anyone feel uncomfortable.

During the Hanford battle, a change had come over Bailie and his neighbors. Over those seven years, as the value of their farmland was threatened and their faith in America was shaken, the people of Franklin County had become divided. Many still insisted that nothing serious had happened. Others feared there was something in their land, or even in their bodies, that would bring tragedy one day. All of them must have sensed that their community had been forever changed. Their patriotic innocence had been betrayed, and life in this once idyllic, rural place would never again feel so secure.

Tom Bailie would be remembered as the man who had started asking the questions. Whether he was right or wrong, many people resented the fact that he had pushed so hard to bring a disturbing truth into the open. Most of all, they must have wished that what Bailie had said about Hanford had turned out to be untrue.

For Bailie, the truth had long been evident in the broken animals and suffering people he had known. Leaning against the graveyard fence, tears mingling with the raindrops that hit his face, Bailie thought about the bitter harvest Hanford had created for his community. He remembered visiting with Leon and Juanita Andrewjeski on the day he took Karen Dorn Steele on that first tour of Franklin County. They had been so open and trusting. All they wanted, they had said, were answers to their questions. He also thought about Dr. Chen, who for thirty years had fearfully kept silent about the irradiated river water and fish. And he recalled the many farm families who had mourned their own mysterious losses in silence.

In the meantime, Tom Bailie also wished that he had been wrong. After all, Hanford had ruined his health when he was a child, ruined many friendships, and opened a chasm between him and his wife. Yet wishing wouldn't make the truth about Hanford disappear. Bailie accepted the truth. But as he mourned Leon Andrewjeski, he couldn't help thinking about the grief that could have been avoided if the government hadn't hidden the truth. He feared the pain and death that waited in the future. And the tears he cried were tears of both sorrow and rage.

# INDEX